GALILEO! GALILEO!

TO APRIL -- ARCHIVIST, ARCHITECT, APIARIST, FRIEND

OTHER BOOKS BY THE AUTHORS

ESME DOOLEY

ESME DOOLEY & THE KIRKKOMAKI CIRCUS

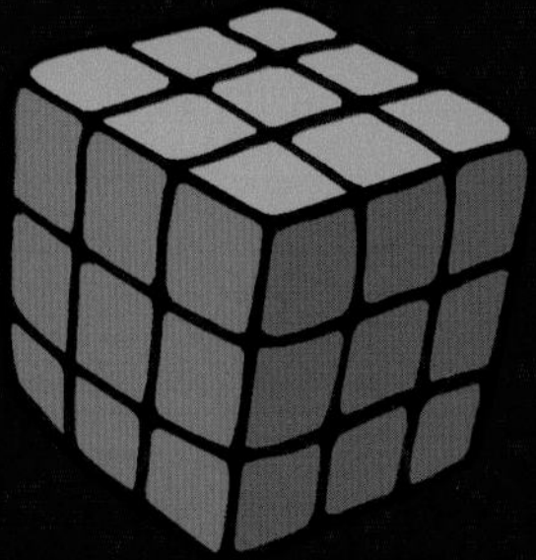

GALILEO! GALILEO!

WRITTEN AND ILLUSTRATED BY

HOLLY TRECHTER AND JANE DONOVAN

SKY CANDLE PRESS

ZUMBRO FALLS, MINNESOTA

GALILEO! GALILEO!

COPYRIGHT © 2020 BY HOLLY TRECHTER AND JANE DONOVAN

PUBLISHED 2020 BY SKY CANDLE PRESS
PRINTED IN THE UNITED STATES OF AMERICA

FIRST EDITION
ISBN 978-1-939360-08-3
LIBRARY OF CONGRESS CONTROL NUMBER: 2020900969

MY NAME IS GALILEO, AND SOME PEOPLE SAY I CHANGED THE WORLD.

YOU SEE, I BUILT A POWERFUL TELESCOPE,
AND ONE NIGHT I TURNED IT TOWARDS JUPITER.

NEAR THE PLANET, I SPOTTED THREE BRIGHT STARS.

1

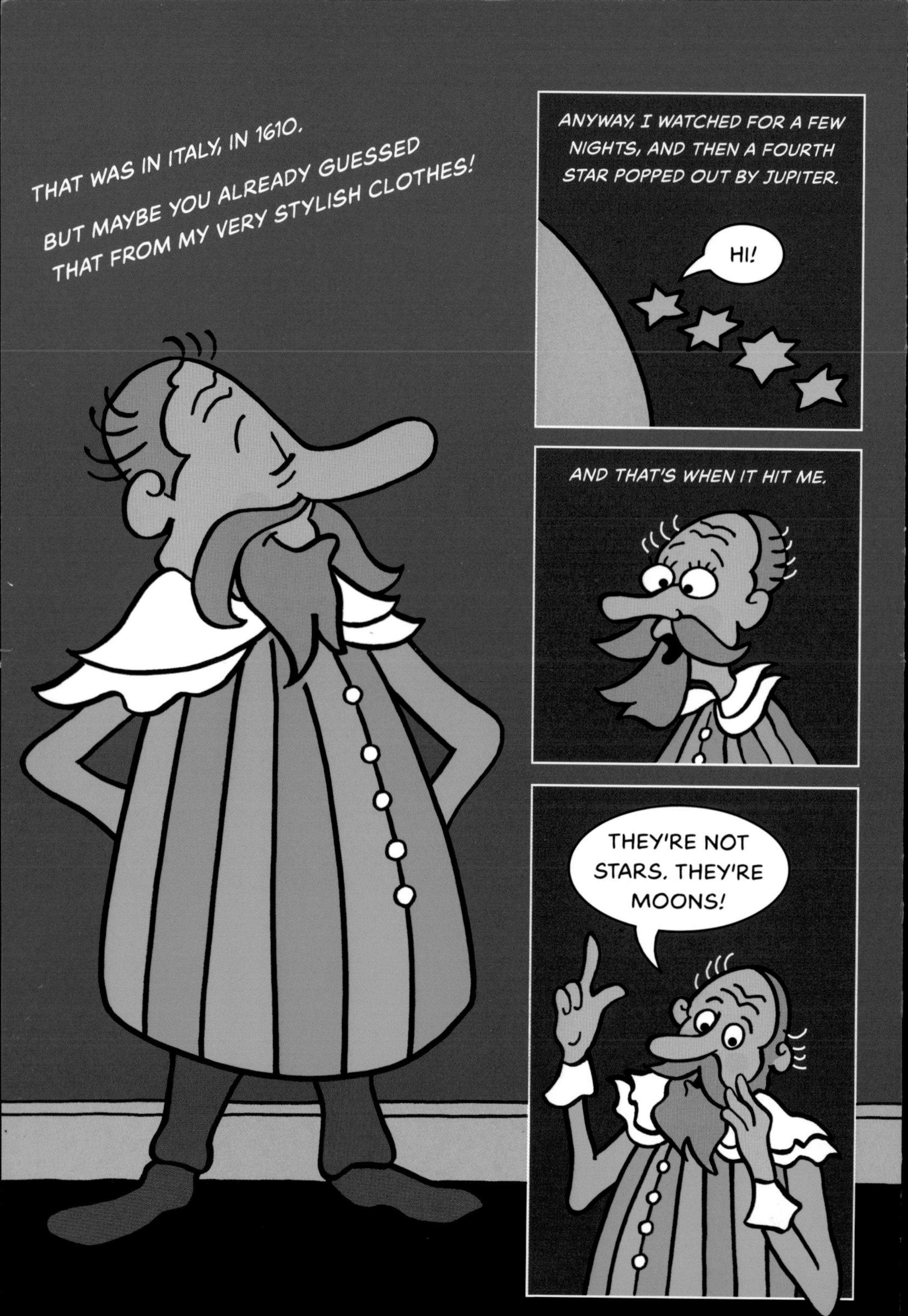
THAT WAS IN ITALY, IN 1610.
BUT MAYBE YOU ALREADY GUESSED THAT FROM MY VERY STYLISH CLOTHES!
ANYWAY, I WATCHED FOR A FEW NIGHTS, AND THEN A FOURTH STAR POPPED OUT BY JUPITER.
HI!
AND THAT'S WHEN IT HIT ME.
THEY'RE NOT STARS. THEY'RE MOONS!

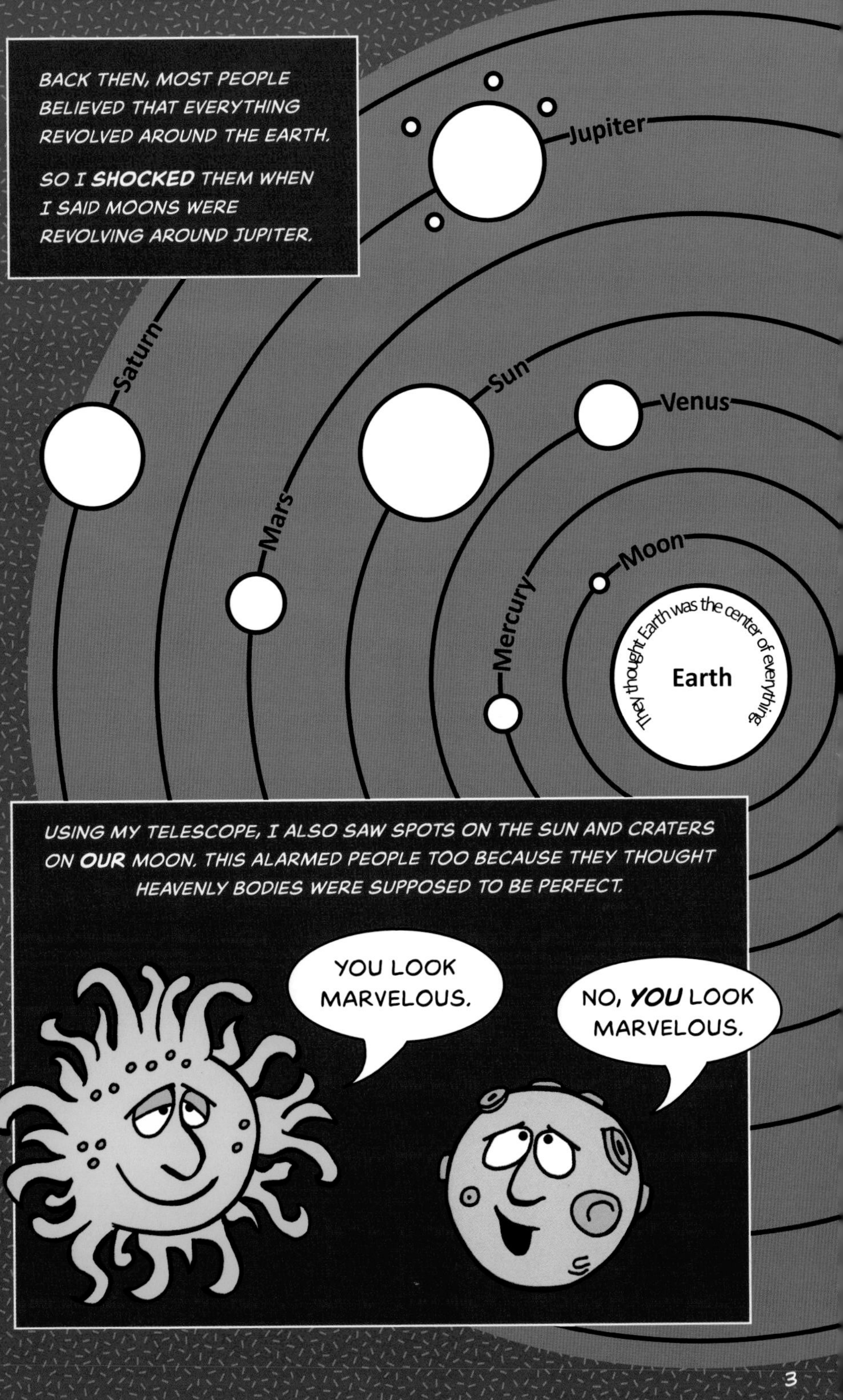
BACK THEN, MOST PEOPLE BELIEVED THAT EVERYTHING REVOLVED AROUND THE EARTH.
SO I **SHOCKED** THEM WHEN I SAID MOONS WERE REVOLVING AROUND JUPITER.
Jupiter
Saturn
Sun
Venus
Mars
Moon
Mercury
They thought Earth was the center of everything.
Earth
USING MY TELESCOPE, I ALSO SAW SPOTS ON THE SUN AND CRATERS ON **OUR** MOON. THIS ALARMED PEOPLE TOO BECAUSE THEY THOUGHT HEAVENLY BODIES WERE SUPPOSED TO BE PERFECT.
YOU LOOK MARVELOUS.
NO, ***YOU*** LOOK MARVELOUS.

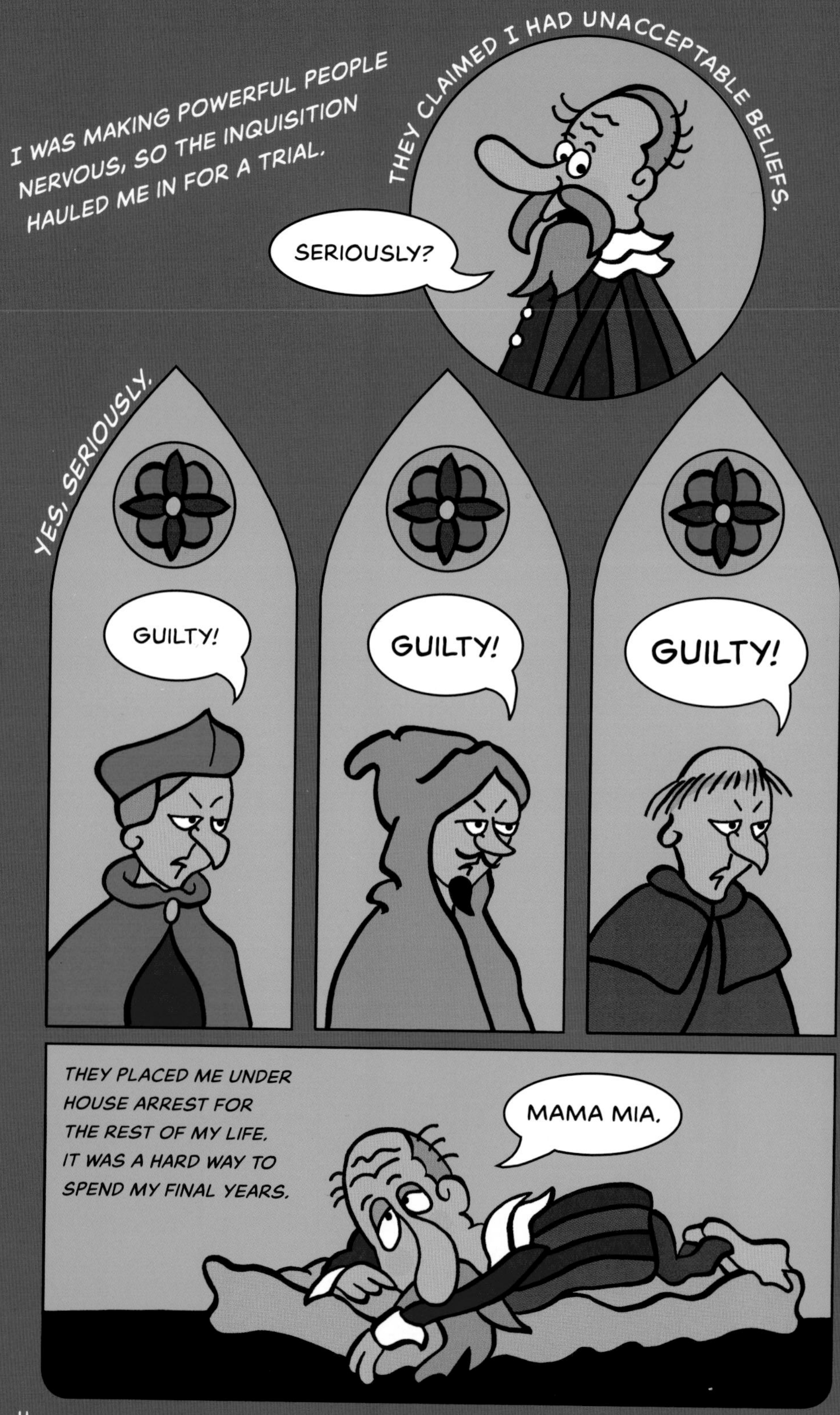
I WAS MAKING POWERFUL PEOPLE NERVOUS, SO THE INQUISITION HAULED ME IN FOR A TRIAL.
THEY CLAIMED I HAD UNACCEPTABLE BELIEFS.
SERIOUSLY?
YES, SERIOUSLY.
GUILTY!
GUILTY!
GUILTY!
THEY PLACED ME UNDER HOUSE ARREST FOR THE REST OF MY LIFE. IT WAS A HARD WAY TO SPEND MY FINAL YEARS.
MAMA MIA.

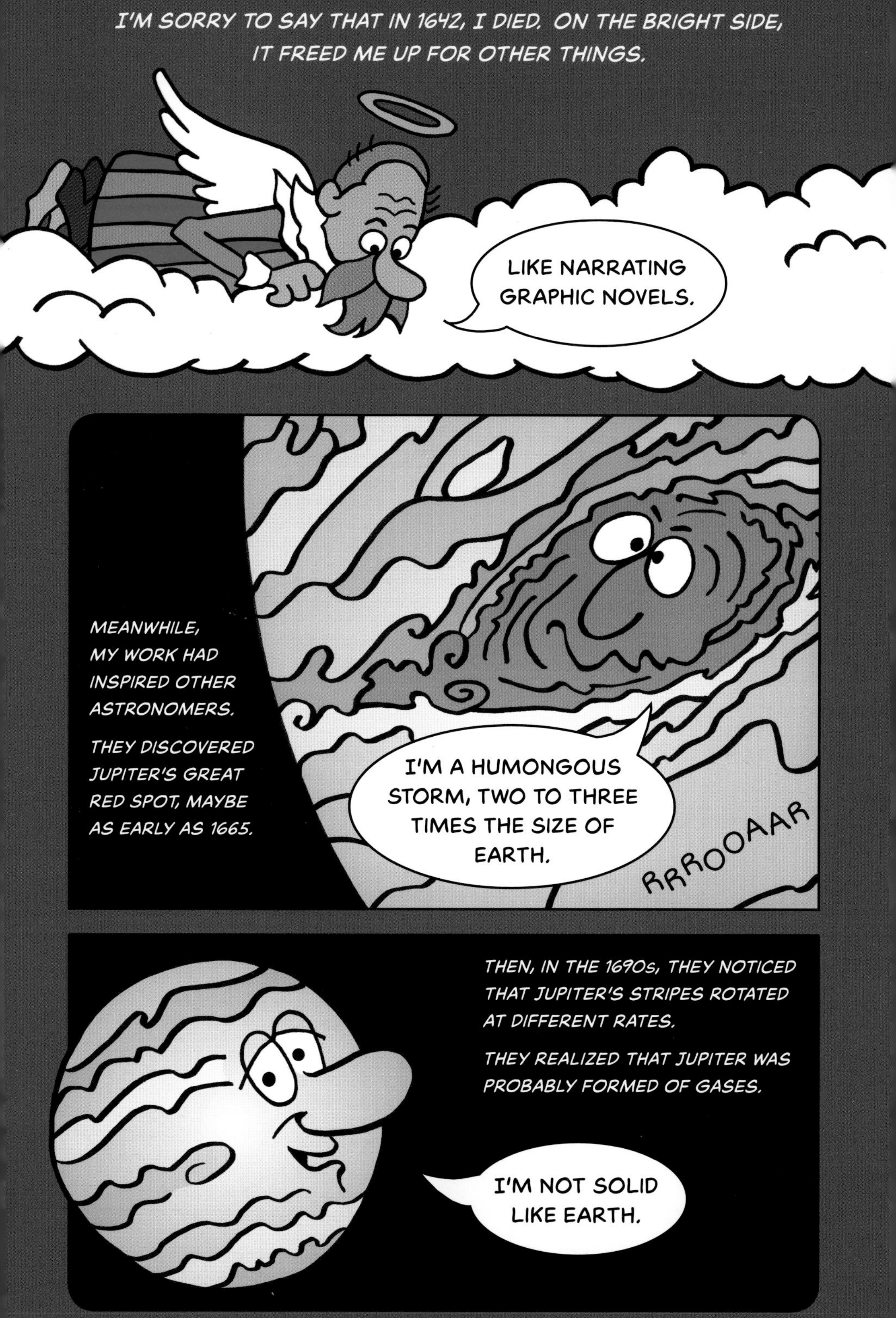
I'M SORRY TO SAY THAT IN 1642, I DIED. ON THE BRIGHT SIDE, IT FREED ME UP FOR OTHER THINGS.
LIKE NARRATING GRAPHIC NOVELS.
MEANWHILE, MY WORK HAD INSPIRED OTHER ASTRONOMERS.
THEY DISCOVERED JUPITER'S GREAT RED SPOT, MAYBE AS EARLY AS 1665.
I'M A HUMONGOUS STORM, TWO TO THREE TIMES THE SIZE OF EARTH.
RRROOAAR
THEN, IN THE 1690s, THEY NOTICED THAT JUPITER'S STRIPES ROTATED AT DIFFERENT RATES.
THEY REALIZED THAT JUPITER WAS PROBABLY FORMED OF GASES.
I'M NOT SOLID LIKE EARTH.

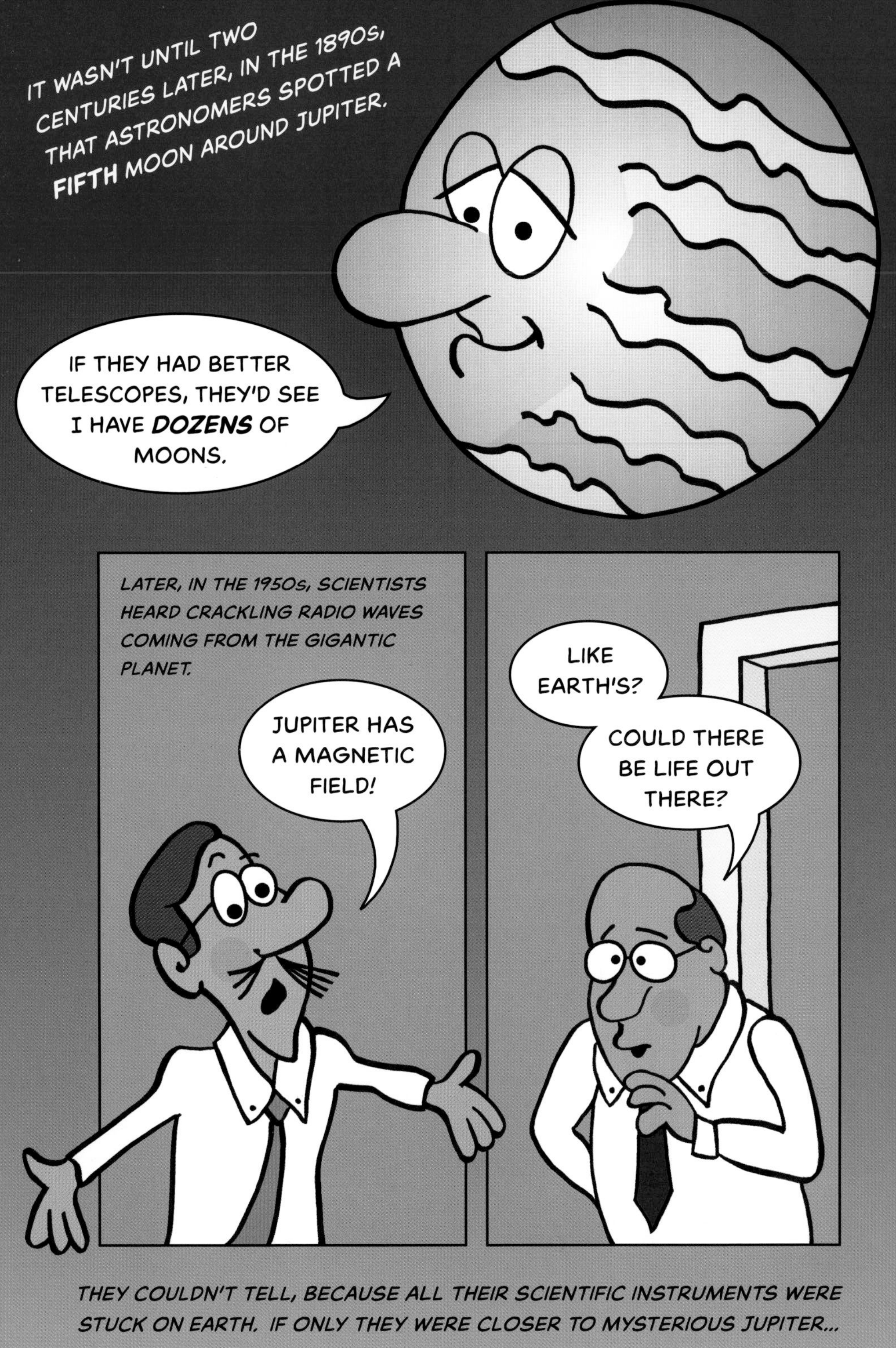

IT WASN'T UNTIL TWO CENTURIES LATER, IN THE 1890s, THAT ASTRONOMERS SPOTTED A FIFTH MOON AROUND JUPITER.
IF THEY HAD BETTER TELESCOPES, THEY'D SEE I HAVE DOZENS OF MOONS.
LATER, IN THE 1950s, SCIENTISTS HEARD CRACKLING RADIO WAVES COMING FROM THE GIGANTIC PLANET.
JUPITER HAS A MAGNETIC FIELD!
LIKE EARTH'S?
COULD THERE BE LIFE OUT THERE?
THEY COULDN'T TELL, BECAUSE ALL THEIR SCIENTIFIC INSTRUMENTS WERE STUCK ON EARTH. IF ONLY THEY WERE CLOSER TO MYSTERIOUS JUPITER...

SO NASA (THE NATIONAL AERONAUTICS AND SPACE ADMINISTRATION) BEGAN TO THINK ABOUT A JUPITER MISSION.

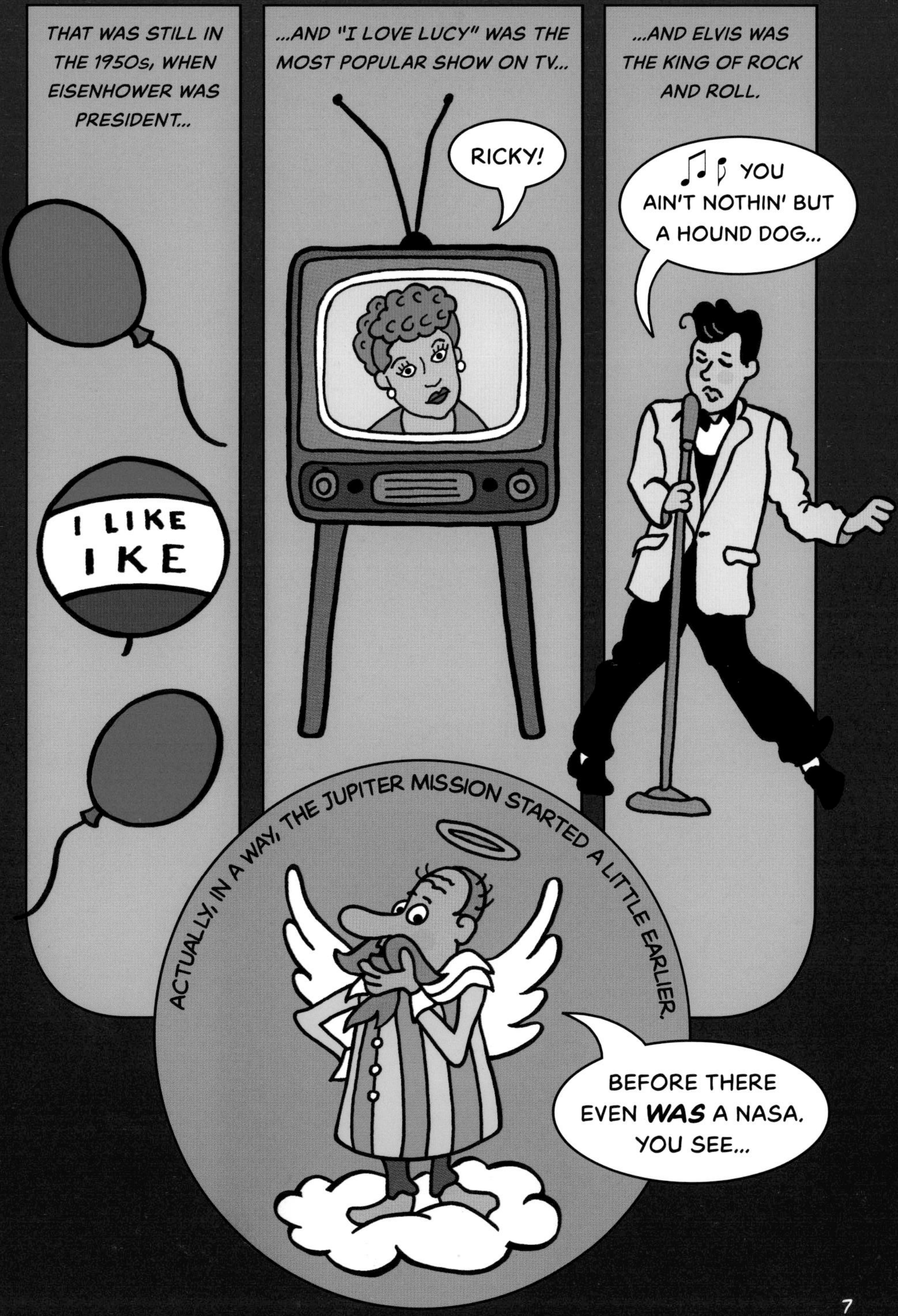
THAT WAS STILL IN THE 1950s, WHEN EISENHOWER WAS PRESIDENT...
I LIKE IKE
...AND "I LOVE LUCY" WAS THE MOST POPULAR SHOW ON TV...
RICKY!
...AND ELVIS WAS THE KING OF ROCK AND ROLL.
♫♪ YOU AIN'T NOTHIN' BUT A HOUND DOG...
ACTUALLY, IN A WAY, THE JUPITER MISSION STARTED A LITTLE EARLIER.
BEFORE THERE EVEN **WAS** A NASA. YOU SEE...

...AFTER WORLD WAR II, GERMAN SCIENTISTS WERE BROUGHT TO THE UNITED STATES TO KEEP THEIR SKILLS AWAY FROM GERMANY AND THE SOVIET UNION.

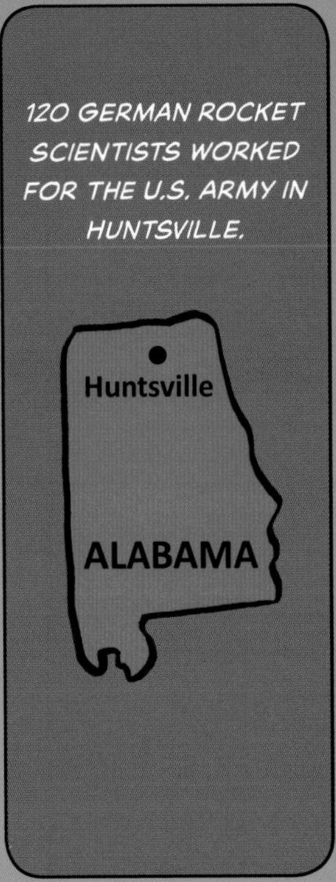
120 GERMAN ROCKET SCIENTISTS WORKED FOR THE U.S. ARMY IN HUNTSVILLE.
Huntsville
ALABAMA

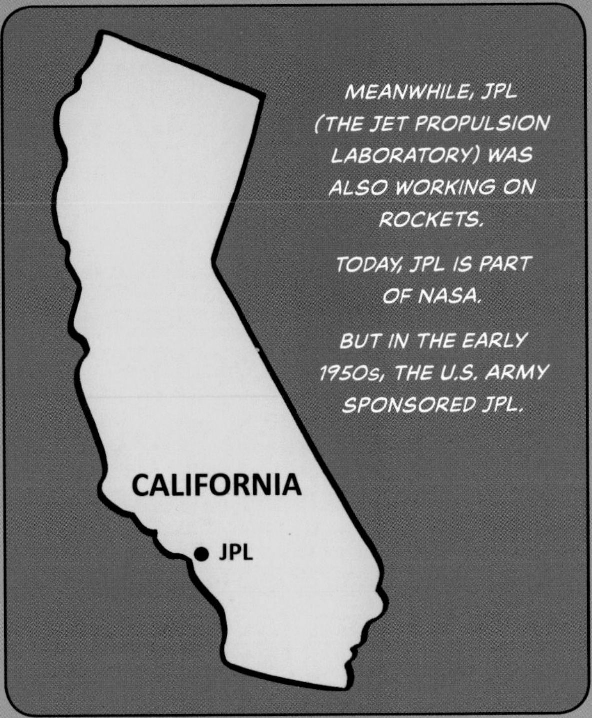
MEANWHILE, JPL (THE JET PROPULSION LABORATORY) WAS ALSO WORKING ON ROCKETS.
TODAY, JPL IS PART OF NASA.
BUT IN THE EARLY 1950s, THE U.S. ARMY SPONSORED JPL.
CALIFORNIA
JPL

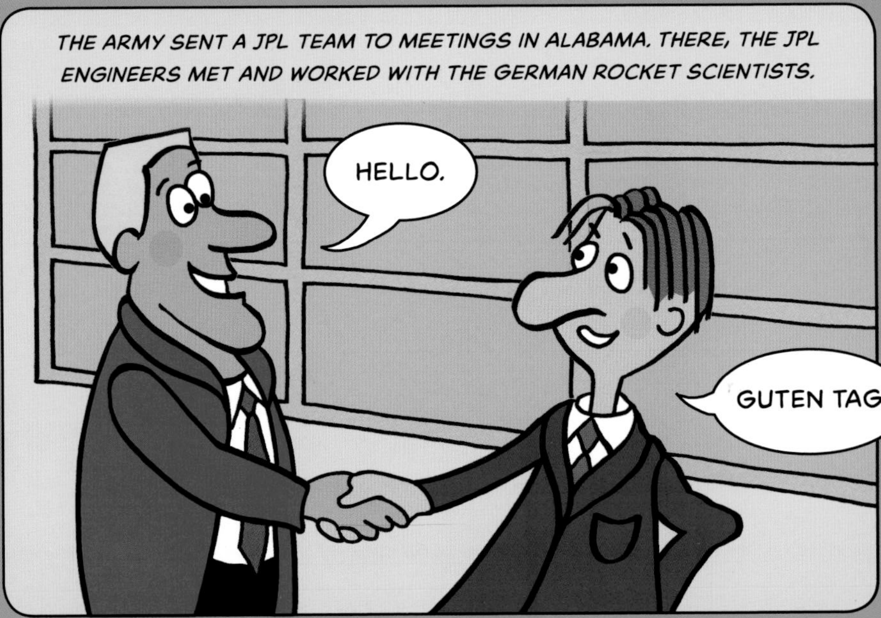
THE ARMY SENT A JPL TEAM TO MEETINGS IN ALABAMA. THERE, THE JPL ENGINEERS MET AND WORKED WITH THE GERMAN ROCKET SCIENTISTS.
HELLO.
GUTEN TAG.

THEY FORMED GOOD RELATIONSHIPS WHICH WOULD HELP NASA WHEN IT STARTED IN 1958.

TIME PASSED, AND THE WORLD GREW FASCINATED WITH SPACE TRAVEL.

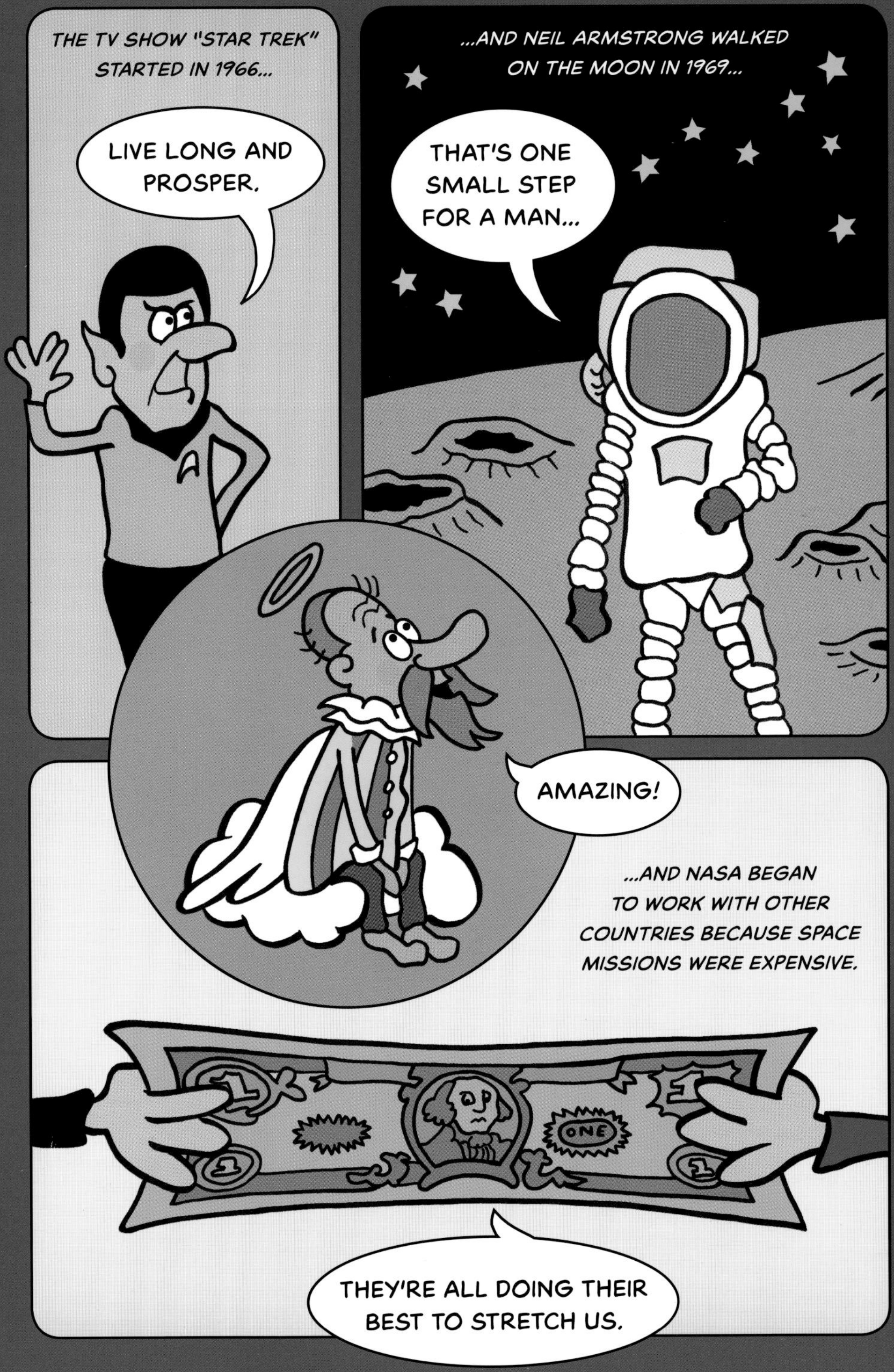
THE TV SHOW "STAR TREK" STARTED IN 1966...
LIVE LONG AND PROSPER.
...AND NEIL ARMSTRONG WALKED ON THE MOON IN 1969...
THAT'S ONE SMALL STEP FOR A MAN...
AMAZING!
...AND NASA BEGAN TO WORK WITH OTHER COUNTRIES BECAUSE SPACE MISSIONS WERE EXPENSIVE.
ONE
THEY'RE ALL DOING THEIR BEST TO STRETCH US.

IN 1974, THE UNITED STATES AND GERMANY DECIDED TO WORK TOGETHER ON A JUPITER MISSION.

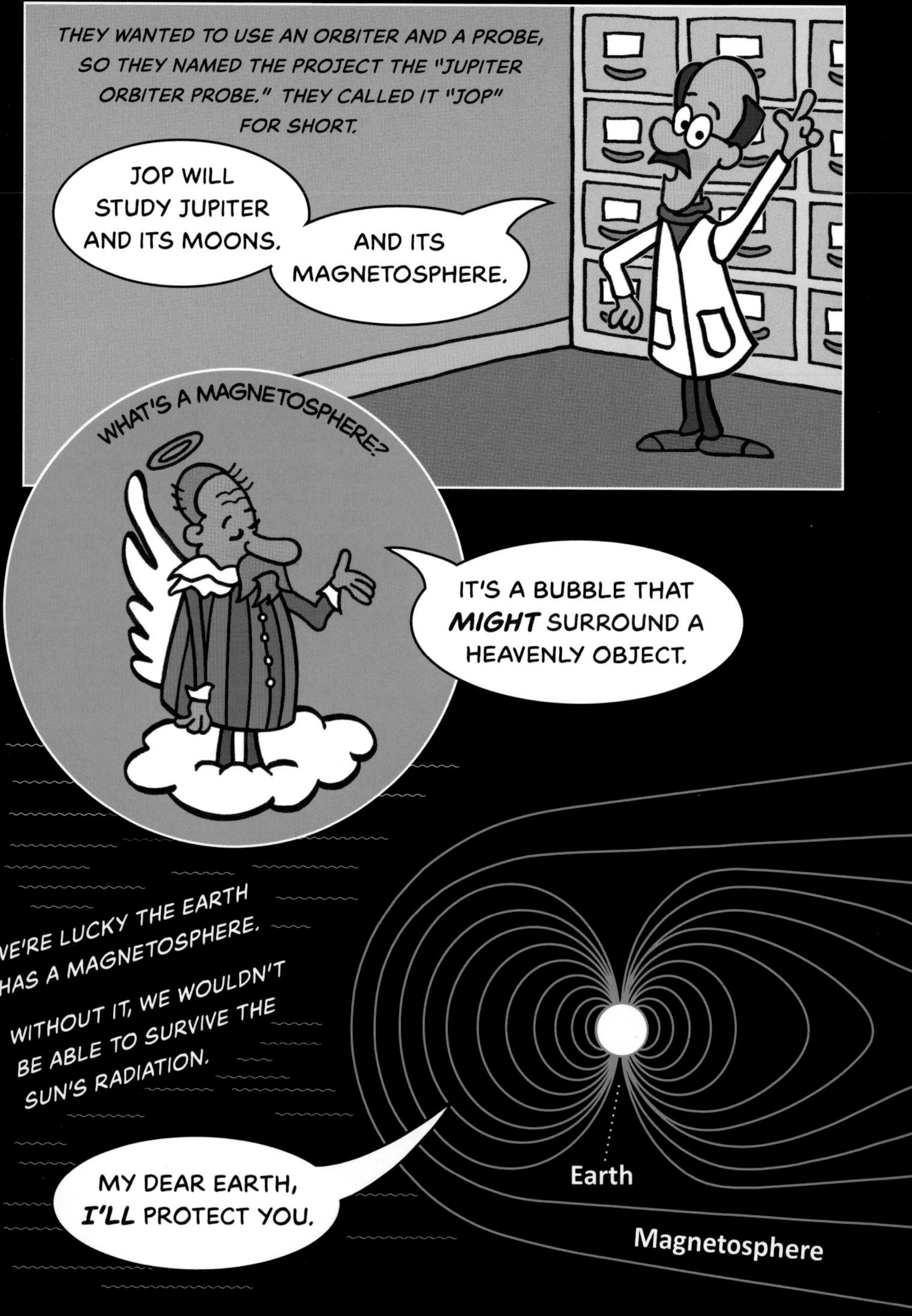
THEY WANTED TO USE AN ORBITER AND A PROBE, SO THEY NAMED THE PROJECT THE "JUPITER ORBITER PROBE." THEY CALLED IT "JOP" FOR SHORT.
JOP WILL STUDY JUPITER AND ITS MOONS.
AND ITS MAGNETOSPHERE.
WHAT'S A MAGNETOSPHERE?
IT'S A BUBBLE THAT ***MIGHT*** SURROUND A HEAVENLY OBJECT.
WE'RE LUCKY THE EARTH HAS A MAGNETOSPHERE.
WITHOUT IT, WE WOULDN'T BE ABLE TO SURVIVE THE SUN'S RADIATION.
MY DEAR EARTH, ***I'LL*** PROTECT YOU.
Earth
Magnetosphere

FOR THE JOP PROJECT, THE ENGINEERS WANTED TO BUILD A SPINNING SPACECRAFT BECAUSE THEY THOUGHT IT WOULD BE MORE STABLE IF IT SPUN.

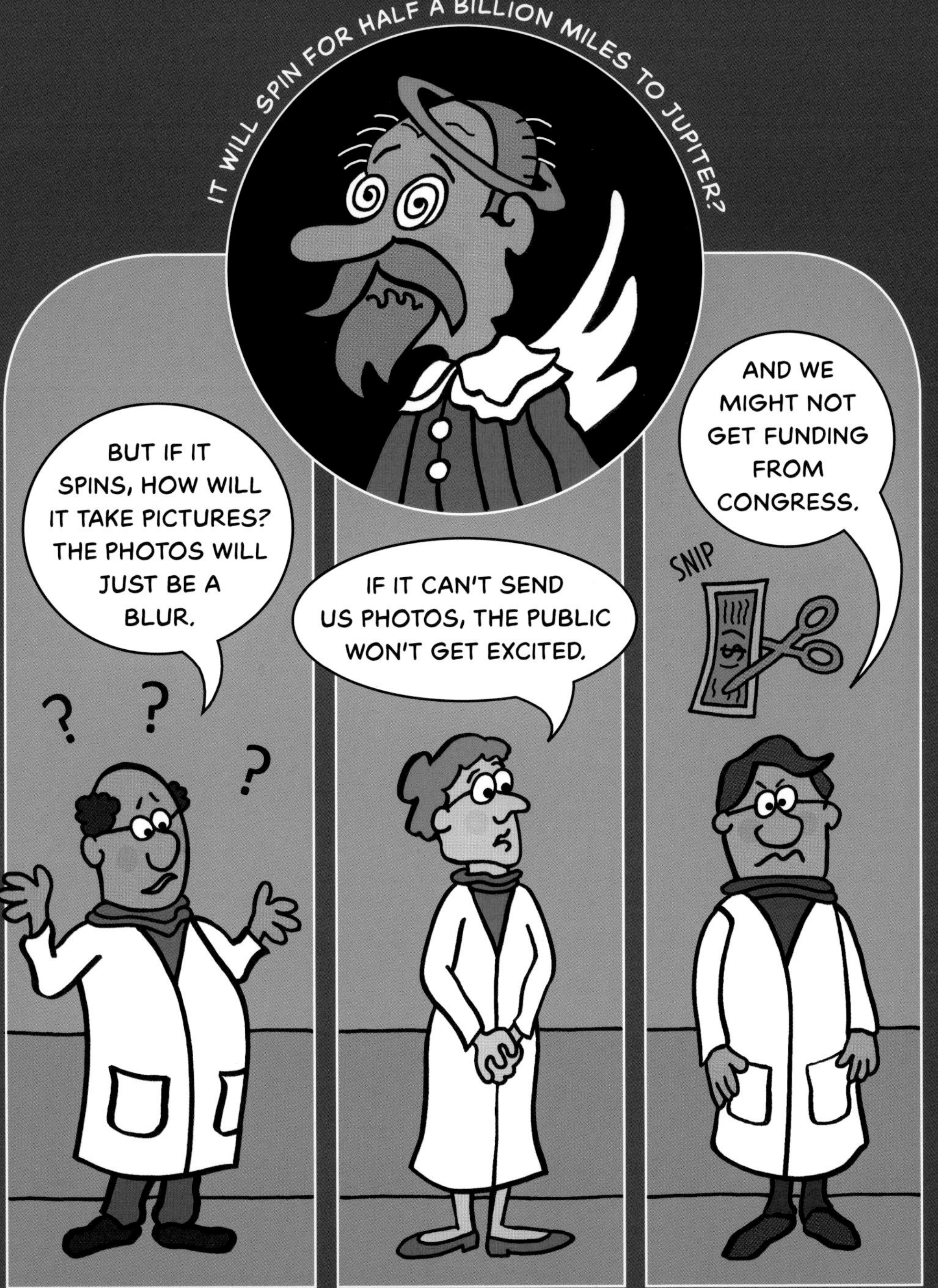
IT WILL SPIN FOR HALF A BILLION MILES TO JUPITER?
BUT IF IT SPINS, HOW WILL IT TAKE PICTURES? THE PHOTOS WILL JUST BE A BLUR.
IF IT CAN'T SEND US PHOTOS, THE PUBLIC WON'T GET EXCITED.
AND WE MIGHT NOT GET FUNDING FROM CONGRESS.
SNIP

SO THE ENGINEERS CAME UP WITH A CLEVER DESIGN.

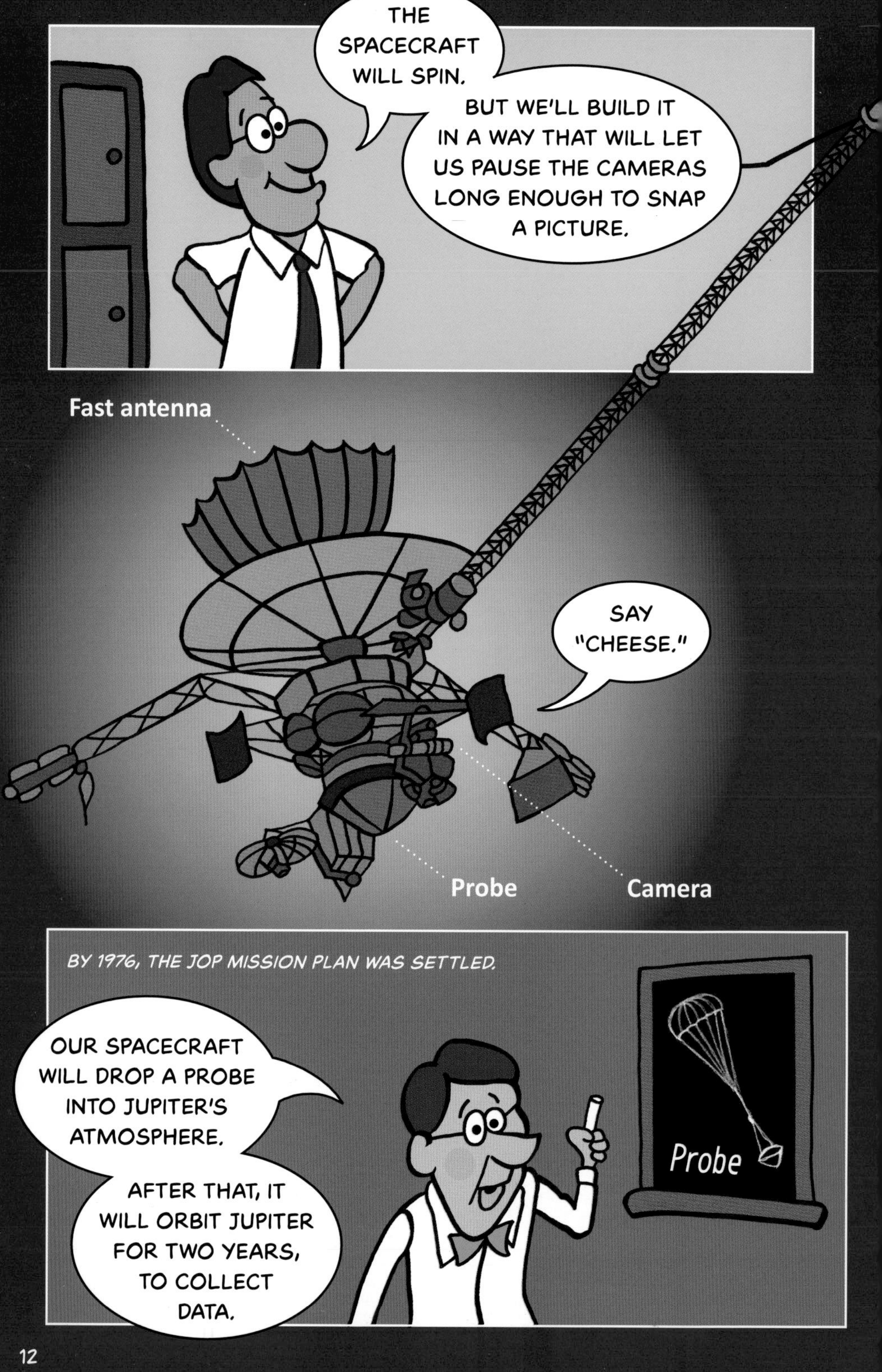
THE SPACECRAFT WILL SPIN.
BUT WE'LL BUILD IT IN A WAY THAT WILL LET US PAUSE THE CAMERAS LONG ENOUGH TO SNAP A PICTURE.
Fast antenna
SAY "CHEESE."
Probe
Camera
BY 1976, THE JOP MISSION PLAN WAS SETTLED.
OUR SPACECRAFT WILL DROP A PROBE INTO JUPITER'S ATMOSPHERE.
AFTER THAT, IT WILL ORBIT JUPITER FOR TWO YEARS, TO COLLECT DATA.
Probe

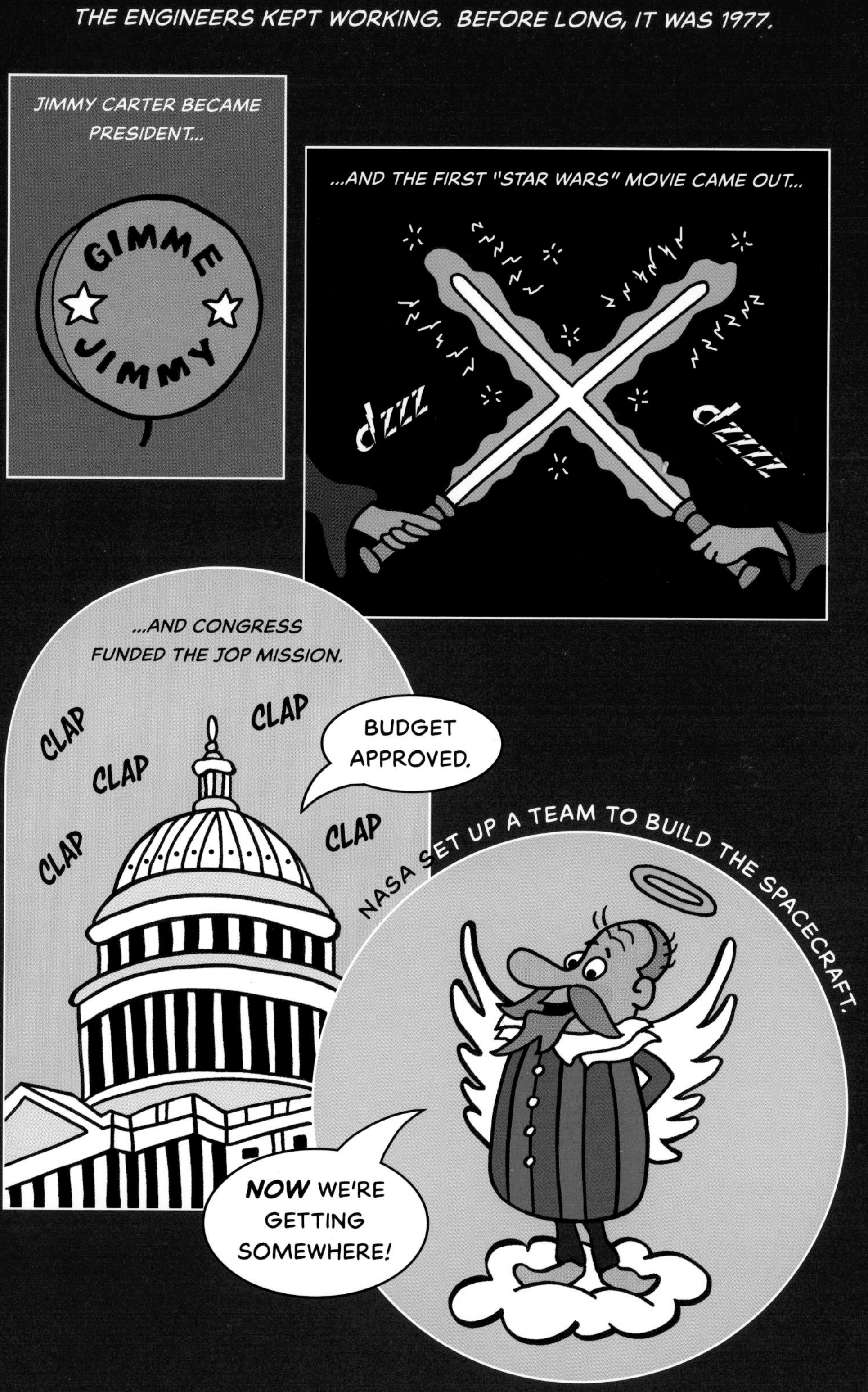
THE ENGINEERS KEPT WORKING. BEFORE LONG, IT WAS 1977.
JIMMY CARTER BECAME PRESIDENT...
GIMME JIMMY
...AND THE FIRST "STAR WARS" MOVIE CAME OUT...
dzzz
dzzzz
...AND CONGRESS FUNDED THE JOP MISSION.
CLAP
CLAP
CLAP
CLAP
CLAP
BUDGET APPROVED.
NASA SET UP A TEAM TO BUILD THE SPACECRAFT.
NOW WE'RE GETTING SOMEWHERE!

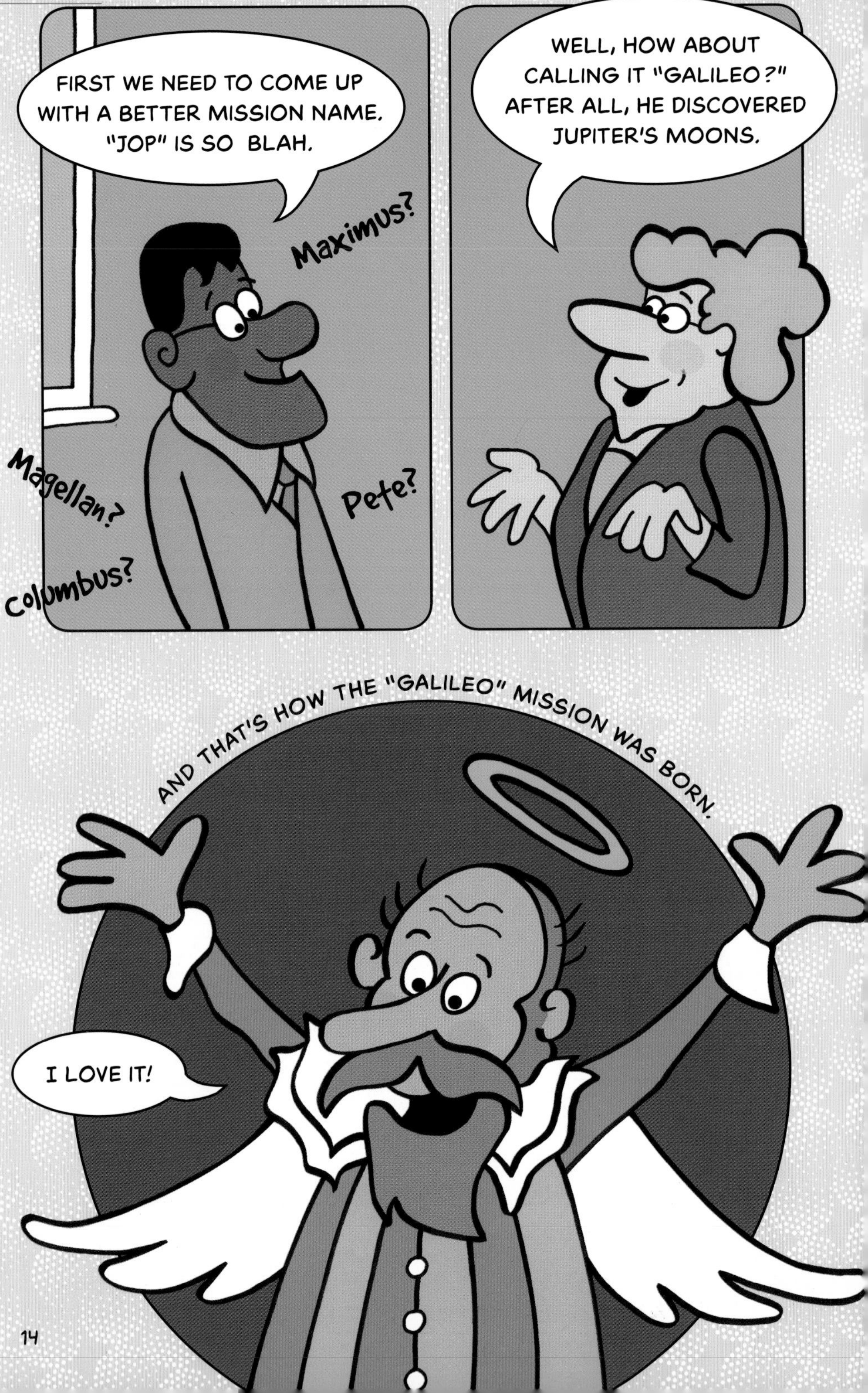
FIRST WE NEED TO COME UP WITH A BETTER MISSION NAME. "JOP" IS SO BLAH.
Maximus?
Magellan?
Pete?
Columbus?
WELL, HOW ABOUT CALLING IT "GALILEO?" AFTER ALL, HE DISCOVERED JUPITER'S MOONS.
AND THAT'S HOW THE "GALILEO" MISSION WAS BORN.
I LOVE IT!

THE AMERICANS AND THEIR GERMAN PARTNERS ON THE GALILEO MISSION HAD TO FIGURE OUT WHO WOULD BE DOING WHAT.

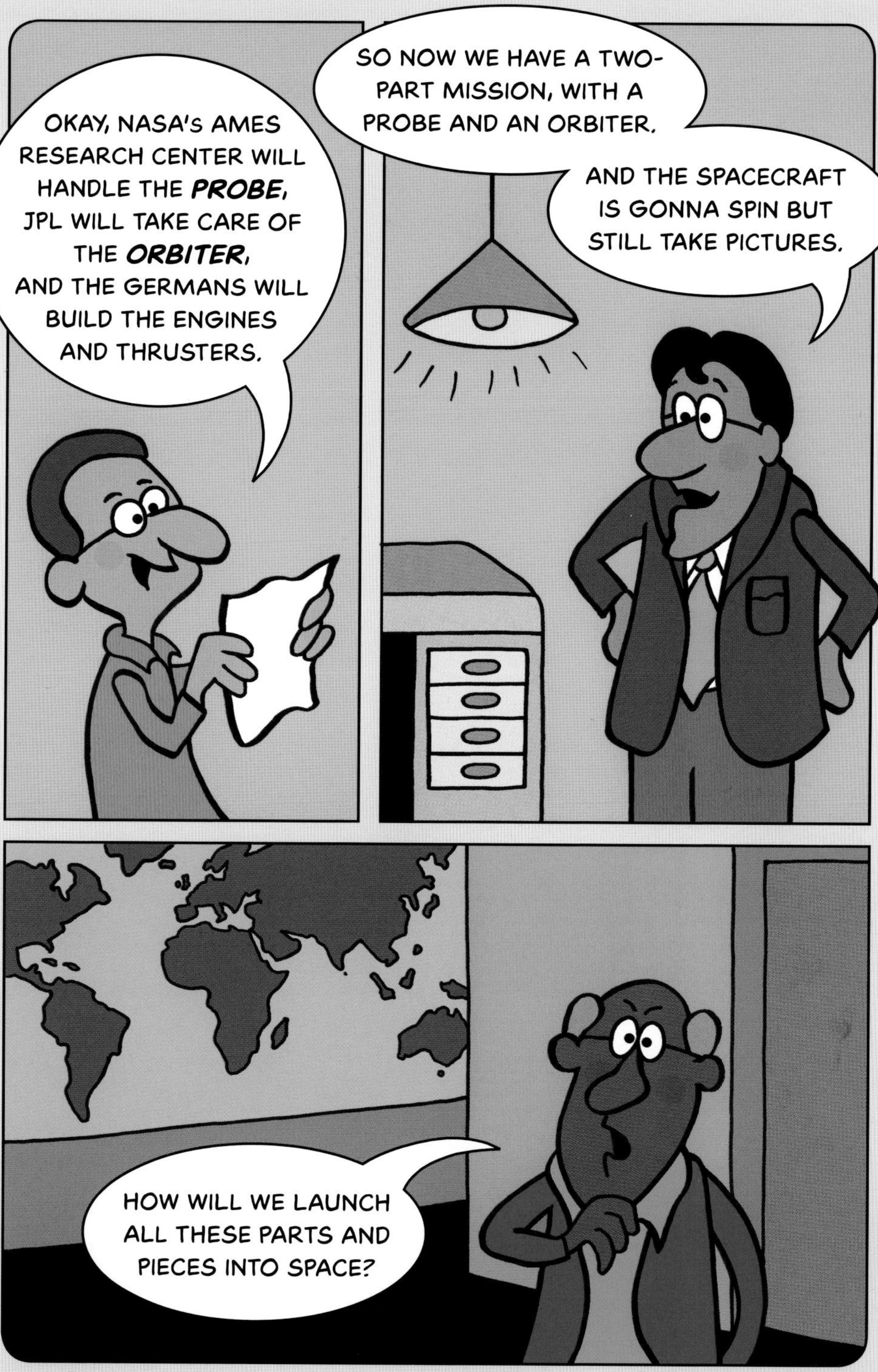
OKAY, NASA's AMES RESEARCH CENTER WILL HANDLE THE PROBE, JPL WILL TAKE CARE OF THE ORBITER, AND THE GERMANS WILL BUILD THE ENGINES AND THRUSTERS.
SO NOW WE HAVE A TWO-PART MISSION, WITH A PROBE AND AN ORBITER.
AND THE SPACECRAFT IS GONNA SPIN BUT STILL TAKE PICTURES.
HOW WILL WE LAUNCH ALL THESE PARTS AND PIECES INTO SPACE?

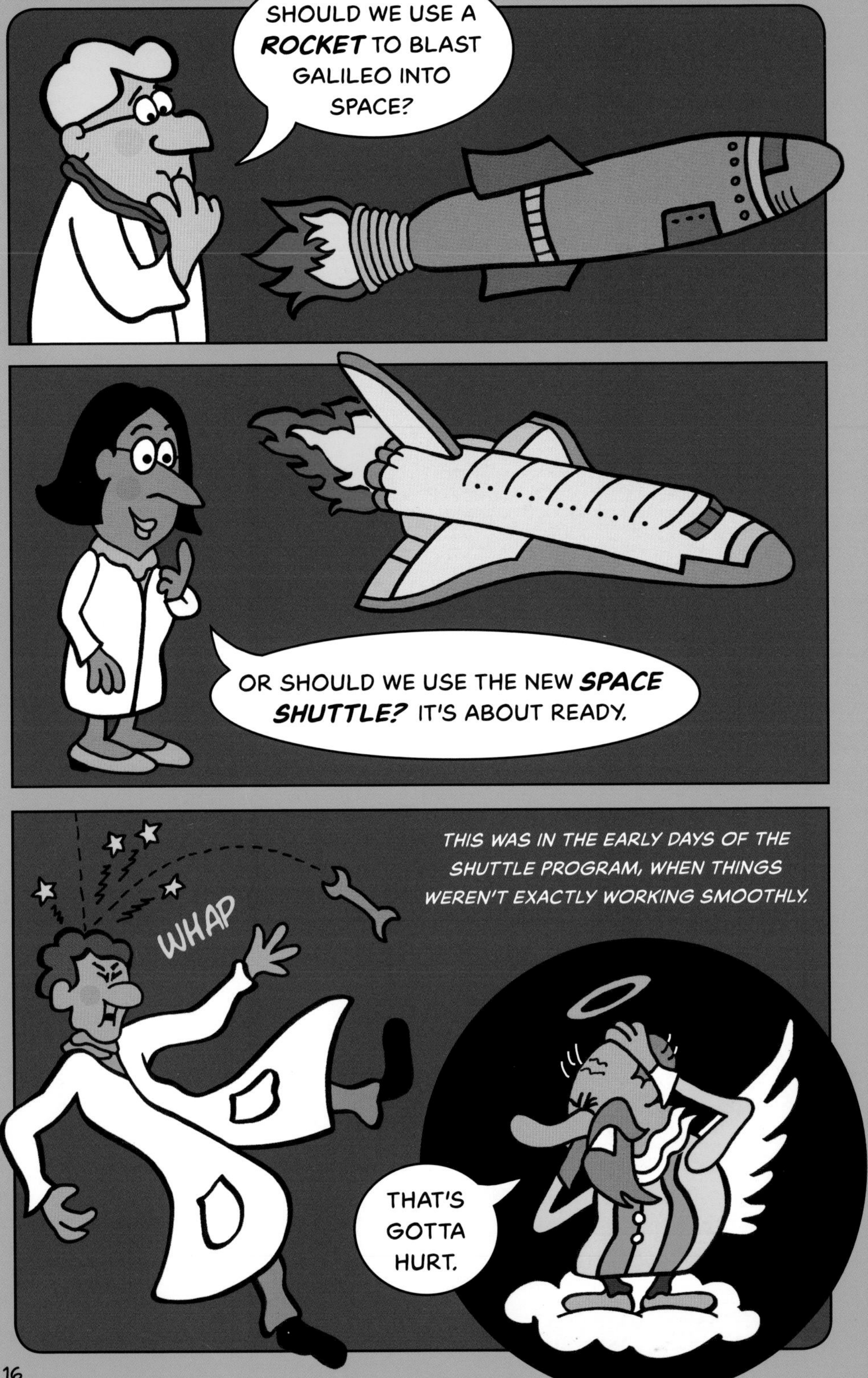
SHOULD WE USE A **ROCKET** TO BLAST GALILEO INTO SPACE?
OR SHOULD WE USE THE NEW **SPACE SHUTTLE?** IT'S ABOUT READY.
THIS WAS IN THE EARLY DAYS OF THE SHUTTLE PROGRAM, WHEN THINGS WEREN'T EXACTLY WORKING SMOOTHLY.
WHAP
THAT'S GOTTA HURT.

THE GALILEO TEAM WENT BACK AND FORTH,
TRYING TO DECIDE BETWEEN A ROCKET
AND THE SHUTTLE.

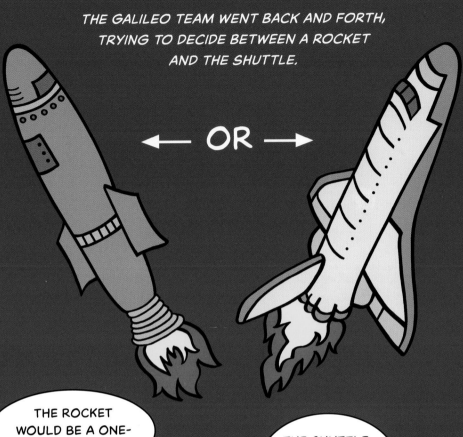

← OR →

THE ROCKET WOULD BE A ONE-SHOT DEAL.

AFTER THE LAUNCH, ITS PARTS WOULD FALL AWAY, AND WE WOULDN'T BE ABLE TO USE THEM AGAIN.

THE SHUTTLE, ON THE OTHER HAND, WOULD BE REUSABLE.

WE COULD FLY IT UP HIGH AND PUSH GALILEO OUT OF ITS CARGO HOLD. THEN THE SHUTTLE COULD COME BACK TO EARTH.

ALSO, THERE WAS **ANOTHER** PART TO THE PUZZLE...

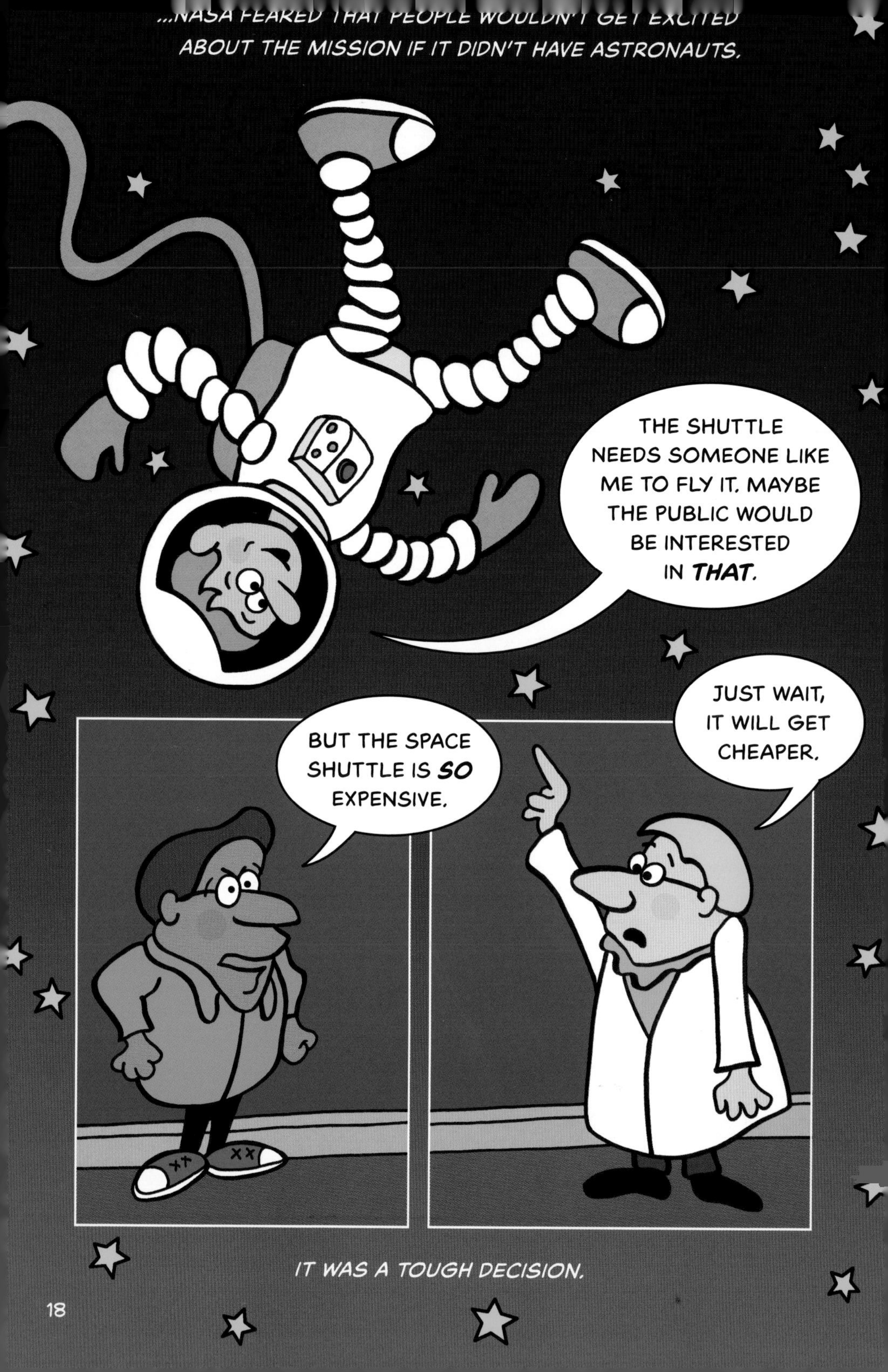
...NASA FEARED THAT PEOPLE WOULDN'T GET EXCITED ABOUT THE MISSION IF IT DIDN'T HAVE ASTRONAUTS.
THE SHUTTLE NEEDS SOMEONE LIKE ME TO FLY IT. MAYBE THE PUBLIC WOULD BE INTERESTED IN *THAT*.
BUT THE SPACE SHUTTLE IS *SO* EXPENSIVE.
JUST WAIT, IT WILL GET CHEAPER.
IT WAS A TOUGH DECISION.

NASA FINALLY DECIDED TO USE THE SPACE SHUTTLE TO LAUNCH GALILEO.

THEY HAD NO IDEA HOW HARD IT WAS GOING TO BE.

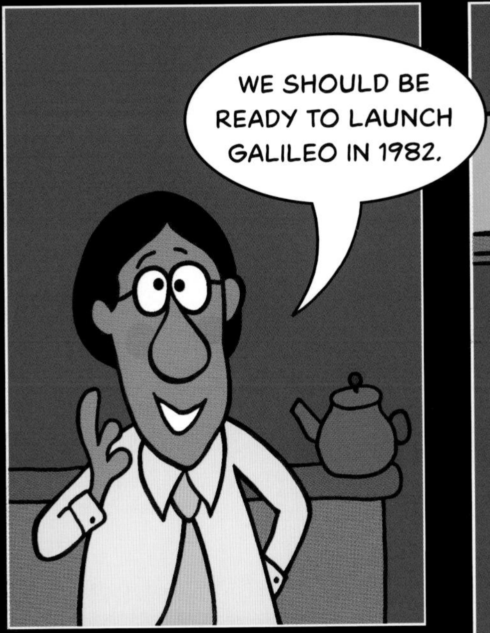
WE SHOULD BE READY TO LAUNCH GALILEO IN 1982.

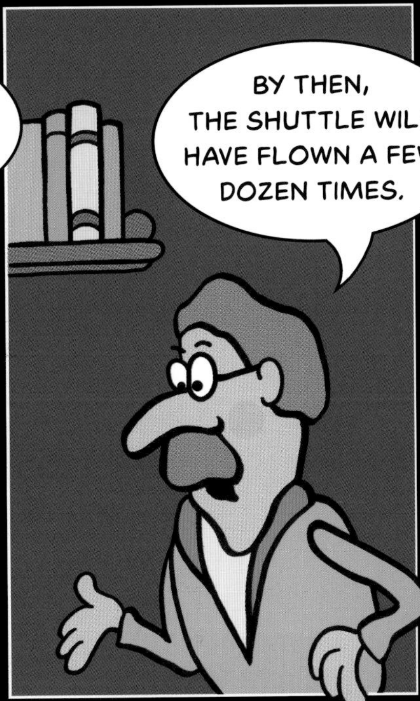
BY THEN, THE SHUTTLE WILL HAVE FLOWN A FEW DOZEN TIMES.

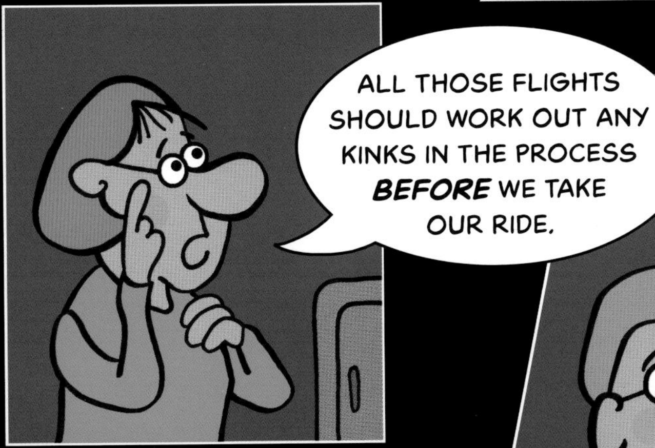
ALL THOSE FLIGHTS SHOULD WORK OUT ANY KINKS IN THE PROCESS ***BEFORE*** WE TAKE OUR RIDE.

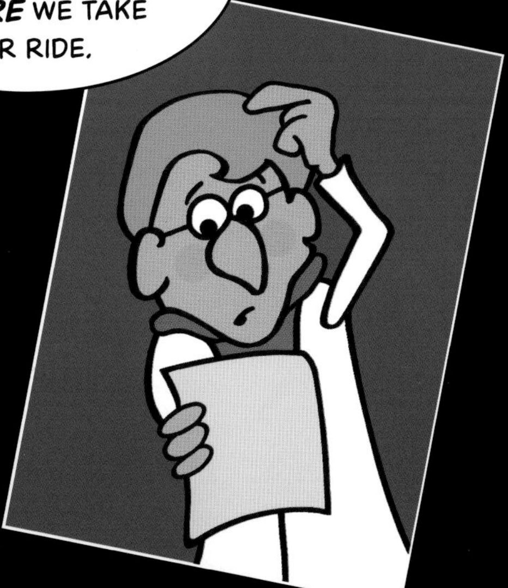

BUT THE SHUTTLE PROGRAM KEPT HAVING PROBLEMS.

SO THEY POSTPONED GALILEO'S LAUNCH FOR TWO YEARS, TO GIVE THE SHUTTLE A CHANCE TO CATCH UP.

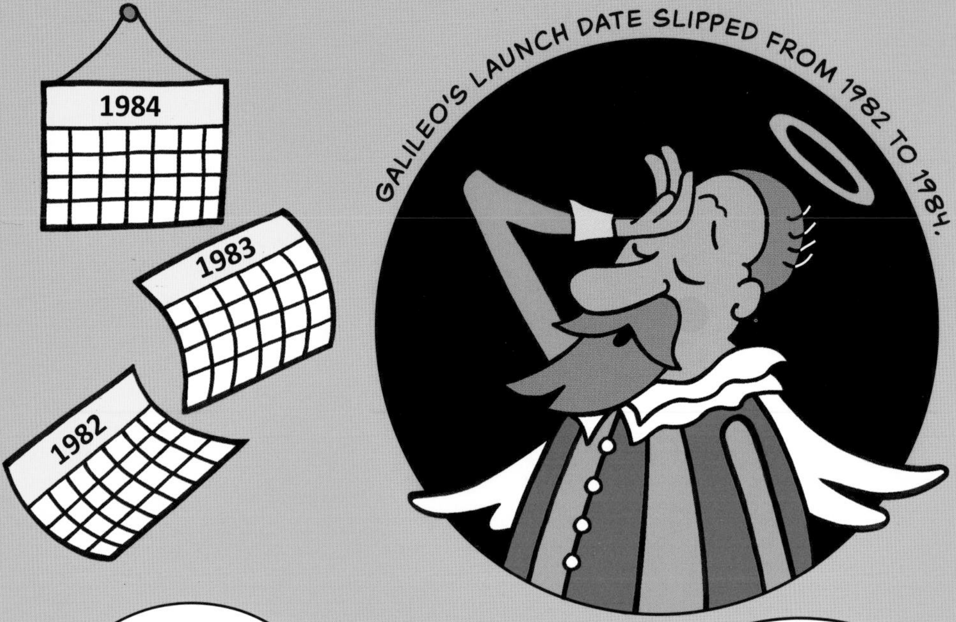
1984
1983
1982
GALILEO'S LAUNCH DATE SLIPPED FROM 1982 TO 1984.

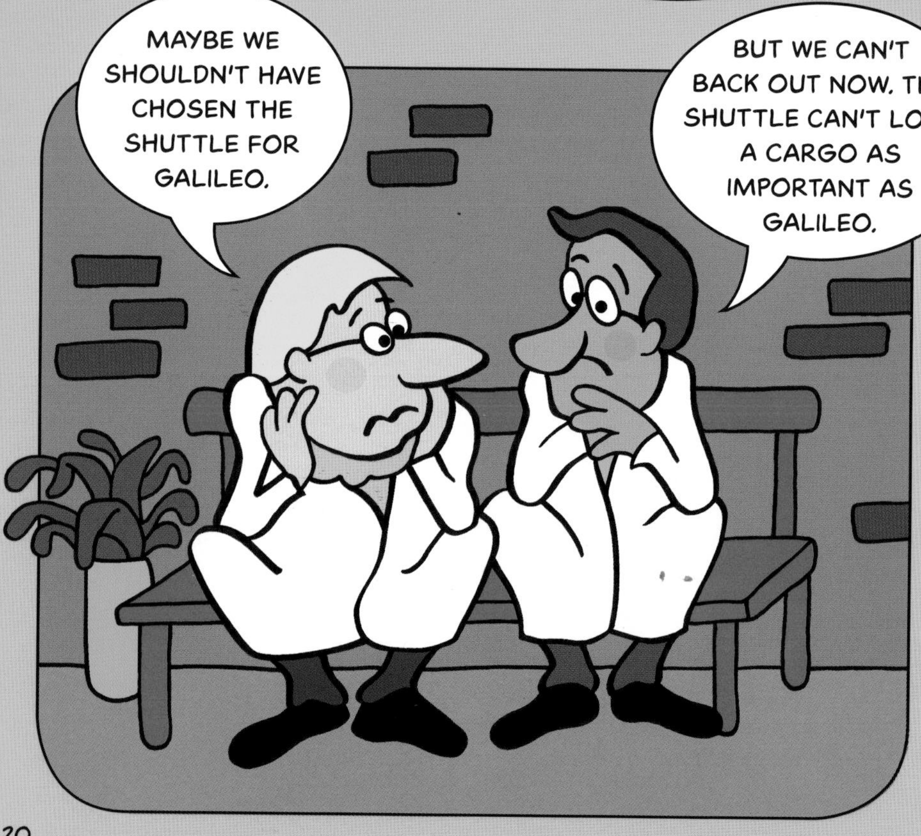
MAYBE WE SHOULDN'T HAVE CHOSEN THE SHUTTLE FOR GALILEO.
BUT WE CAN'T BACK OUT NOW. THE SHUTTLE CAN'T LOSE A CARGO AS IMPORTANT AS GALILEO.

AS THE GALILEO TEAM WAITED FOR THEIR SHUTTLE RIDE, THEY WORKED ON WHAT THEY CALLED THE "UPPER STAGE."

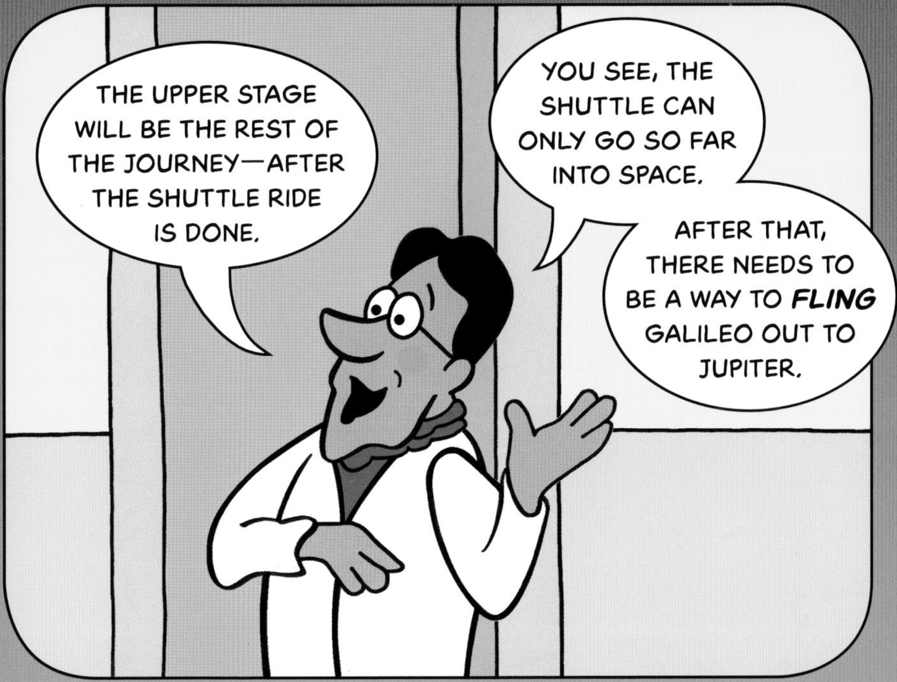
THE UPPER STAGE WILL BE THE REST OF THE JOURNEY—AFTER THE SHUTTLE RIDE IS DONE.
YOU SEE, THE SHUTTLE CAN ONLY GO SO FAR INTO SPACE.
AFTER THAT, THERE NEEDS TO BE A WAY TO **FLING** GALILEO OUT TO JUPITER.

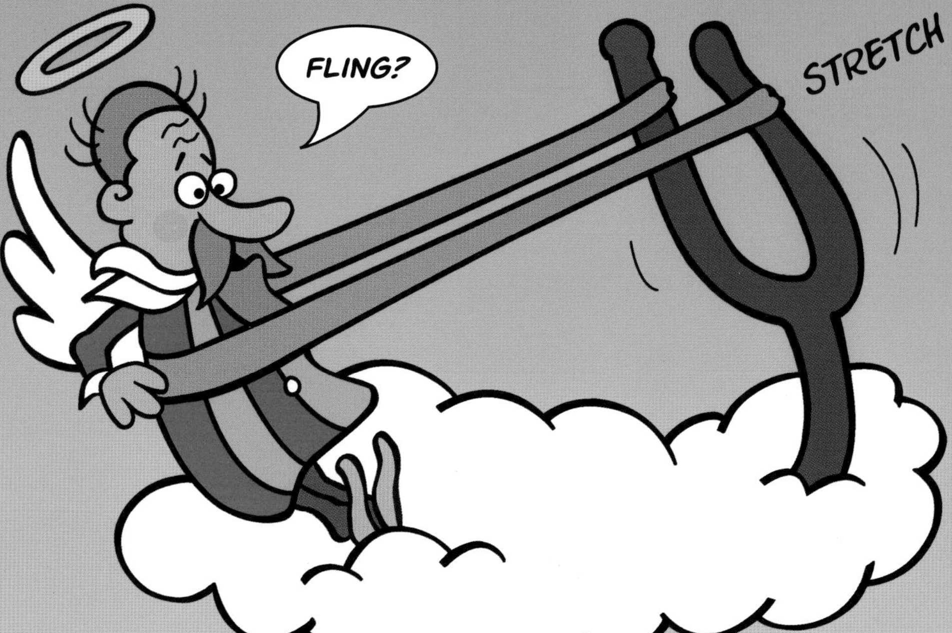
FLING?
STRETCH

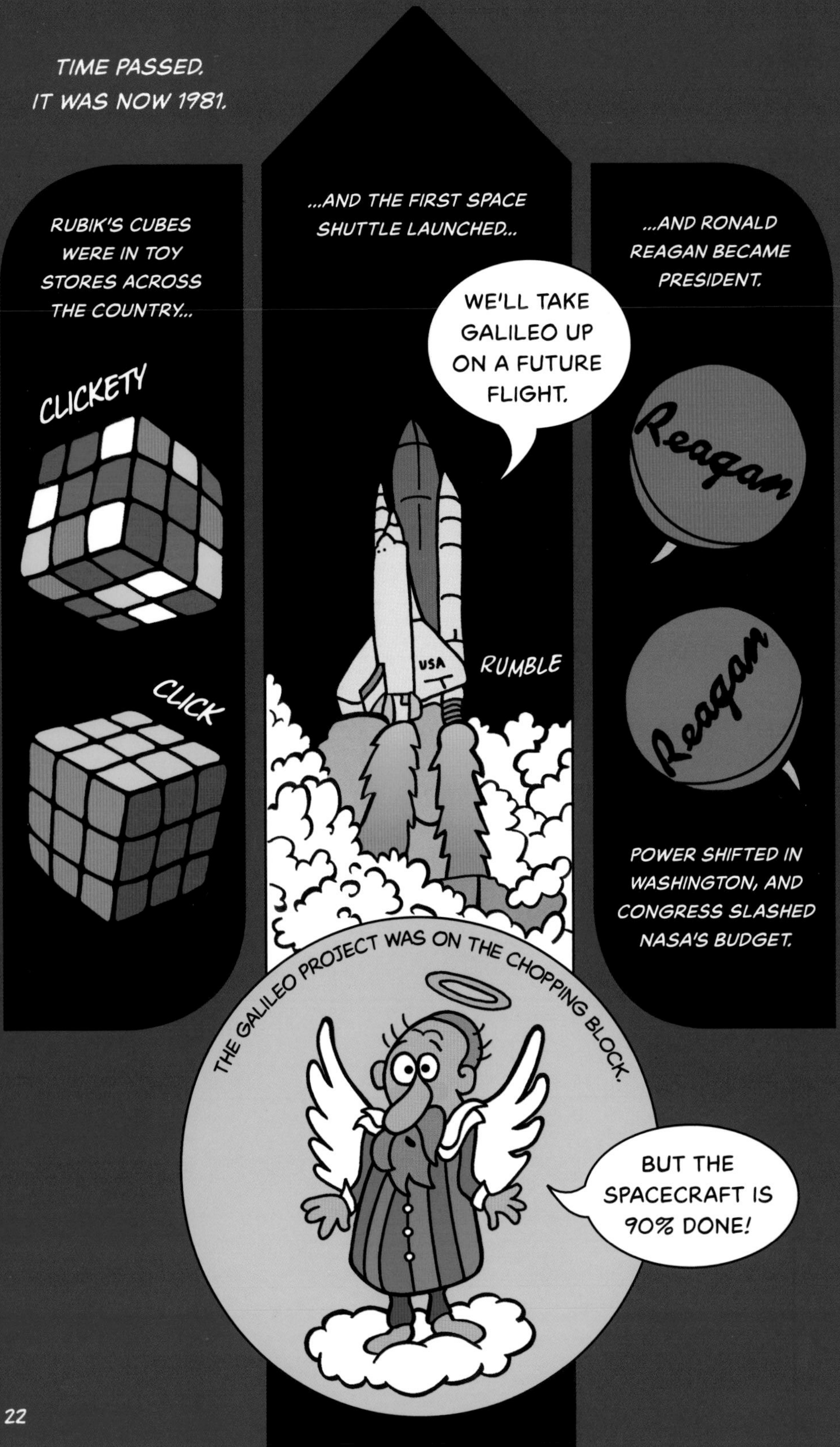
TIME PASSED. IT WAS NOW 1981.
RUBIK'S CUBES WERE IN TOY STORES ACROSS THE COUNTRY...
CLICKETY
CLICK
...AND THE FIRST SPACE SHUTTLE LAUNCHED...
WE'LL TAKE GALILEO UP ON A FUTURE FLIGHT.
USA
RUMBLE
...AND RONALD REAGAN BECAME PRESIDENT.
Reagan
Reagan
POWER SHIFTED IN WASHINGTON, AND CONGRESS SLASHED NASA'S BUDGET.
THE GALILEO PROJECT WAS ON THE CHOPPING BLOCK.
BUT THE SPACECRAFT IS 90% DONE!

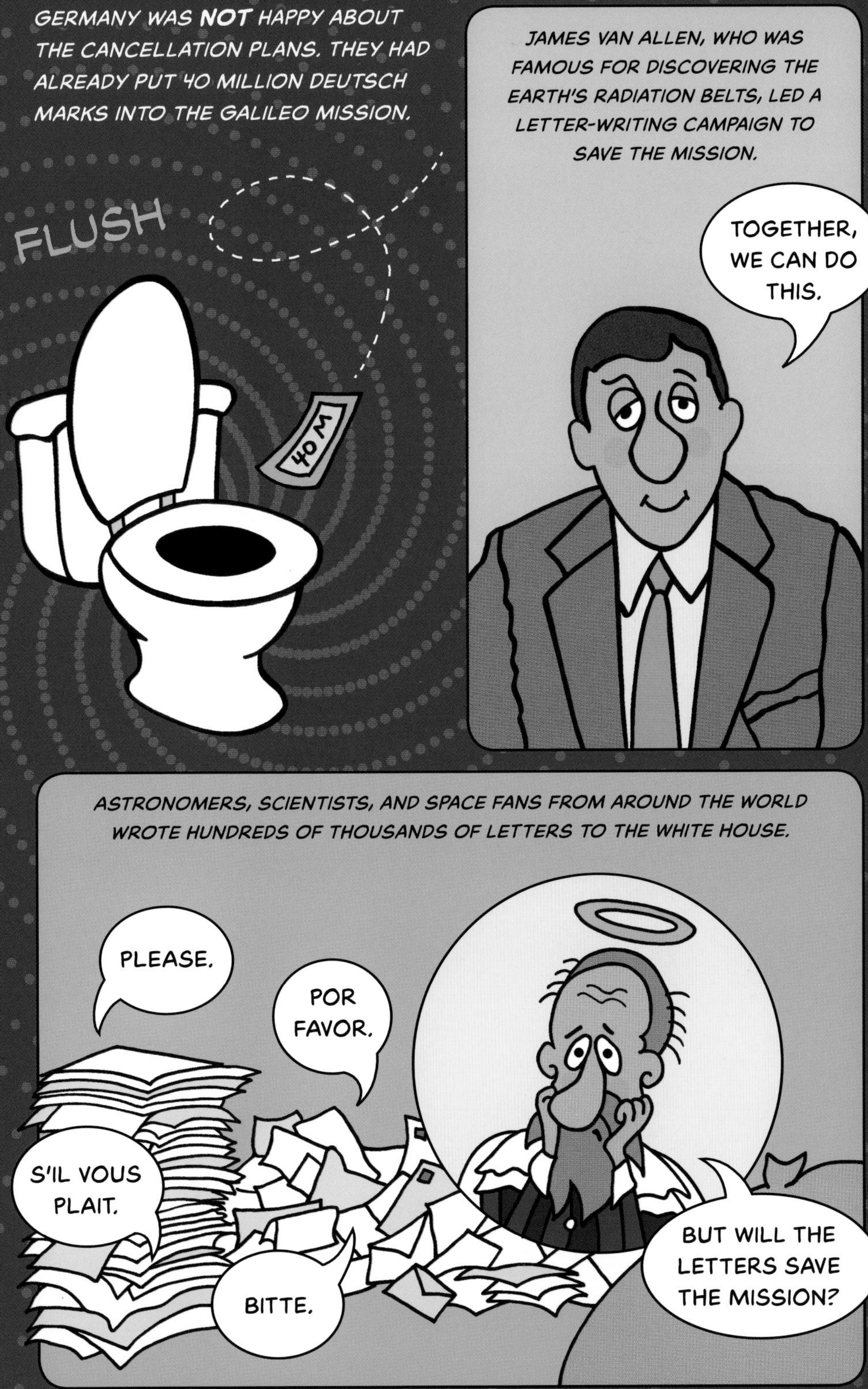
GERMANY WAS **NOT** HAPPY ABOUT THE CANCELLATION PLANS. THEY HAD ALREADY PUT 40 MILLION DEUTSCH MARKS INTO THE GALILEO MISSION.
FLUSH
40 M
JAMES VAN ALLEN, WHO WAS FAMOUS FOR DISCOVERING THE EARTH'S RADIATION BELTS, LED A LETTER-WRITING CAMPAIGN TO SAVE THE MISSION.
TOGETHER, WE CAN DO THIS.
ASTRONOMERS, SCIENTISTS, AND SPACE FANS FROM AROUND THE WORLD WROTE HUNDREDS OF THOUSANDS OF LETTERS TO THE WHITE HOUSE.
PLEASE.
POR FAVOR.
S'IL VOUS PLAIT.
BITTE.
BUT WILL THE LETTERS SAVE THE MISSION?

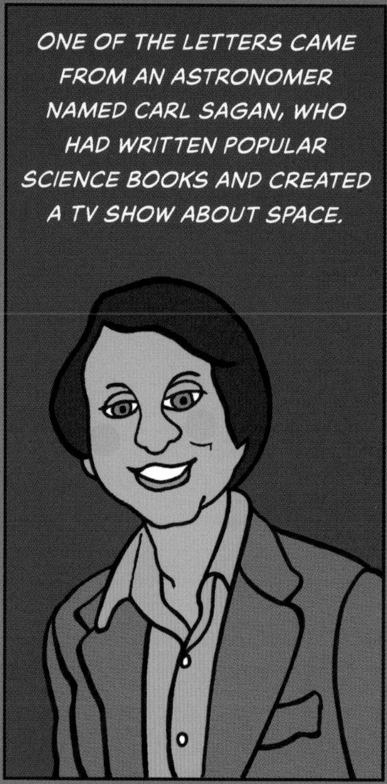
ONE OF THE LETTERS CAME FROM AN ASTRONOMER NAMED CARL SAGAN, WHO HAD WRITTEN POPULAR SCIENCE BOOKS AND CREATED A TV SHOW ABOUT SPACE.

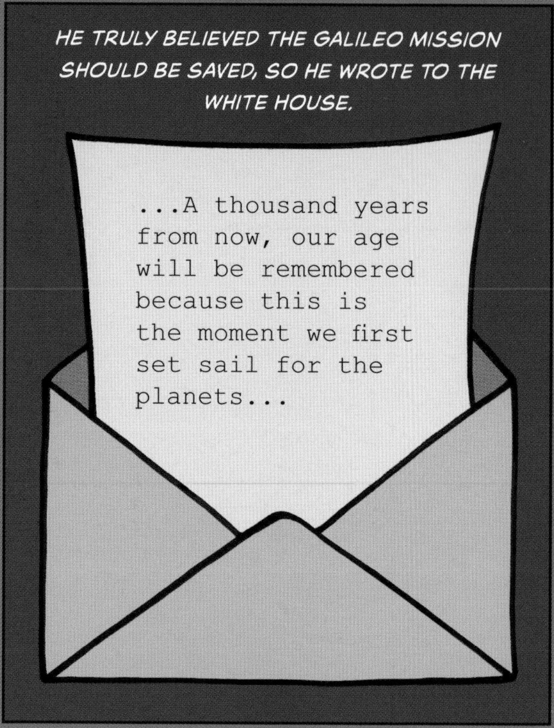
HE TRULY BELIEVED THE GALILEO MISSION SHOULD BE SAVED, SO HE WROTE TO THE WHITE HOUSE.
...A thousand years from now, our age will be remembered because this is the moment we first set sail for the planets...

THE MANY LETTERS DID THE TRICK, AND IN 1983, THE MISSION WAS SAVED FROM CANCELLATION.

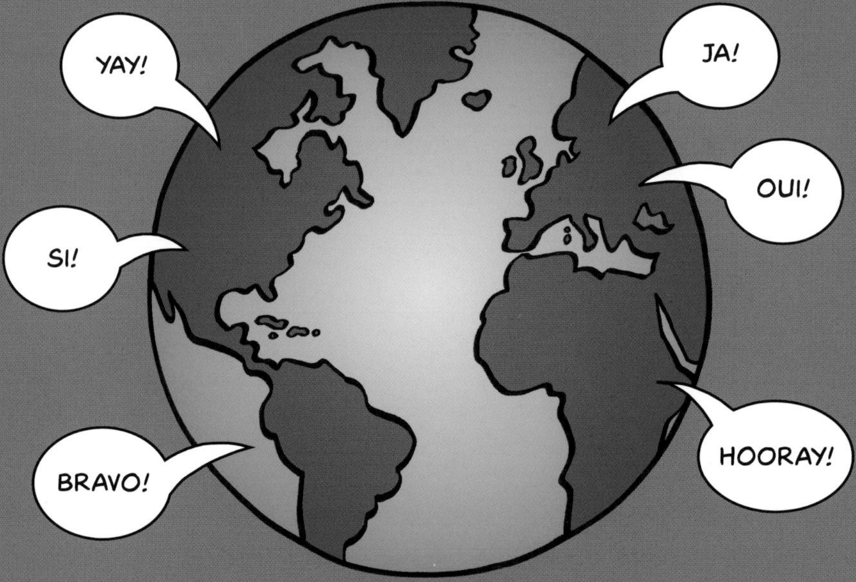
YAY!
JA!
OUI!
SI!
HOORAY!
BRAVO!

NASA **NOW** HOPED IT WOULD BE ABLE TO LAUNCH GALILEO IN 1986.

DURING THE NEXT THREE YEARS...

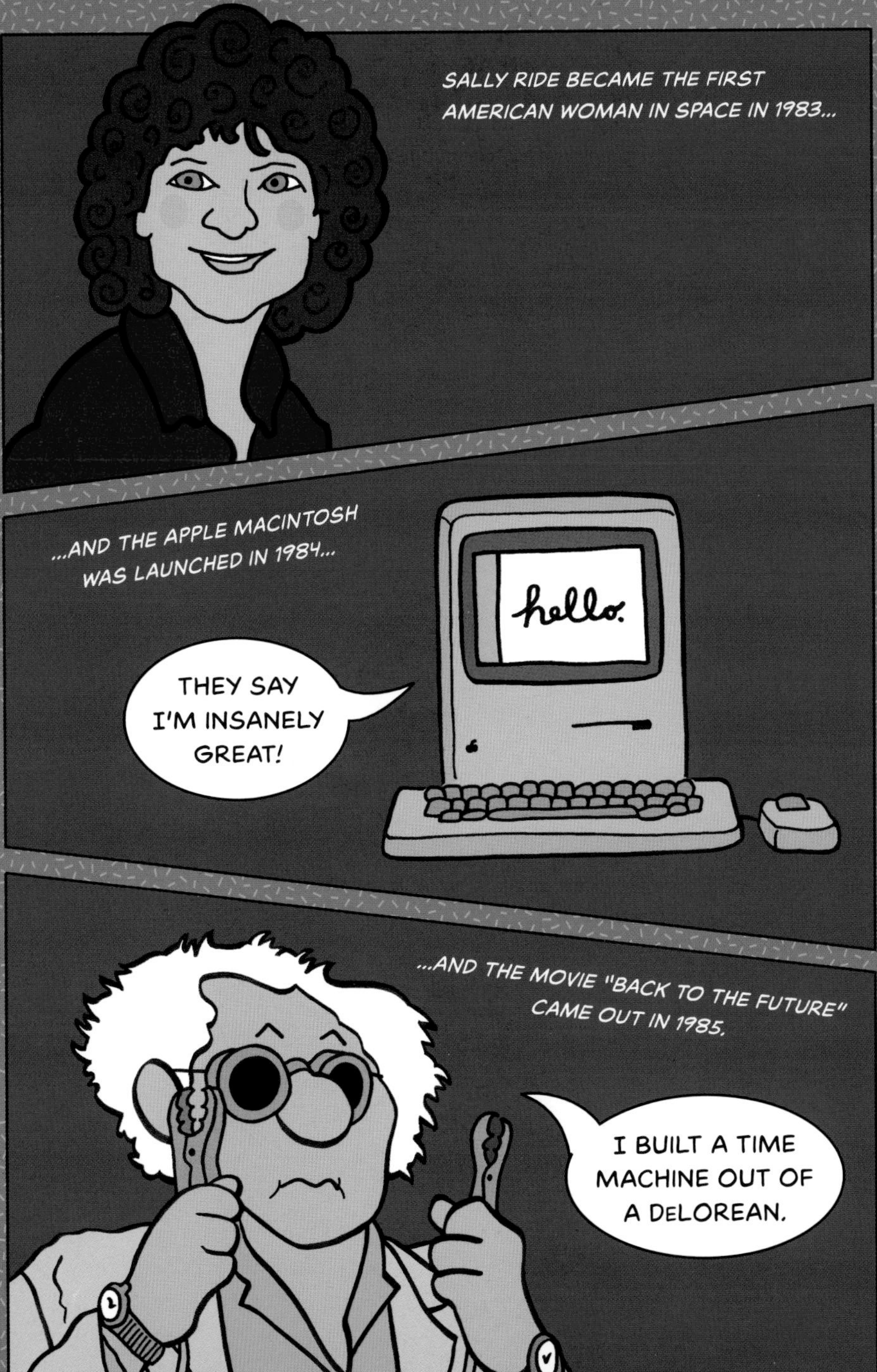
SALLY RIDE BECAME THE FIRST AMERICAN WOMAN IN SPACE IN 1983...
...AND THE APPLE MACINTOSH WAS LAUNCHED IN 1984...
hello.
THEY SAY I'M INSANELY GREAT!
...AND THE MOVIE "BACK TO THE FUTURE" CAME OUT IN 1985.
I BUILT A TIME MACHINE OUT OF A DeLOREAN.

GALILEO'S LAUNCH DATE WAS GETTING CLOSER!

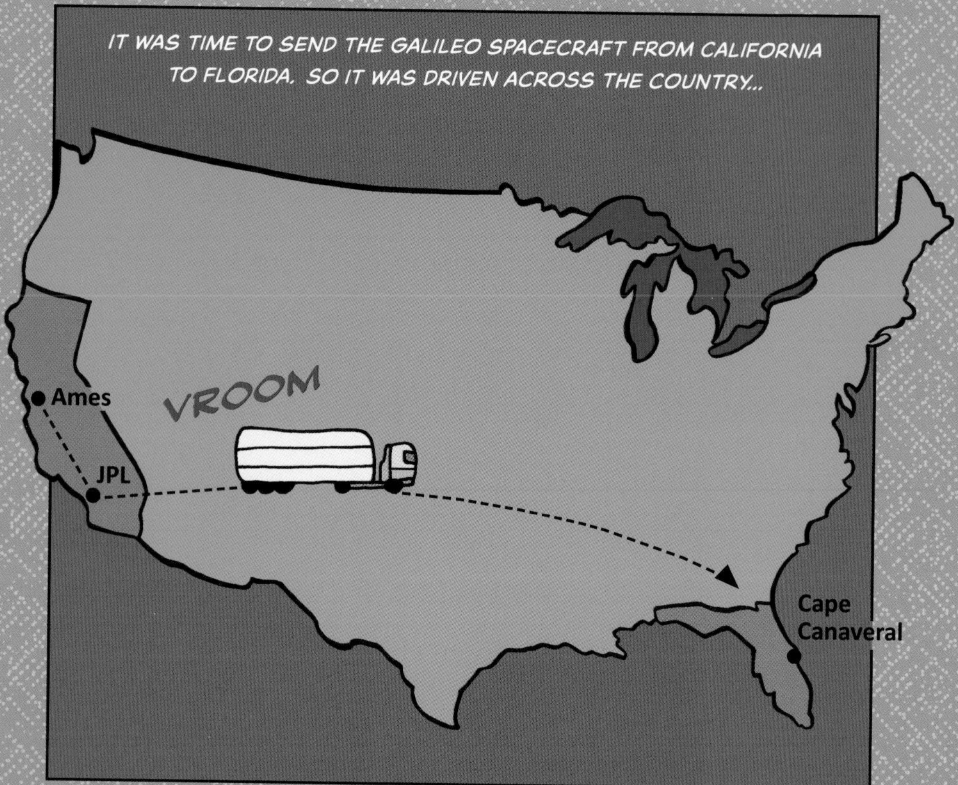
IT WAS TIME TO SEND THE GALILEO SPACECRAFT FROM CALIFORNIA TO FLORIDA. SO IT WAS DRIVEN ACROSS THE COUNTRY...
Ames
VROOM
JPL
Cape Canaveral

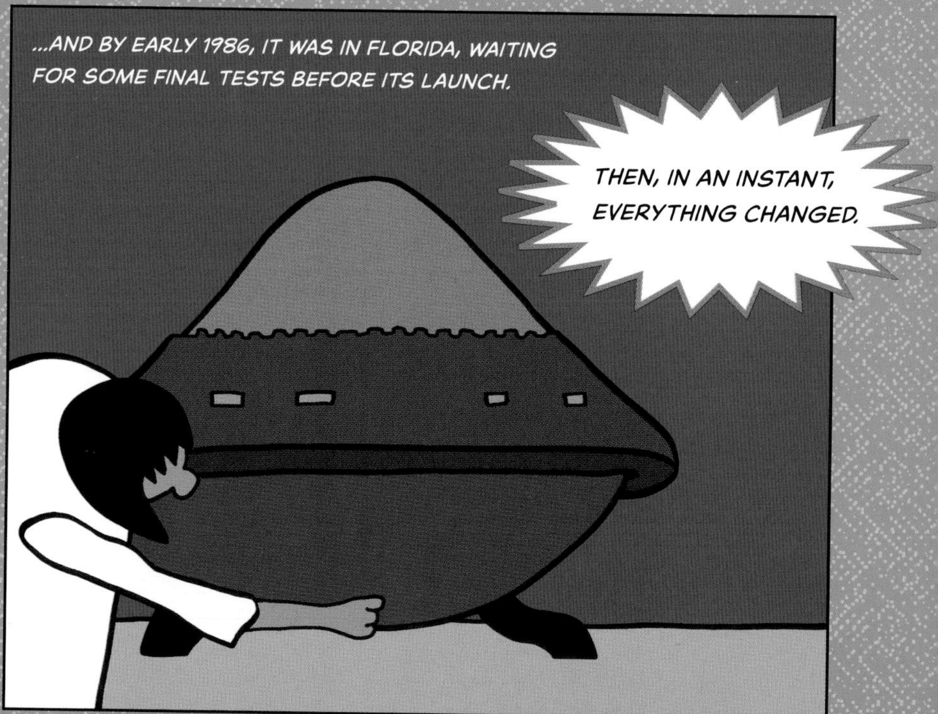
...AND BY EARLY 1986, IT WAS IN FLORIDA, WAITING FOR SOME FINAL TESTS BEFORE ITS LAUNCH.
THEN, IN AN INSTANT, EVERYTHING CHANGED.

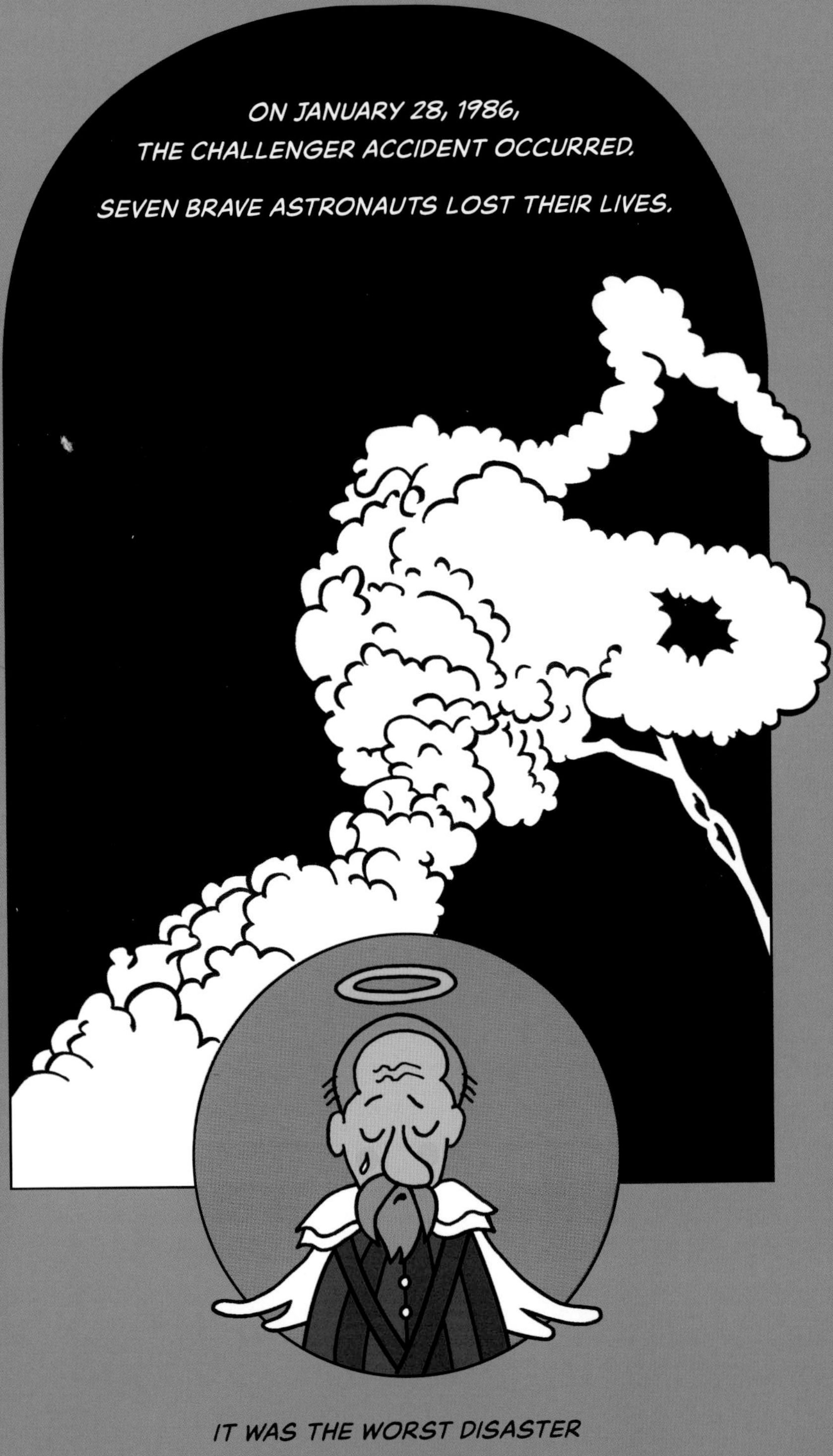
ON JANUARY 28, 1986,
THE CHALLENGER ACCIDENT OCCURRED.
SEVEN BRAVE ASTRONAUTS LOST THEIR LIVES.
IT WAS THE WORST DISASTER
THAT NASA HAD EVER HAD.

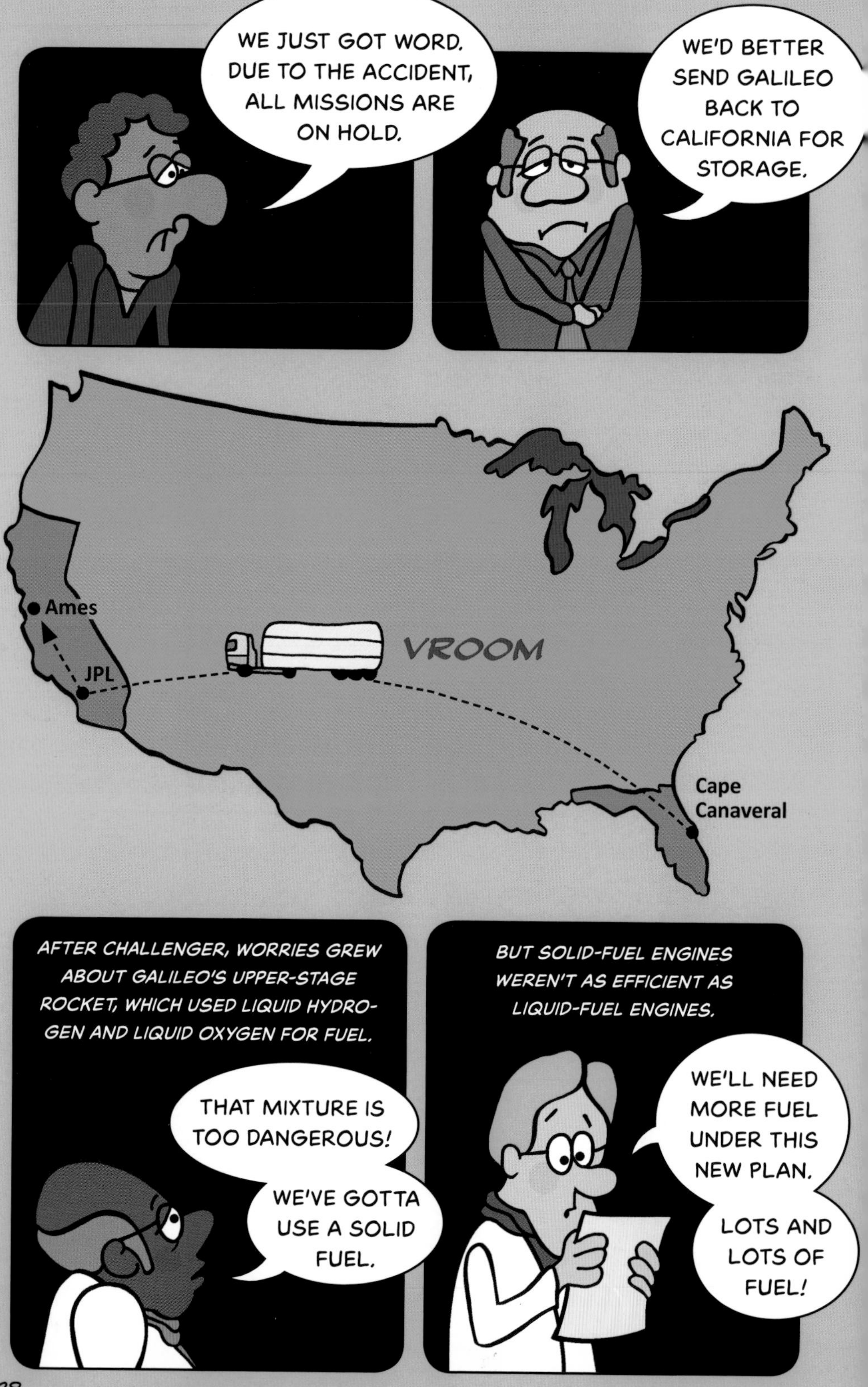
WE JUST GOT WORD. DUE TO THE ACCIDENT, ALL MISSIONS ARE ON HOLD.
WE'D BETTER SEND GALILEO BACK TO CALIFORNIA FOR STORAGE.
Ames
JPL
VROOM
Cape Canaveral
AFTER CHALLENGER, WORRIES GREW ABOUT GALILEO'S UPPER-STAGE ROCKET, WHICH USED LIQUID HYDROGEN AND LIQUID OXYGEN FOR FUEL.
THAT MIXTURE IS TOO DANGEROUS!
WE'VE GOTTA USE A SOLID FUEL.
BUT SOLID-FUEL ENGINES WEREN'T AS EFFICIENT AS LIQUID-FUEL ENGINES.
WE'LL NEED MORE FUEL UNDER THIS NEW PLAN.
LOTS AND LOTS OF FUEL!

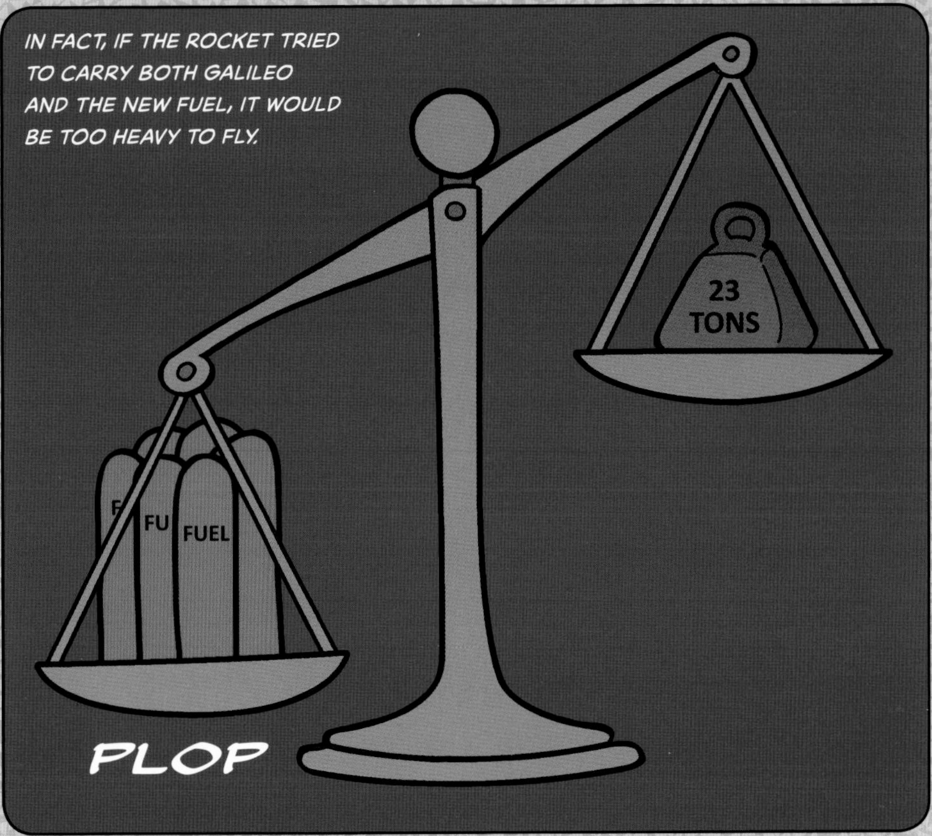
IN FACT, IF THE ROCKET TRIED TO CARRY BOTH GALILEO AND THE NEW FUEL, IT WOULD BE TOO HEAVY TO FLY.
23 TONS
FUEL
PLOP

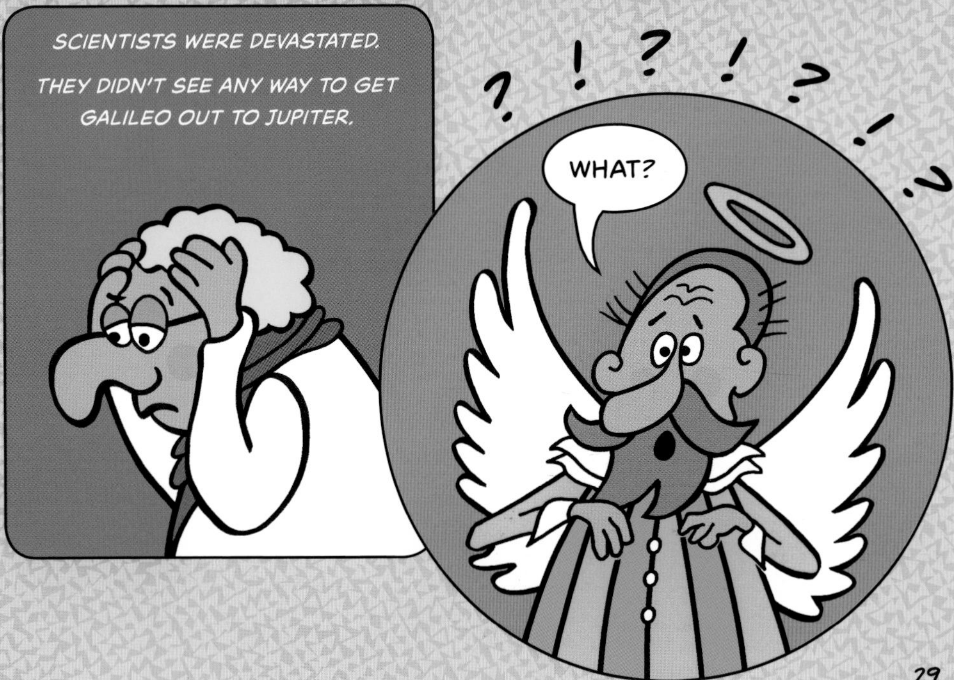
SCIENTISTS WERE DEVASTATED.
THEY DIDN'T SEE ANY WAY TO GET GALILEO OUT TO JUPITER.
WHAT?

AFTER ALL THE YEARS SPENT ON THE PROJECT,
IT LOOKED LIKE THE NEW FUEL RULES WOULD END THE MISSION.

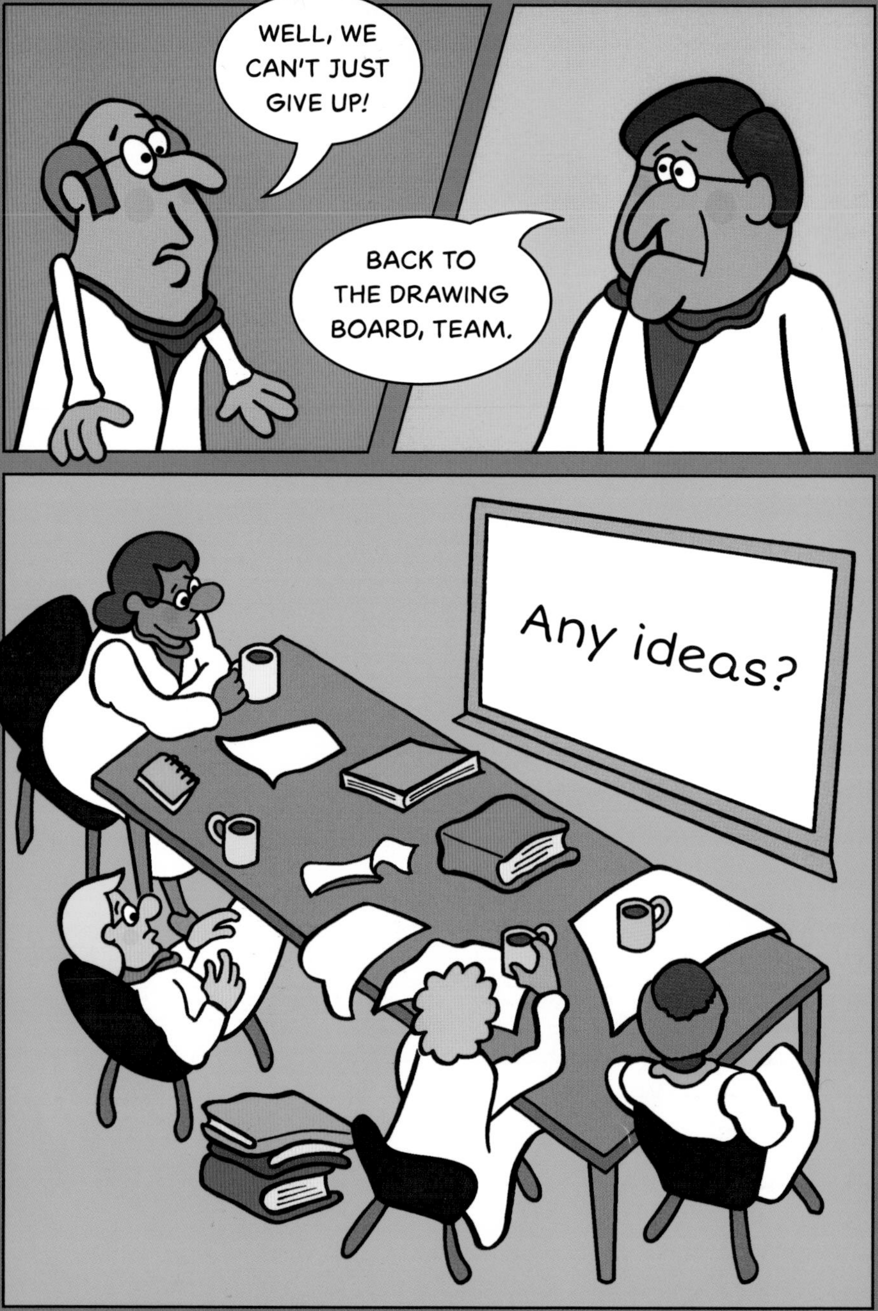
WELL, WE CAN'T JUST GIVE UP!
BACK TO THE DRAWING BOARD, TEAM.
Any ideas?

AFTER MANY MEETINGS, THEY HATCHED A PLAN.
*THEY WOULD USE THE FORCE OF **GRAVITY** TO GET GALILEO TO JUPITER.*

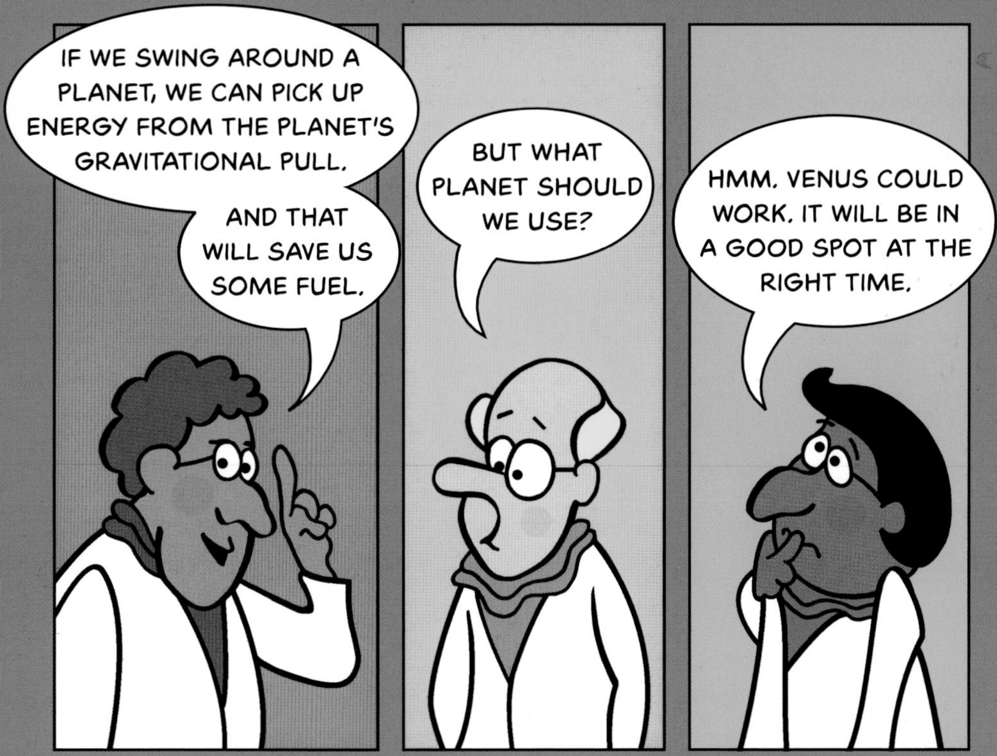
IF WE SWING AROUND A PLANET, WE CAN PICK UP ENERGY FROM THE PLANET'S GRAVITATIONAL PULL.
AND THAT WILL SAVE US SOME FUEL.
BUT WHAT PLANET SHOULD WE USE?
HMM. VENUS COULD WORK. IT WILL BE IN A GOOD SPOT AT THE RIGHT TIME.

SO THEY DECIDED TO GIVE GALILEO ***THREE*** *GRAVITY ASSISTS.*
IT WOULD SWING AROUND VENUS, AND THEN TWICE AROUND EARTH.

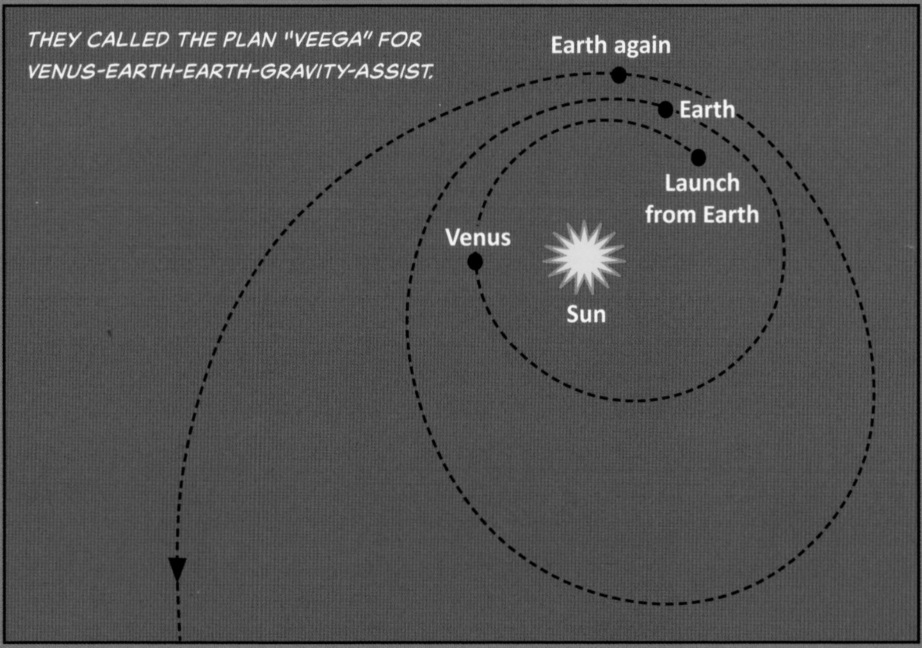
THEY CALLED THE PLAN "VEEGA" FOR VENUS-EARTH-EARTH-GRAVITY-ASSIST.
Earth again
Earth
Launch from Earth
Venus
Sun

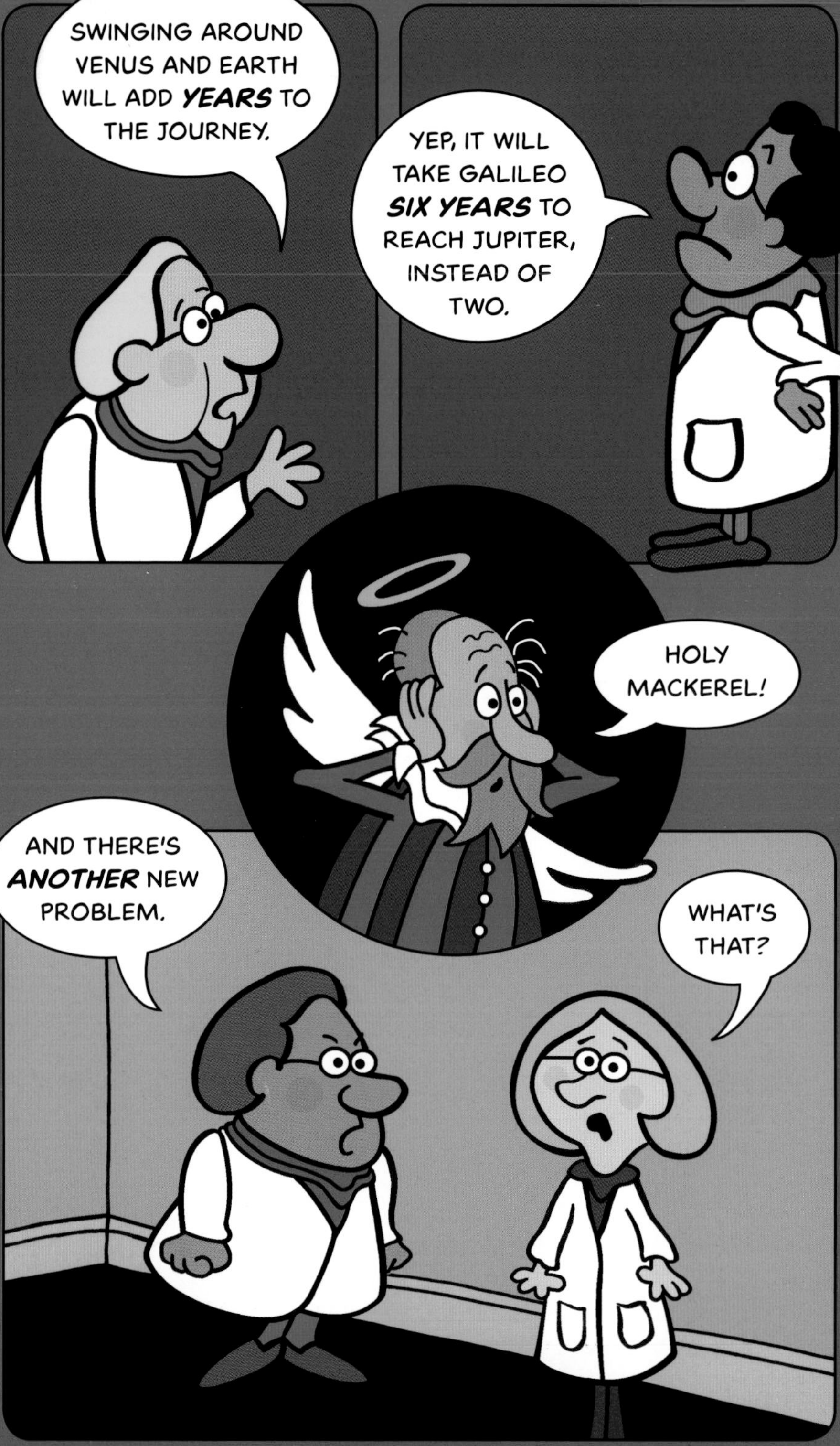
SWINGING AROUND VENUS AND EARTH WILL ADD ***YEARS*** TO THE JOURNEY.
YEP, IT WILL TAKE GALILEO ***SIX YEARS*** TO REACH JUPITER, INSTEAD OF TWO.
HOLY MACKEREL!
AND THERE'S ***ANOTHER*** NEW PROBLEM.
WHAT'S THAT?

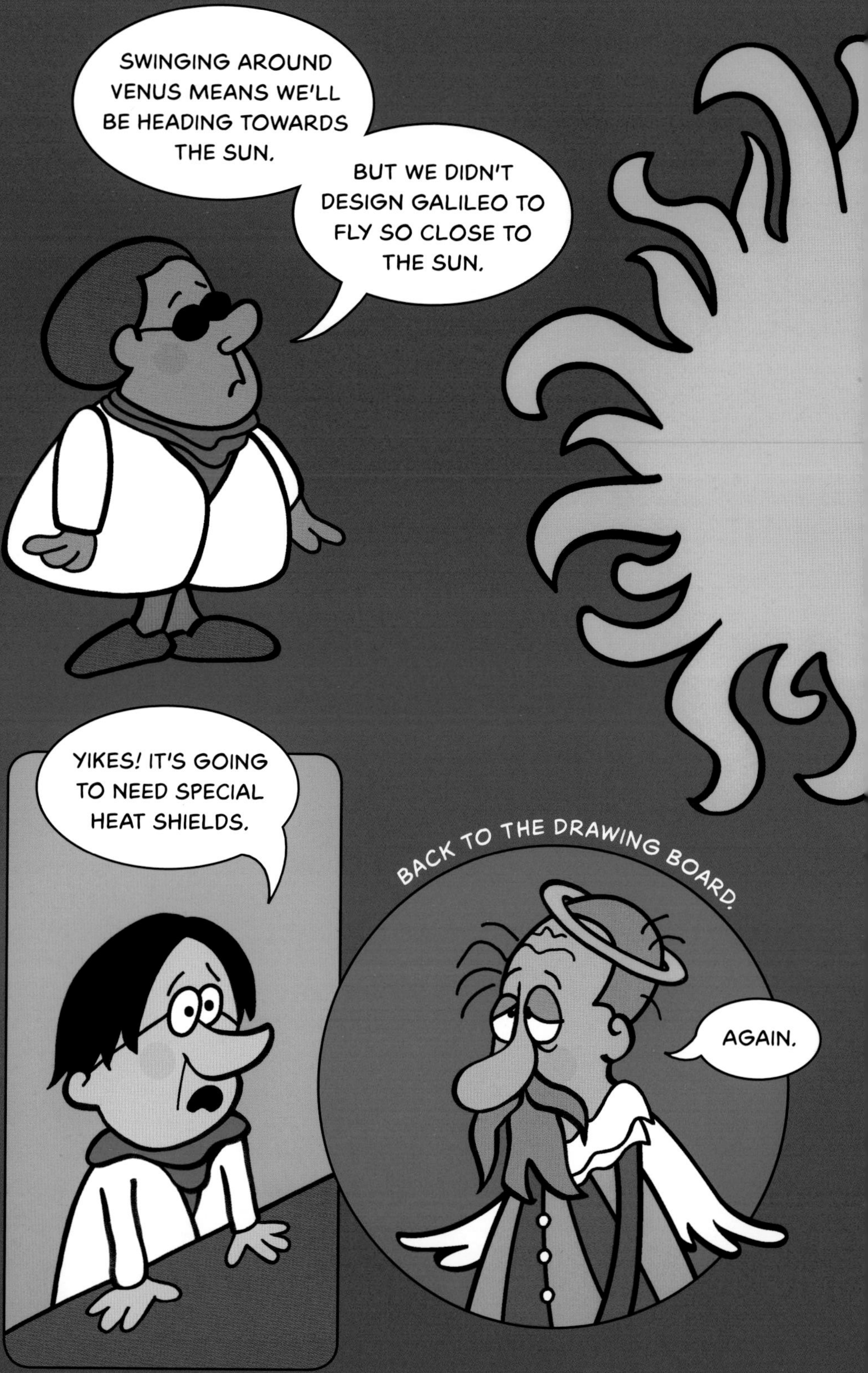
SWINGING AROUND VENUS MEANS WE'LL BE HEADING TOWARDS THE SUN.
BUT WE DIDN'T DESIGN GALILEO TO FLY SO CLOSE TO THE SUN.
YIKES! IT'S GOING TO NEED SPECIAL HEAT SHIELDS.
BACK TO THE DRAWING BOARD.
AGAIN.

IN EARLY 1987, GALILEO WAS BACK IN CALIFORNIA -- IN ABOUT A MILLION PIECES.

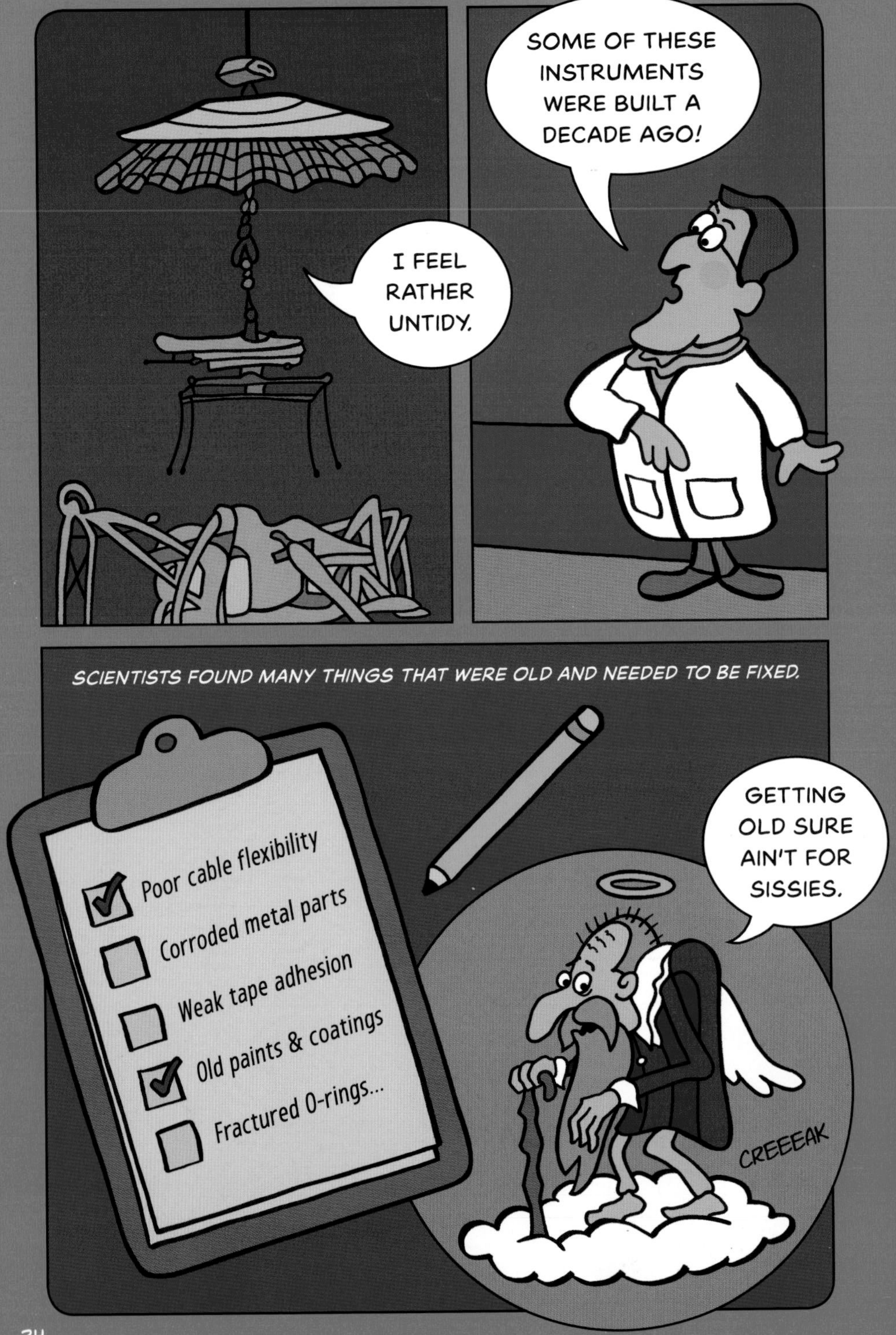
SOME OF THESE INSTRUMENTS WERE BUILT A DECADE AGO!
I FEEL RATHER UNTIDY.
SCIENTISTS FOUND MANY THINGS THAT WERE OLD AND NEEDED TO BE FIXED.
Poor cable flexibility
Corroded metal parts
Weak tape adhesion
Old paints & coatings
Fractured O-rings...
GETTING OLD SURE AIN'T FOR SISSIES.
CREEEAK

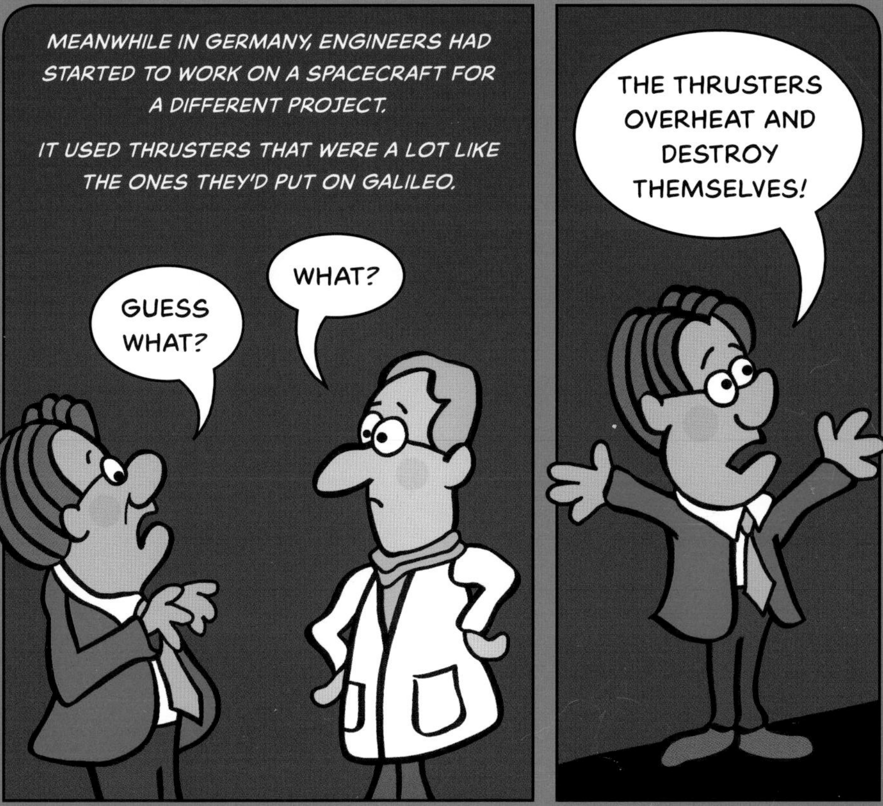
MEANWHILE IN GERMANY, ENGINEERS HAD STARTED TO WORK ON A SPACECRAFT FOR A DIFFERENT PROJECT.
IT USED THRUSTERS THAT WERE A LOT LIKE THE ONES THEY'D PUT ON GALILEO.
GUESS WHAT?
WHAT?
THE THRUSTERS OVERHEAT AND DESTROY THEMSELVES!

THIS WAS A **HUGE** WORRY BECAUSE GALILEO WOULD NEED GOOD THRUSTERS SO NASA COULD EASE IT ONTO THE RIGHT PATHS FOR ITS JOURNEY.

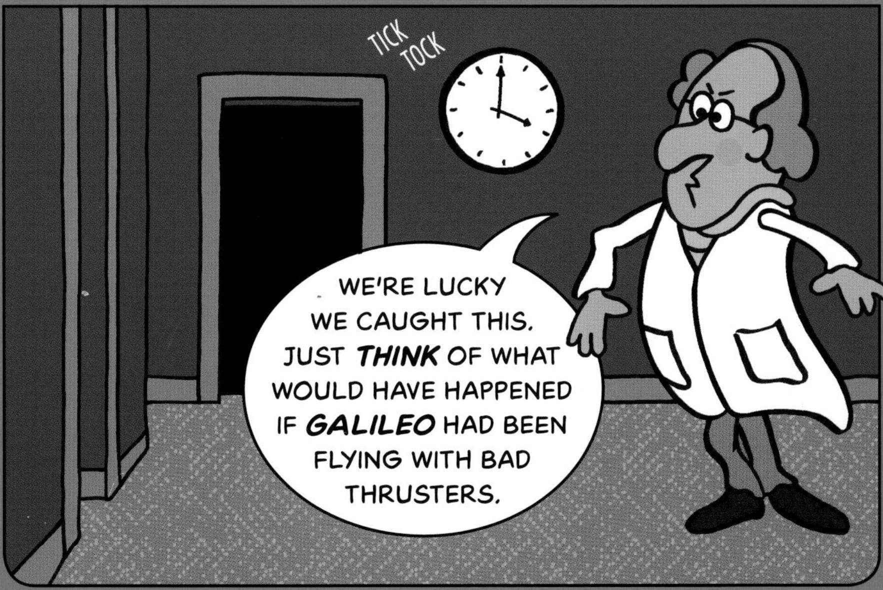
TICK TOCK
WE'RE LUCKY WE CAUGHT THIS. JUST **THINK** OF WHAT WOULD HAVE HAPPENED IF ***GALILEO*** HAD BEEN FLYING WITH BAD THRUSTERS.

JPL RECEIVED NEW THRUSTERS FROM GERMANY IN EARLY 1989.

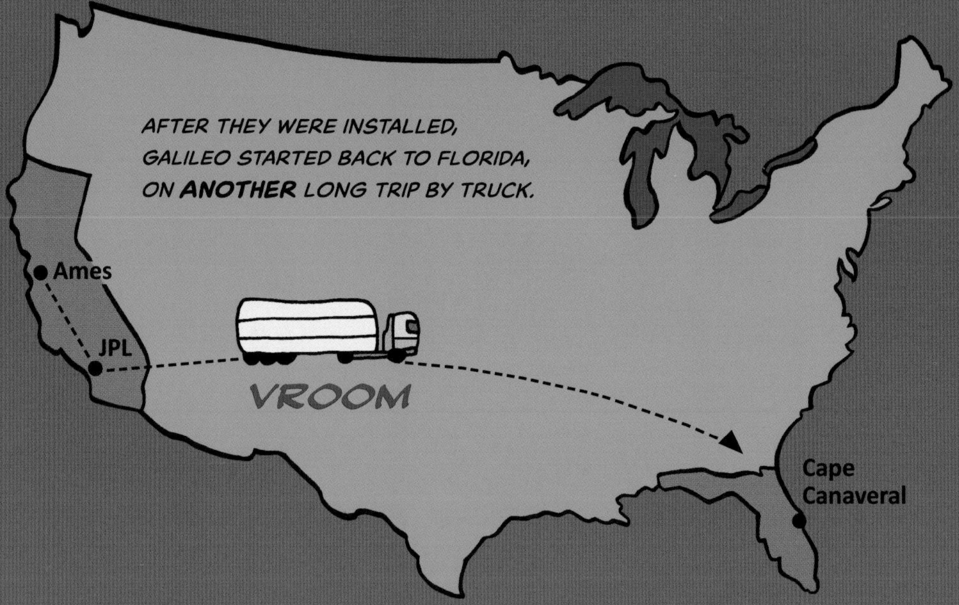

AFTER THEY WERE INSTALLED, GALILEO STARTED BACK TO FLORIDA, ON **ANOTHER** LONG TRIP BY TRUCK.
Ames
JPL
VROOM
Cape Canaveral

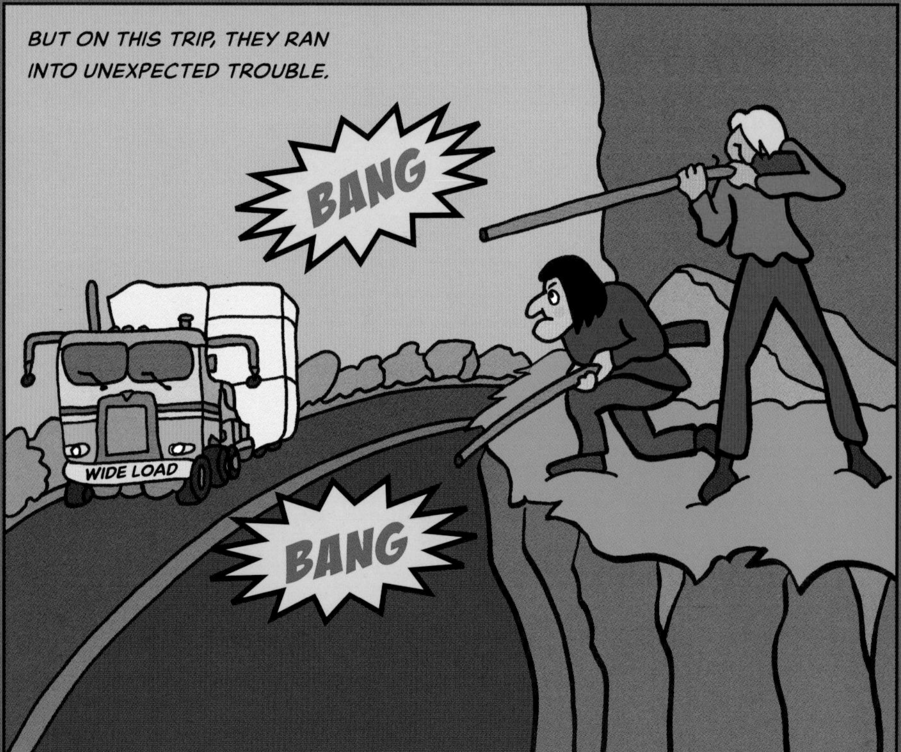

BUT ON THIS TRIP, THEY RAN INTO UNEXPECTED TROUBLE.
BANG
WIDE LOAD
BANG

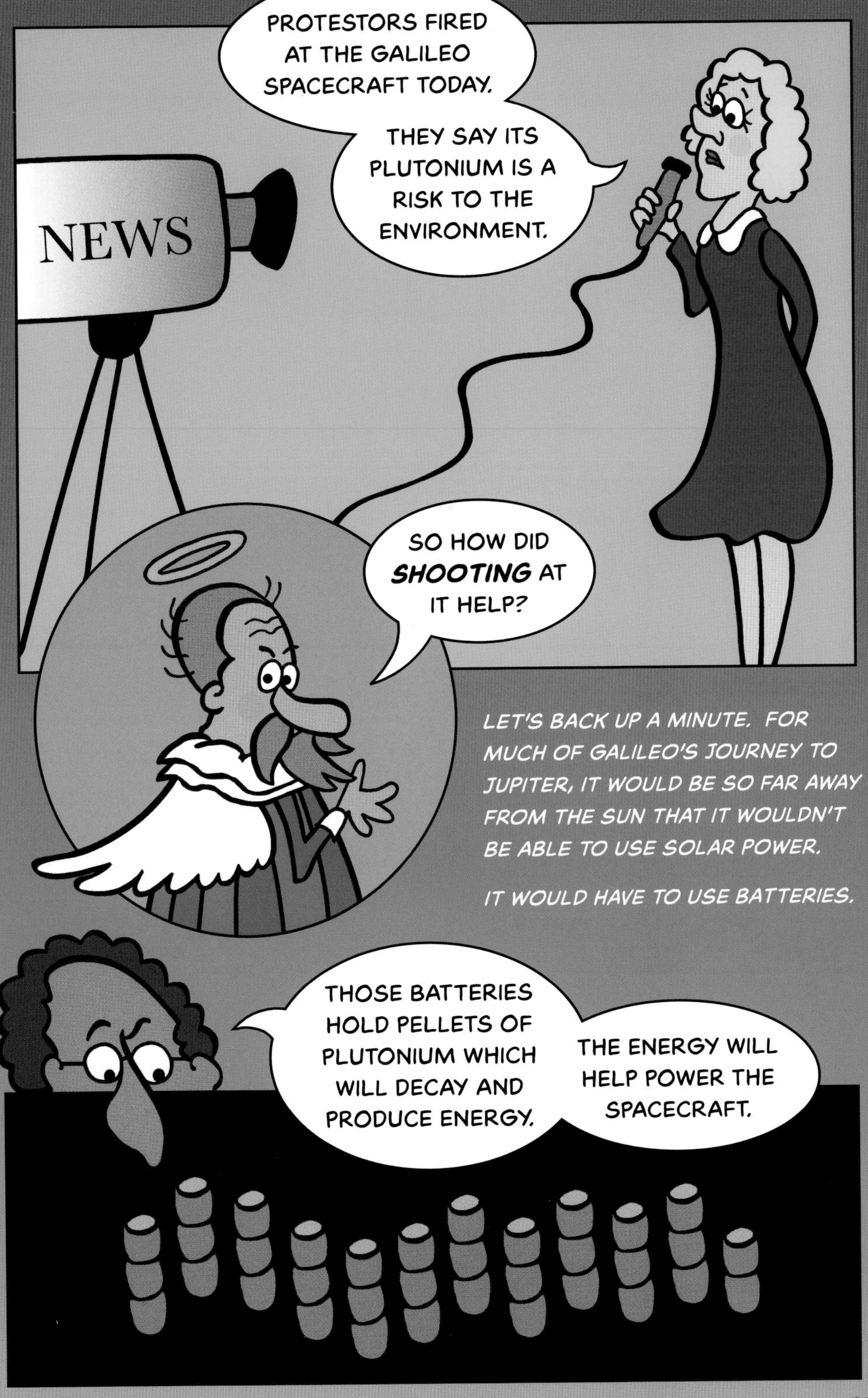
PROTESTORS FIRED AT THE GALILEO SPACECRAFT TODAY.
THEY SAY ITS PLUTONIUM IS A RISK TO THE ENVIRONMENT.
NEWS
SO HOW DID ***SHOOTING*** AT IT HELP?
LET'S BACK UP A MINUTE. FOR MUCH OF GALILEO'S JOURNEY TO JUPITER, IT WOULD BE SO FAR AWAY FROM THE SUN THAT IT WOULDN'T BE ABLE TO USE SOLAR POWER.
IT WOULD HAVE TO USE BATTERIES.
THOSE BATTERIES HOLD PELLETS OF PLUTONIUM WHICH WILL DECAY AND PRODUCE ENERGY.
THE ENERGY WILL HELP POWER THE SPACECRAFT.

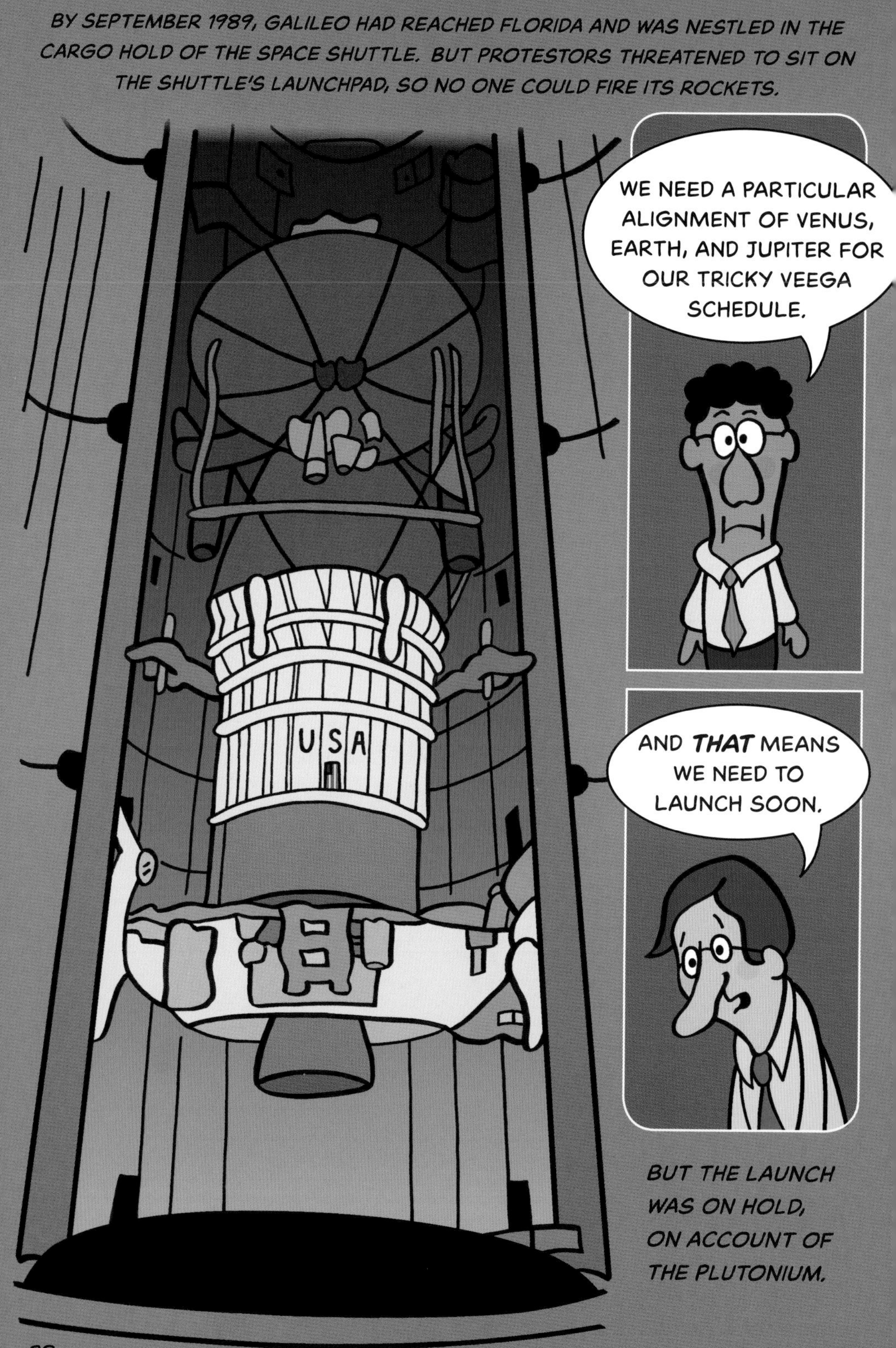
BY SEPTEMBER 1989, GALILEO HAD REACHED FLORIDA AND WAS NESTLED IN THE CARGO HOLD OF THE SPACE SHUTTLE. BUT PROTESTORS THREATENED TO SIT ON THE SHUTTLE'S LAUNCHPAD, SO NO ONE COULD FIRE ITS ROCKETS.
WE NEED A PARTICULAR ALIGNMENT OF VENUS, EARTH, AND JUPITER FOR OUR TRICKY VEEGA SCHEDULE.
USA
AND **THAT** MEANS WE NEED TO LAUNCH SOON.
BUT THE LAUNCH WAS ON HOLD, ON ACCOUNT OF THE PLUTONIUM.

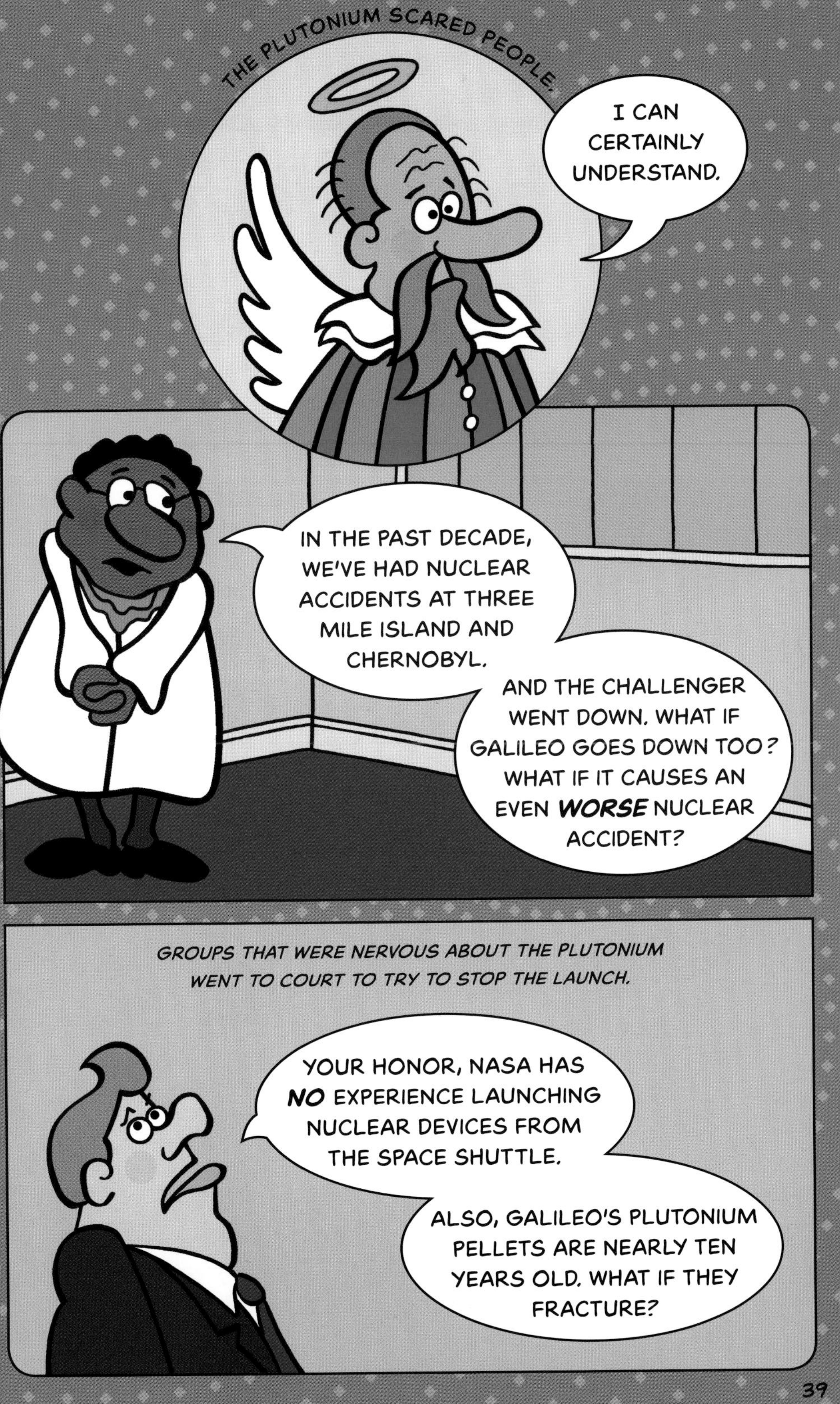

THE PLUTONIUM SCARED PEOPLE.
I CAN CERTAINLY UNDERSTAND.
IN THE PAST DECADE, WE'VE HAD NUCLEAR ACCIDENTS AT THREE MILE ISLAND AND CHERNOBYL.
AND THE CHALLENGER WENT DOWN. WHAT IF GALILEO GOES DOWN TOO? WHAT IF IT CAUSES AN EVEN WORSE NUCLEAR ACCIDENT?
GROUPS THAT WERE NERVOUS ABOUT THE PLUTONIUM WENT TO COURT TO TRY TO STOP THE LAUNCH.
YOUR HONOR, NASA HAS NO EXPERIENCE LAUNCHING NUCLEAR DEVICES FROM THE SPACE SHUTTLE.
ALSO, GALILEO'S PLUTONIUM PELLETS ARE NEARLY TEN YEARS OLD. WHAT IF THEY FRACTURE?

THE FAMOUS ASTRONOMER, CARL SAGAN, STOOD UP FOR GALILEO AGAIN. HE BELIEVED MUCH GOOD COULD COME FROM THE MISSION, AND THE CHANCE OF A PLUTONIUM ACCIDENT WAS SMALL. IN A NEWSPAPER ARTICLE, HE WROTE...

"There is nothing absurd about either side of this argument. But considering the possibility that many more lives might be saved because of Galileo's findings, my personal vote is to launch."

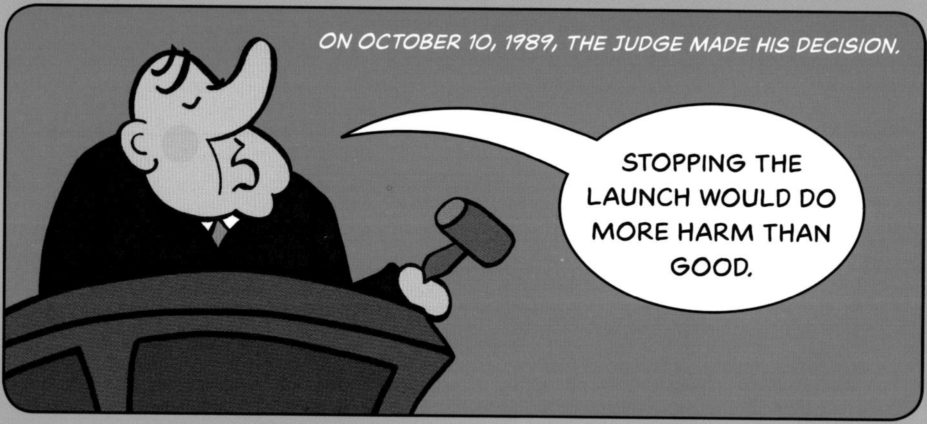

ON OCTOBER 10, 1989, THE JUDGE MADE HIS DECISION.
STOPPING THE LAUNCH WOULD DO MORE HARM THAN GOOD.

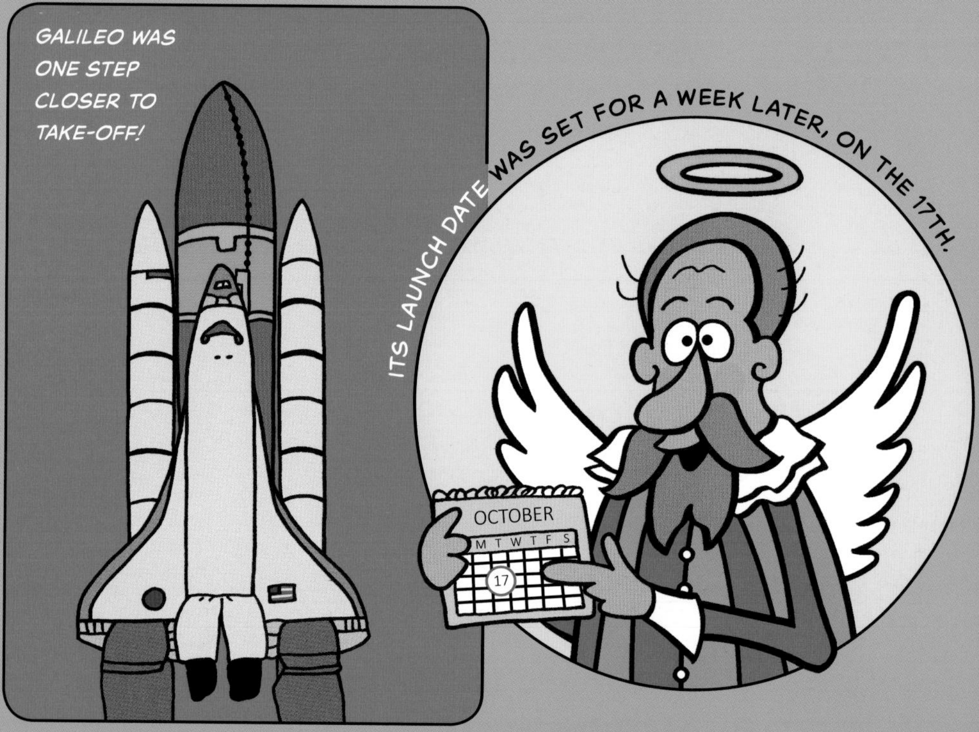

GALILEO WAS ONE STEP CLOSER TO TAKE-OFF!
ITS LAUNCH DATE WAS SET FOR A WEEK LATER, ON THE 17TH.
OCTOBER
M T W T F S
17

HOWEVER, ON OCTOBER 16TH, THE DAY BEFORE THE LAUNCH WAS SUPPOSED TO TAKE PLACE, NASA EMPLOYEES ARRIVED AT THEIR OFFICES TO A HUGE SURPRISE.

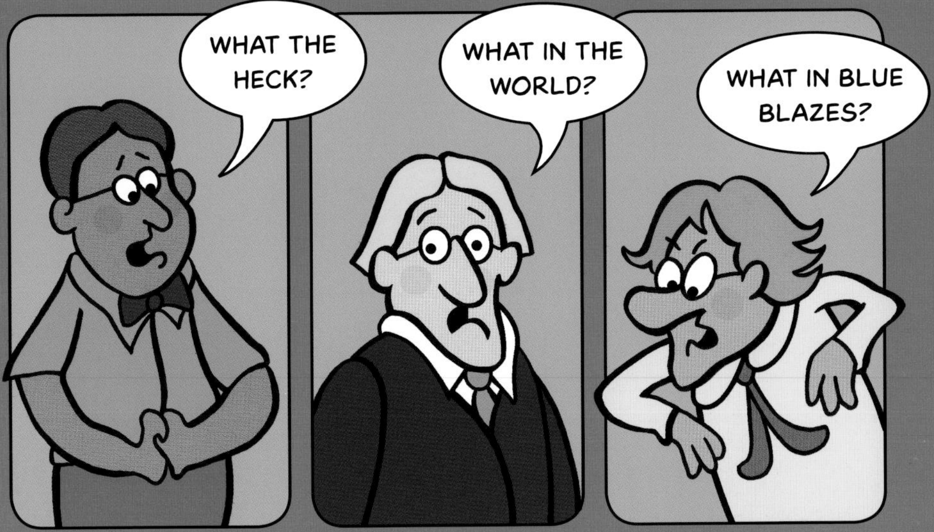
WHAT THE HECK?
WHAT IN THE WORLD?
WHAT IN BLUE BLAZES?

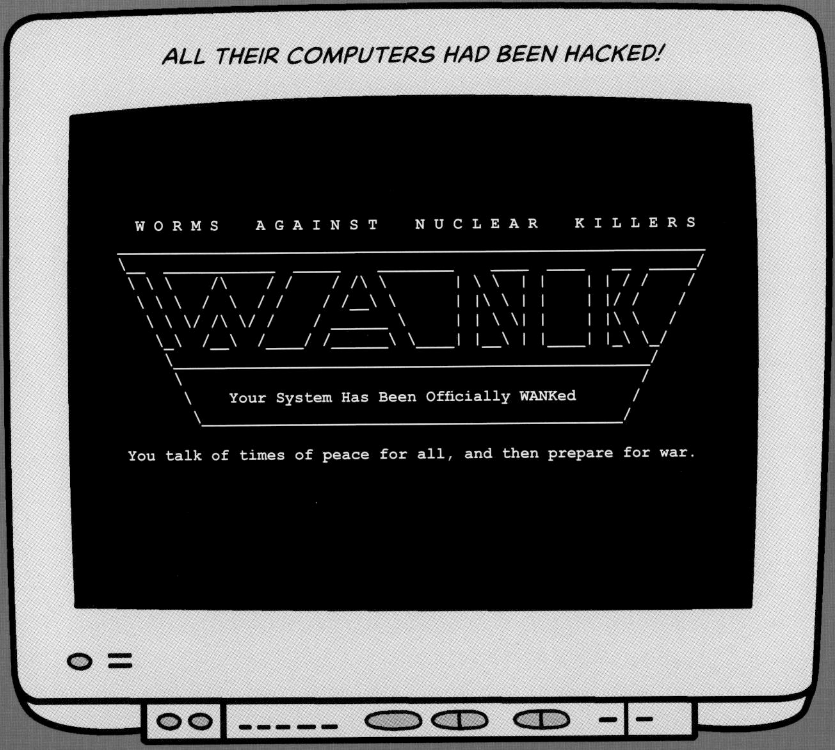
ALL THEIR COMPUTERS HAD BEEN HACKED!
WORMS AGAINST NUCLEAR KILLERS
WANK
Your System Has Been Officially WANKed
You talk of times of peace for all, and then prepare for war.

IT WAS A COMPUTER WORM, AND IT SEEMED TO BE DELETING ALL THEIR FILES. HAD NASA LOST CONTROL OF ITS COMPUTERS?

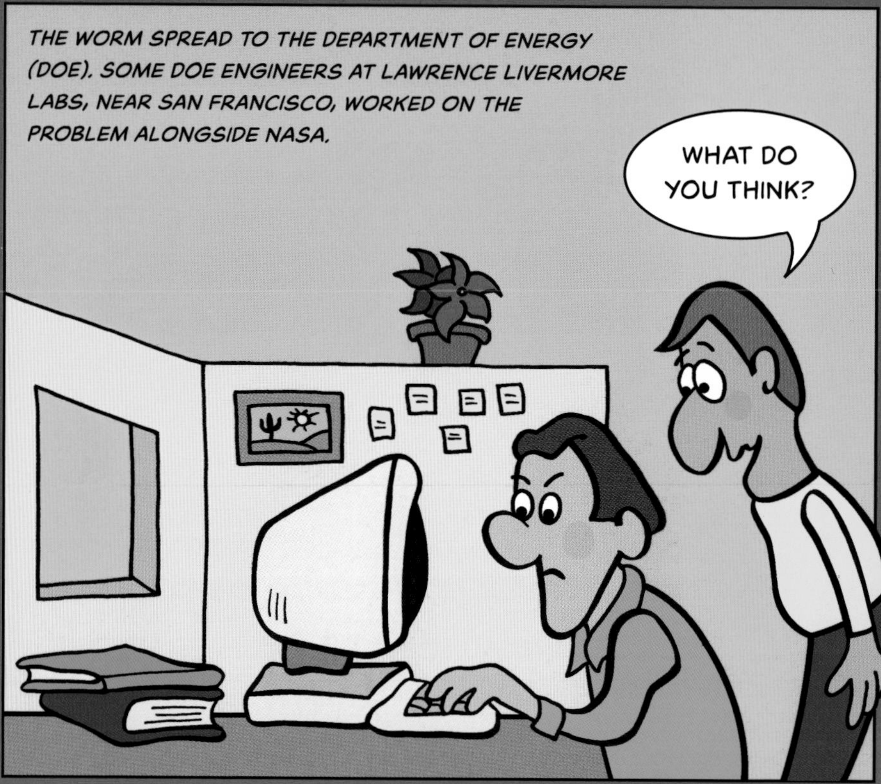
THE WORM SPREAD TO THE DEPARTMENT OF ENERGY (DOE). SOME DOE ENGINEERS AT LAWRENCE LIVERMORE LABS, NEAR SAN FRANCISCO, WORKED ON THE PROBLEM ALONGSIDE NASA.
WHAT DO YOU THINK?

THE NEXT DAY, AS THE WORM CONTINUED TO SPREAD, NASA POSTPONED GALILEO'S LAUNCH.

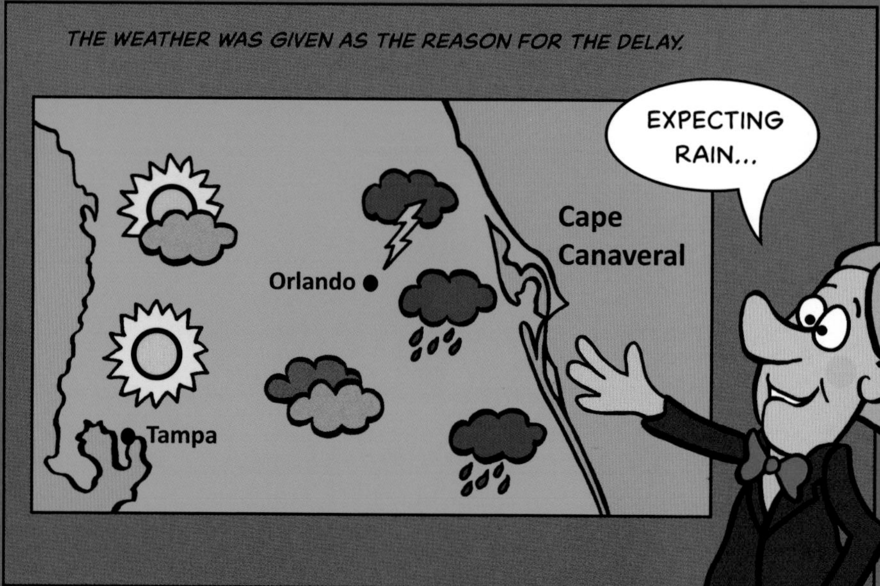
THE WEATHER WAS GIVEN AS THE REASON FOR THE DELAY.
EXPECTING RAIN...
Cape Canaveral
Orlando
Tampa

HOURS AFTER THE LAUNCH WAS CANCELLED, NASA AND DOE CAME UP WITH ANTI-WORM PROGRAMS.

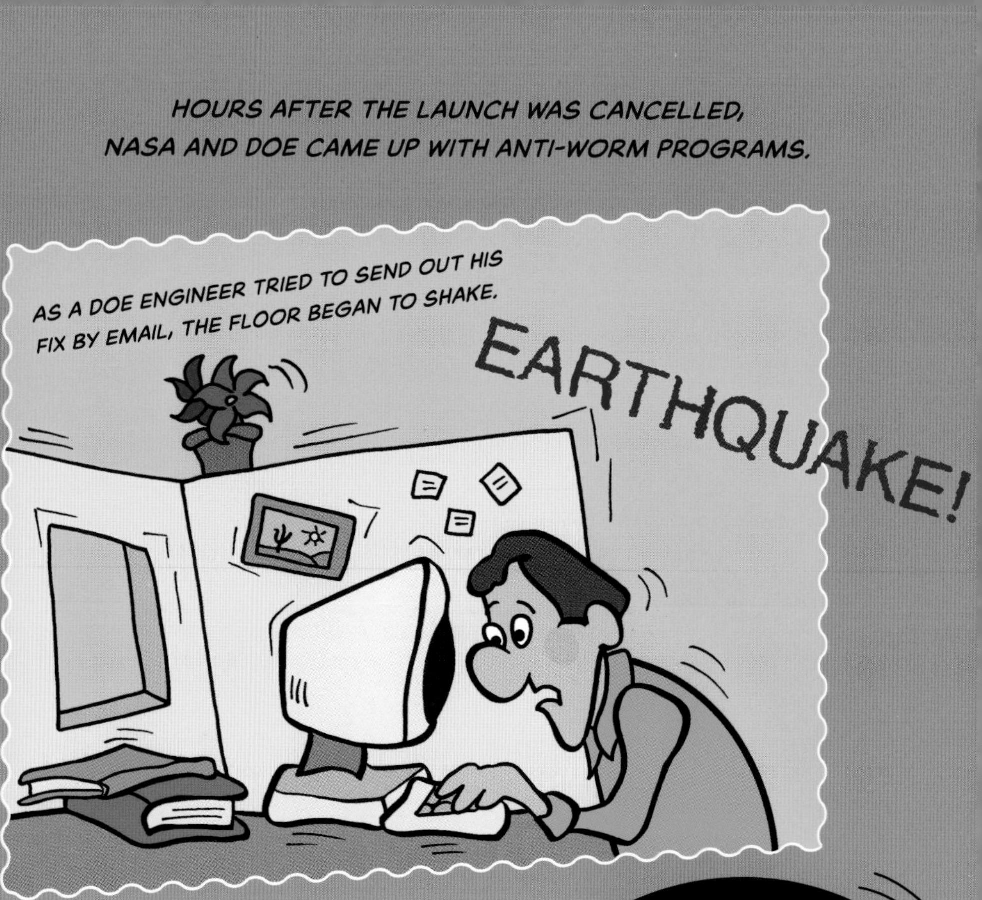
AS A DOE ENGINEER TRIED TO SEND OUT HIS FIX BY EMAIL, THE FLOOR BEGAN TO SHAKE.
EARTHQUAKE!

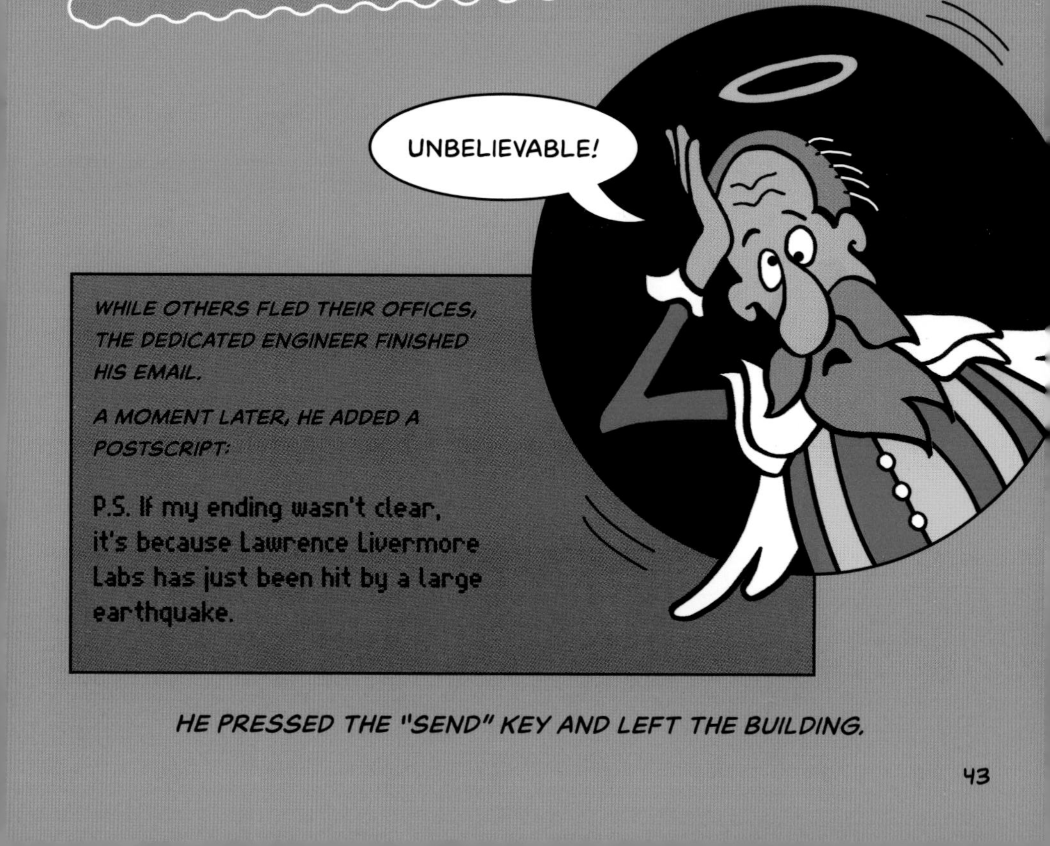
UNBELIEVABLE!

WHILE OTHERS FLED THEIR OFFICES, THE DEDICATED ENGINEER FINISHED HIS EMAIL.

A MOMENT LATER, HE ADDED A POSTSCRIPT:

P.S. If my ending wasn't clear, it's because Lawrence Livermore Labs has just been hit by a large earthquake.

HE PRESSED THE "SEND" KEY AND LEFT THE BUILDING.

SIXTY-THREE PEOPLE DIED. OVER 3,500 WERE INJURED. THE QUAKE'S DESTRUCTION COST BILLIONS.

IT STALLED GALILEO BECAUSE TWO FLIGHT CENTERS IN CALIFORNIA (AMES AND ONIZUKA) WERE DAMAGED.

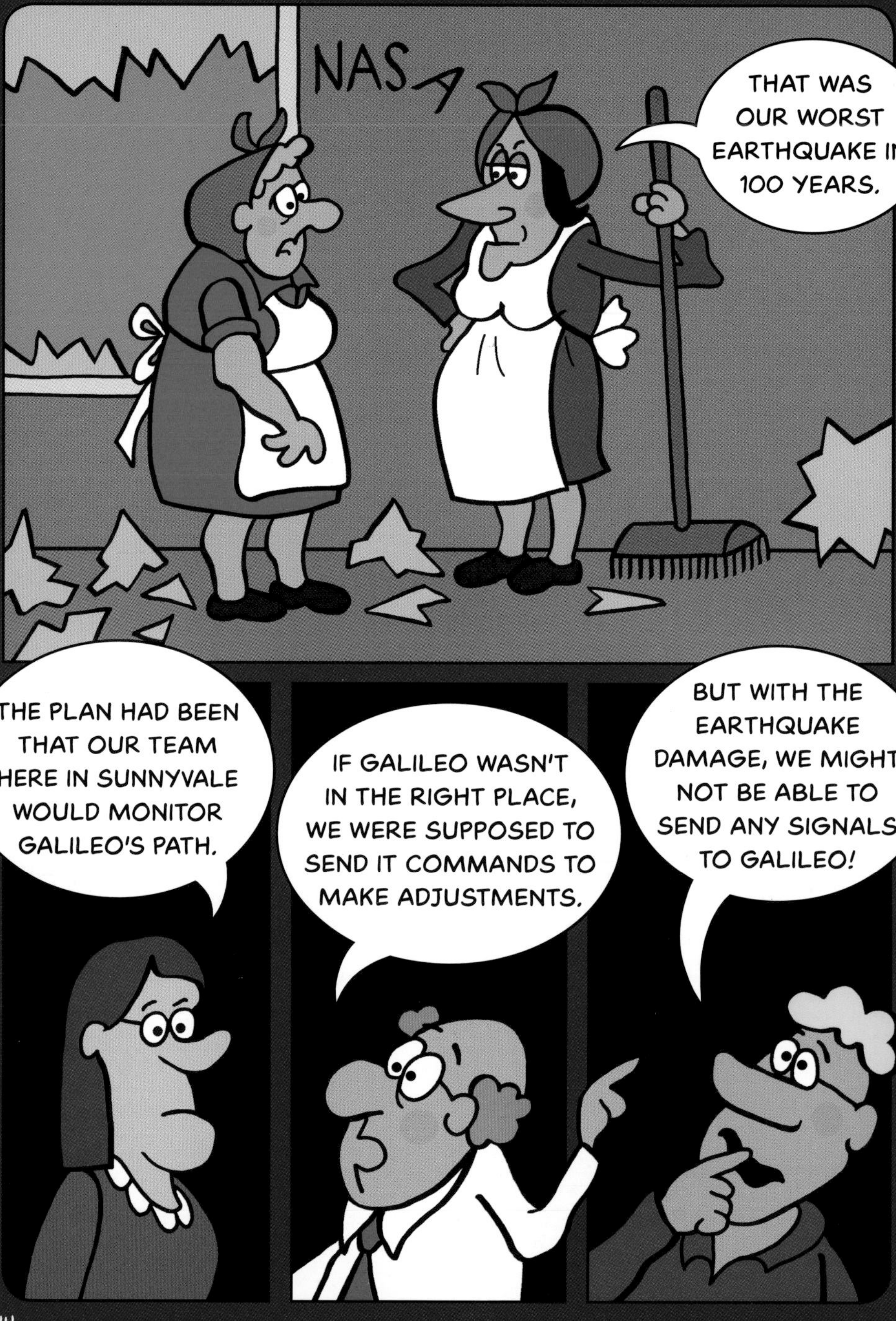
NASA
THAT WAS OUR WORST EARTHQUAKE IN 100 YEARS.
THE PLAN HAD BEEN THAT OUR TEAM HERE IN SUNNYVALE WOULD MONITOR GALILEO'S PATH.
IF GALILEO WASN'T IN THE RIGHT PLACE, WE WERE SUPPOSED TO SEND IT COMMANDS TO MAKE ADJUSTMENTS.
BUT WITH THE EARTHQUAKE DAMAGE, WE MIGHT NOT BE ABLE TO SEND ANY SIGNALS TO GALILEO!

HOWEVER, BY THE NEXT MORNING, THE TWO FLIGHT CENTERS WERE UP AND RUNNING AGAIN.

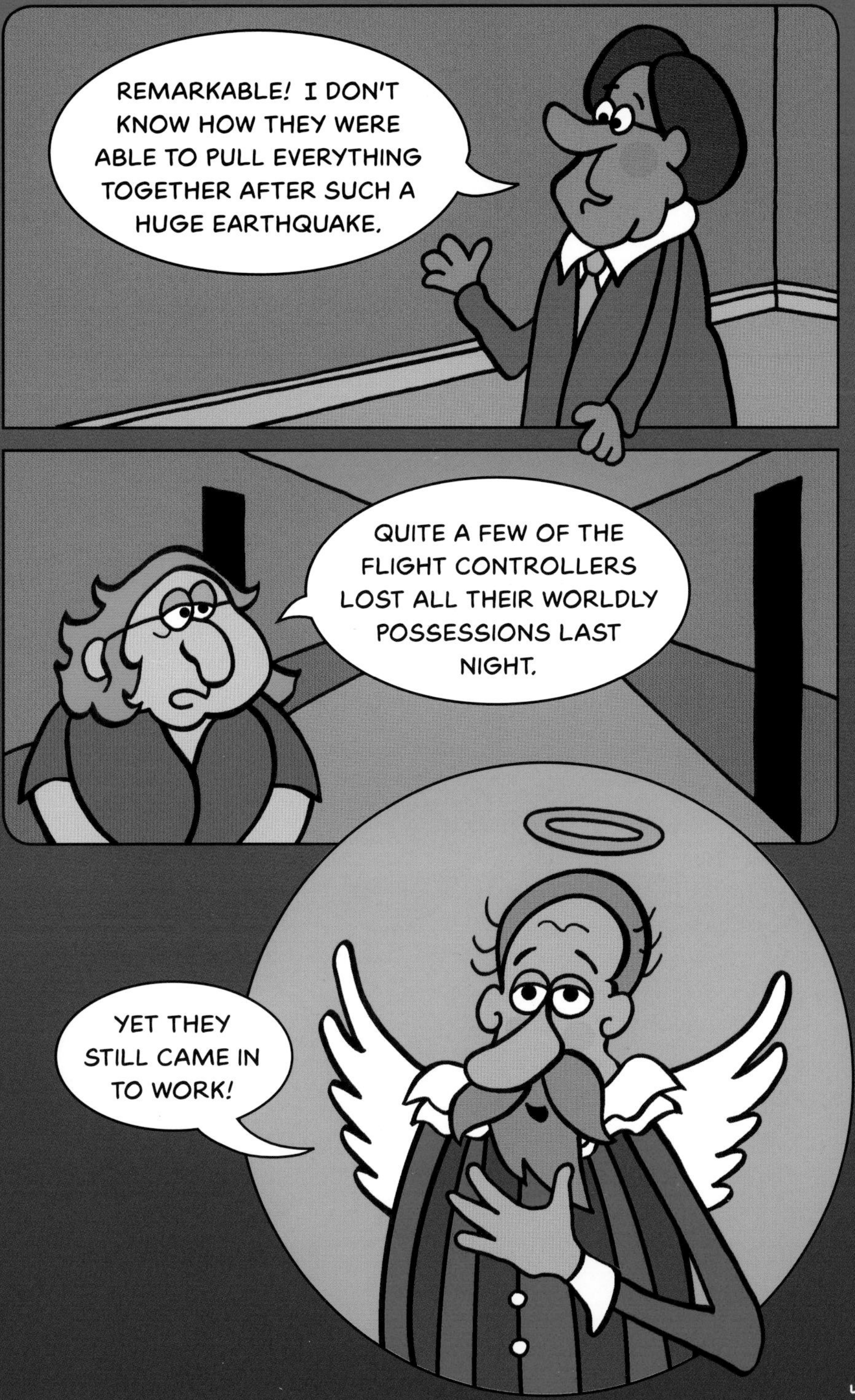
REMARKABLE! I DON'T KNOW HOW THEY WERE ABLE TO PULL EVERYTHING TOGETHER AFTER SUCH A HUGE EARTHQUAKE.
QUITE A FEW OF THE FLIGHT CONTROLLERS LOST ALL THEIR WORLDLY POSSESSIONS LAST NIGHT.
YET THEY STILL CAME IN TO WORK!

AND SO, AFTER YEARS OF TECHNICAL AND POLITICAL PROBLEMS, PLUS SOME FINAL DAYS OF LEGAL BATTLES, HACKERS, AND EVEN A GIGANTIC EARTHQUAKE, GALILEO FINALLY LAUNCHED.

ON OCTOBER 18, 1989, GALILEO LEFT EARTH ON THE SPACE SHUTTLE.

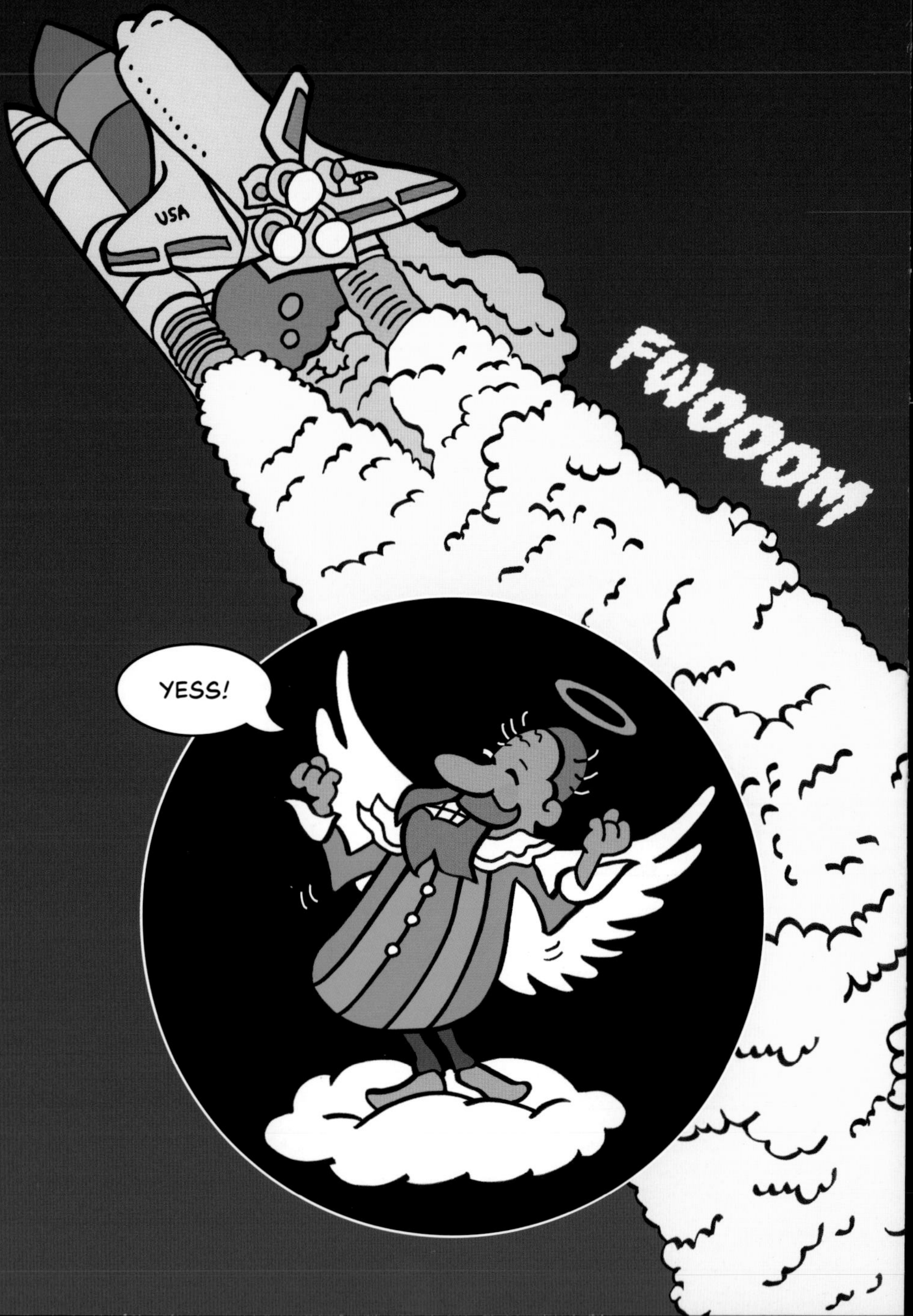
USA
FWOOOM
YESS!

THE GALILEO SPACECRAFT WEIGHED TWO AND A HALF TONS, AND IT SAT IN THE SHUTTLE'S CARGO HOLD, WAITING FOR THE CREW TO FREE IT.

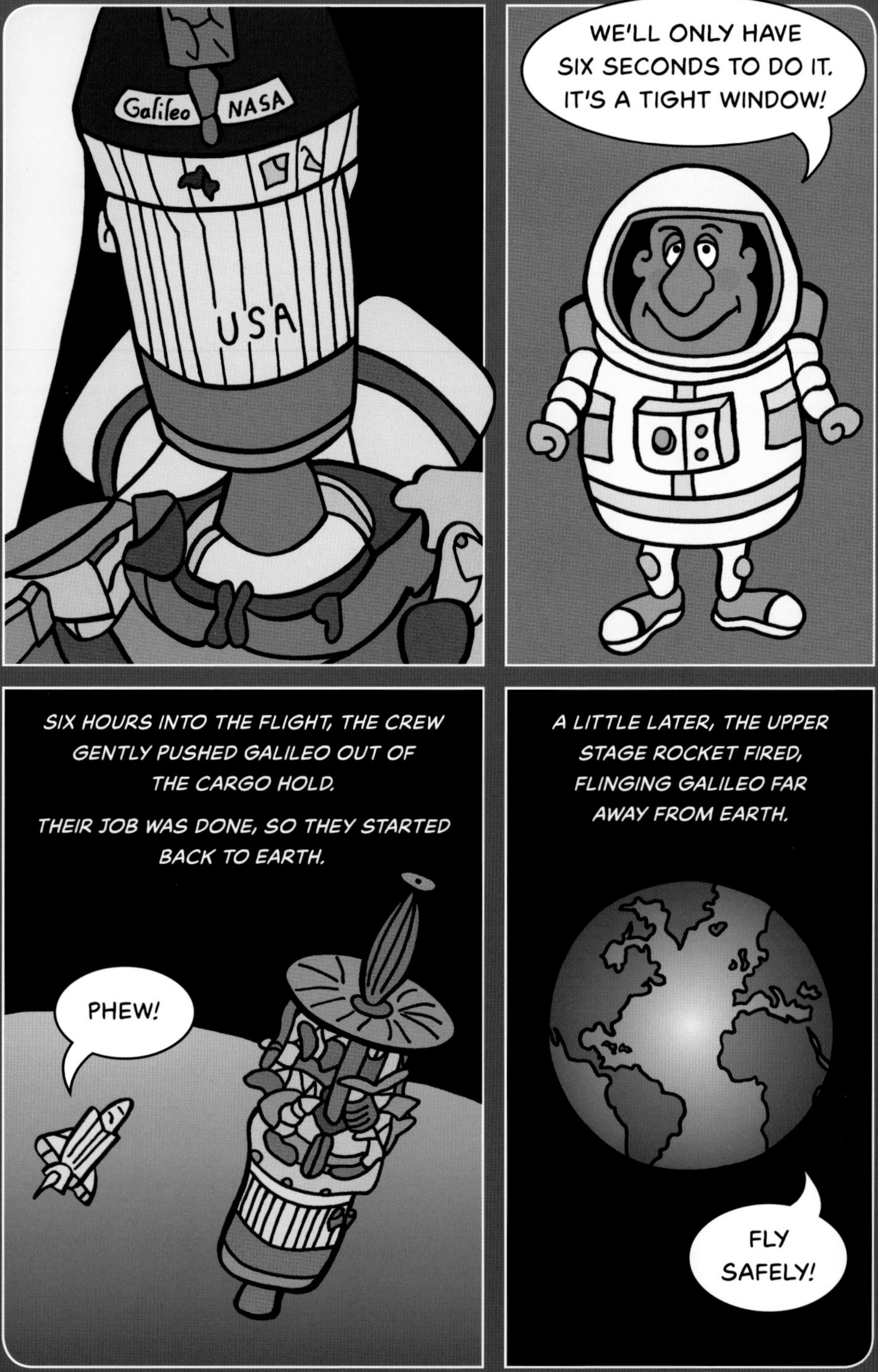
Galileo
NASA
USA
WE'LL ONLY HAVE SIX SECONDS TO DO IT. IT'S A TIGHT WINDOW!
SIX HOURS INTO THE FLIGHT, THE CREW GENTLY PUSHED GALILEO OUT OF THE CARGO HOLD.
THEIR JOB WAS DONE, SO THEY STARTED BACK TO EARTH.
PHEW!
A LITTLE LATER, THE UPPER STAGE ROCKET FIRED, FLINGING GALILEO FAR AWAY FROM EARTH.
FLY SAFELY!

SINCE THERE WERE NO ASTRONAUTS ABOARD THE GALILEO SPACECRAFT, NASA WATCHED AND MANAGED EVERYTHING FROM EARTH.

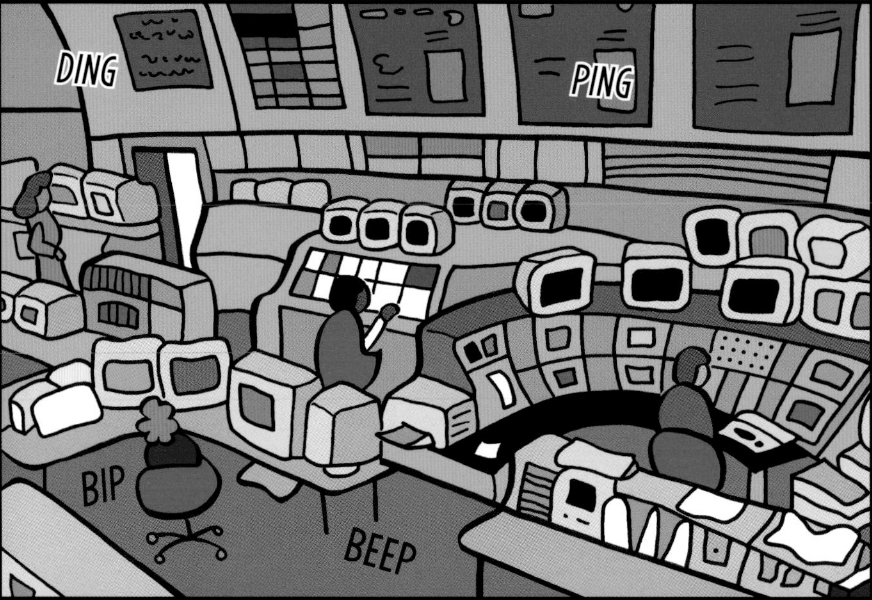
DING
PING
BIP
BEEP

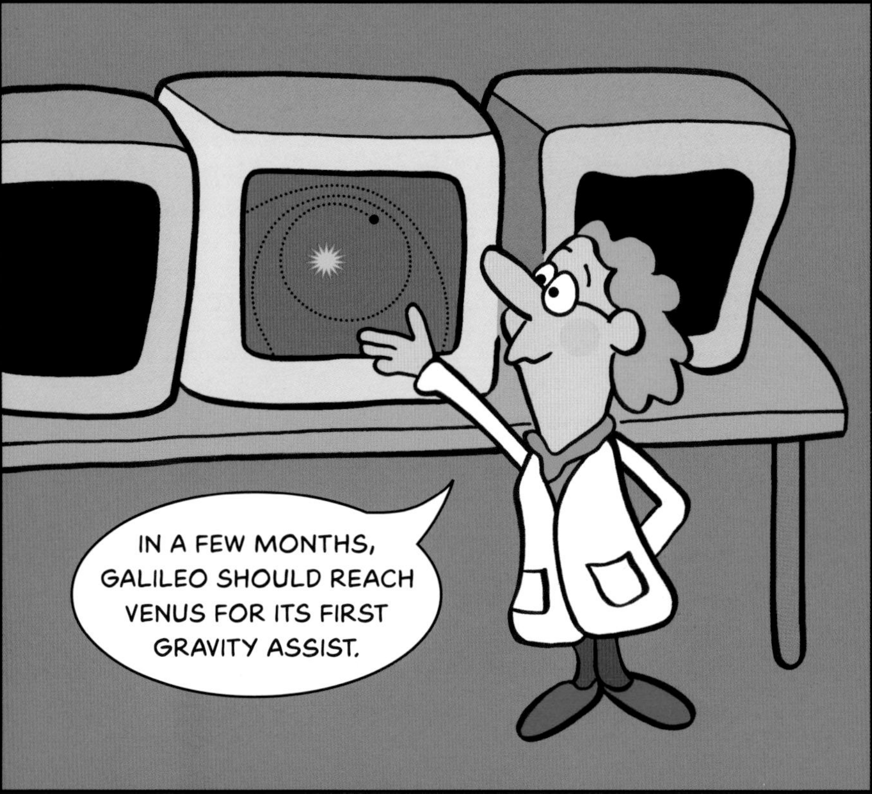
IN A FEW MONTHS, GALILEO SHOULD REACH VENUS FOR ITS FIRST GRAVITY ASSIST.

IT TOOK FOUR MONTHS FOR GALILEO TO REACH VENUS, THE FIRST POINT ON ITS VEEGA PATH.

IT WAS GAINING MOMENTUM THAT WOULD HAVE OTHERWISE COST 150% OF ITS FUEL SUPPLY.

WE'LL TAKE ADVANTAGE OF THE FLY-BY TO COLLECT DATA ABOUT VENUS.

I'M READY FOR MY CLOSE-UP!

Venus

GALILEO'S INSTRUMENTS GAVE SCIENTISTS THEIR FIRST GLIMPSE OF MID-LEVEL CLOUDS ON VENUS.

WOW, THE ATMOSPHERE OF VENUS IS BONE DRY.

AND VENUS HAS LIGHTNING!

Crack

AFTER GALILEO PASSED VENUS, IT STARTED BACK TOWARDS EARTH.

EIGHT MONTHS LATER, IN LATE 1990, IT FLEW BY EARTH AND PICKED UP **MORE** MOMENTUM.

THIS ROBBED EARTH OF A TINY BIT OF ENERGY, WHICH MEANS THAT IN A BILLION YEARS, EARTH WILL BE FIVE INCHES BEHIND, IN ITS ORBIT AROUND THE SUN.

NO BIGGIE.

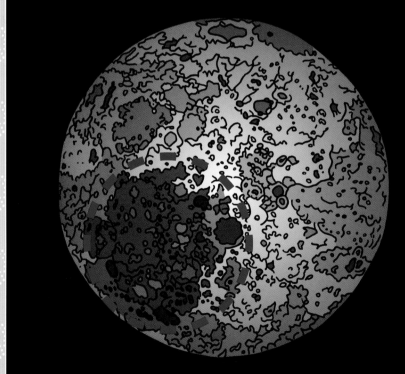

AS GALILEO PASSED EARTH, IT RAN TESTS ON OUR ATMOSPHERE. IT ALSO MAPPED THE SOUTH POLE-AITKEN BASIN ON THE FAR SIDE OF OUR MOON. IT'S ONE OF THE BIGGEST CRATERS IN OUR SOLAR SYSTEM.

THE CRATER IS 1,600 MILES ACROSS. THAT'S NEARLY SIX GRAND CANYONS!

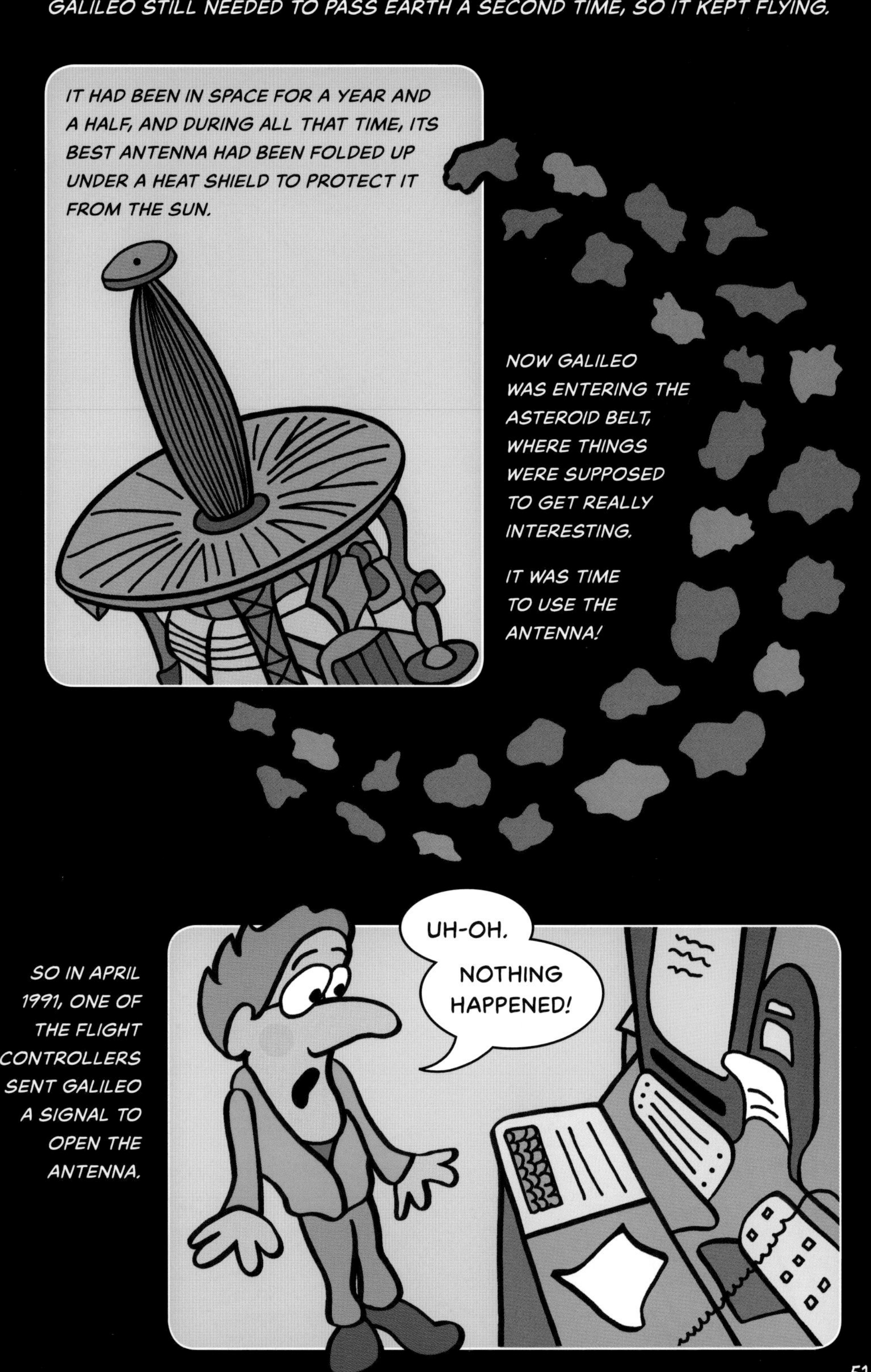
GALILEO STILL NEEDED TO PASS EARTH A SECOND TIME, SO IT KEPT FLYING.
IT HAD BEEN IN SPACE FOR A YEAR AND A HALF, AND DURING ALL THAT TIME, ITS BEST ANTENNA HAD BEEN FOLDED UP UNDER A HEAT SHIELD TO PROTECT IT FROM THE SUN.
NOW GALILEO WAS ENTERING THE ASTEROID BELT, WHERE THINGS WERE SUPPOSED TO GET REALLY INTERESTING.
IT WAS TIME TO USE THE ANTENNA!
SO IN APRIL 1991, ONE OF THE FLIGHT CONTROLLERS SENT GALILEO A SIGNAL TO OPEN THE ANTENNA.
UH-OH.
NOTHING HAPPENED!

NASA WAS COMPLETELY SHOCKED AND CONFUSED! THEY SENT MORE SIGNALS TO GALILEO, TO TEST IT.

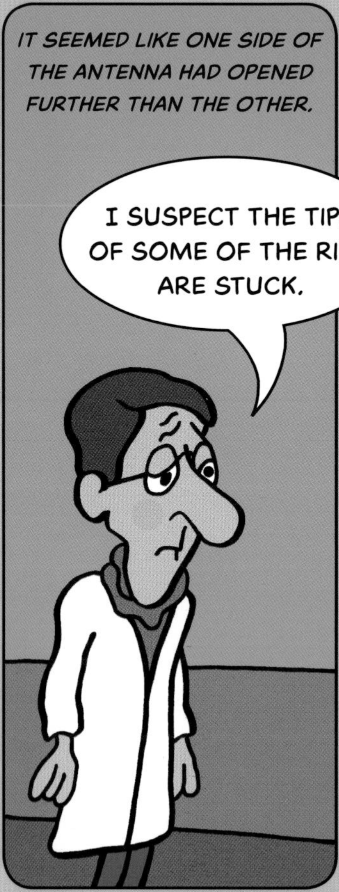
IT SEEMED LIKE ONE SIDE OF THE ANTENNA HAD OPENED FURTHER THAN THE OTHER.
I SUSPECT THE TIPS OF SOME OF THE RIBS ARE STUCK.

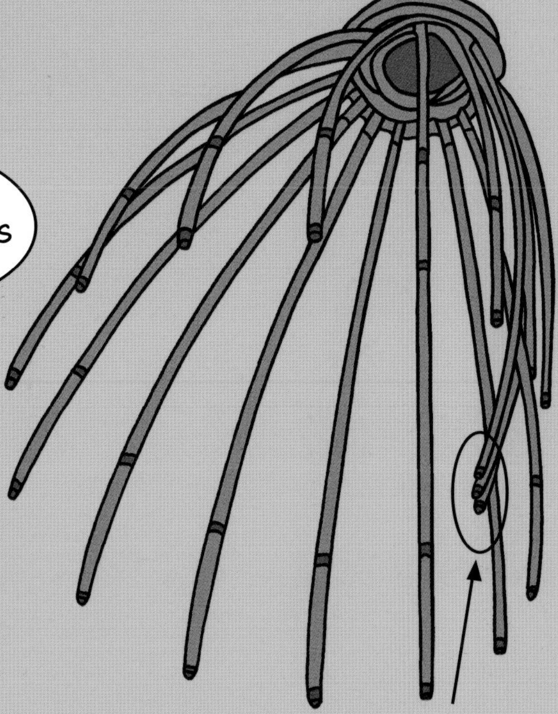

THEIR THEORIES WERE CONFIRMED WHEN THEY RAN THE SAME TESTS ON A DUPLICATE ANTENNA THAT WAS STILL ON EARTH.

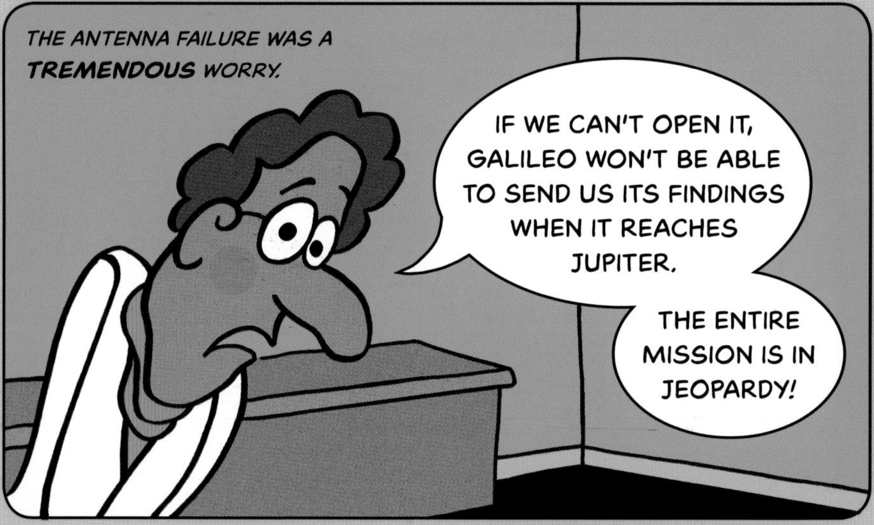
THE ANTENNA FAILURE WAS A TREMENDOUS WORRY.
IF WE CAN'T OPEN IT, GALILEO WON'T BE ABLE TO SEND US ITS FINDINGS WHEN IT REACHES JUPITER.
THE ENTIRE MISSION IS IN JEOPARDY!

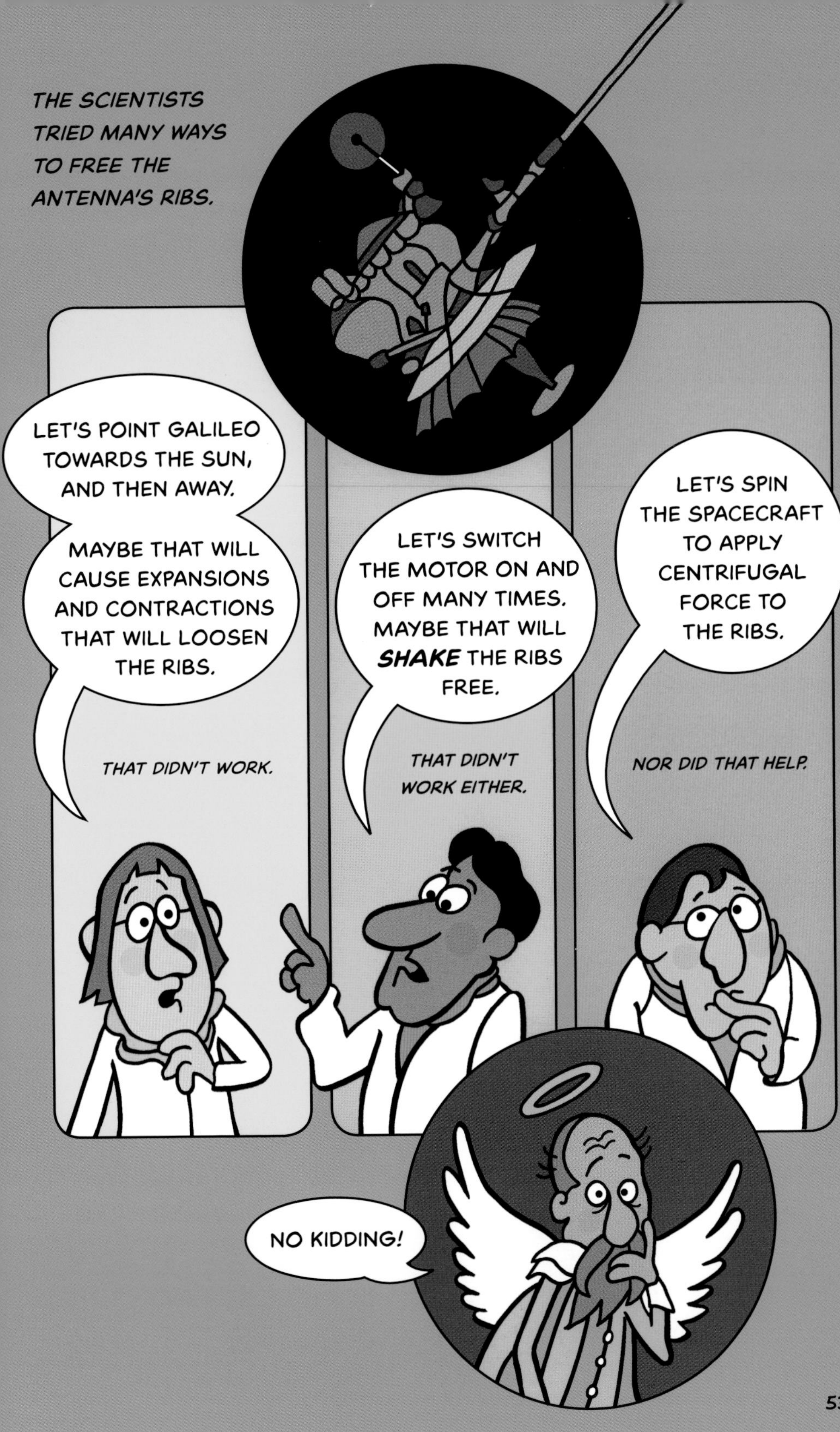
THE SCIENTISTS TRIED MANY WAYS TO FREE THE ANTENNA'S RIBS.
LET'S POINT GALILEO TOWARDS THE SUN, AND THEN AWAY.
MAYBE THAT WILL CAUSE EXPANSIONS AND CONTRACTIONS THAT WILL LOOSEN THE RIBS.
THAT DIDN'T WORK.
LET'S SWITCH THE MOTOR ON AND OFF MANY TIMES. MAYBE THAT WILL *SHAKE* THE RIBS FREE.
THAT DIDN'T WORK EITHER.
LET'S SPIN THE SPACECRAFT TO APPLY CENTRIFUGAL FORCE TO THE RIBS.
NOR DID THAT HELP.
NO KIDDING!

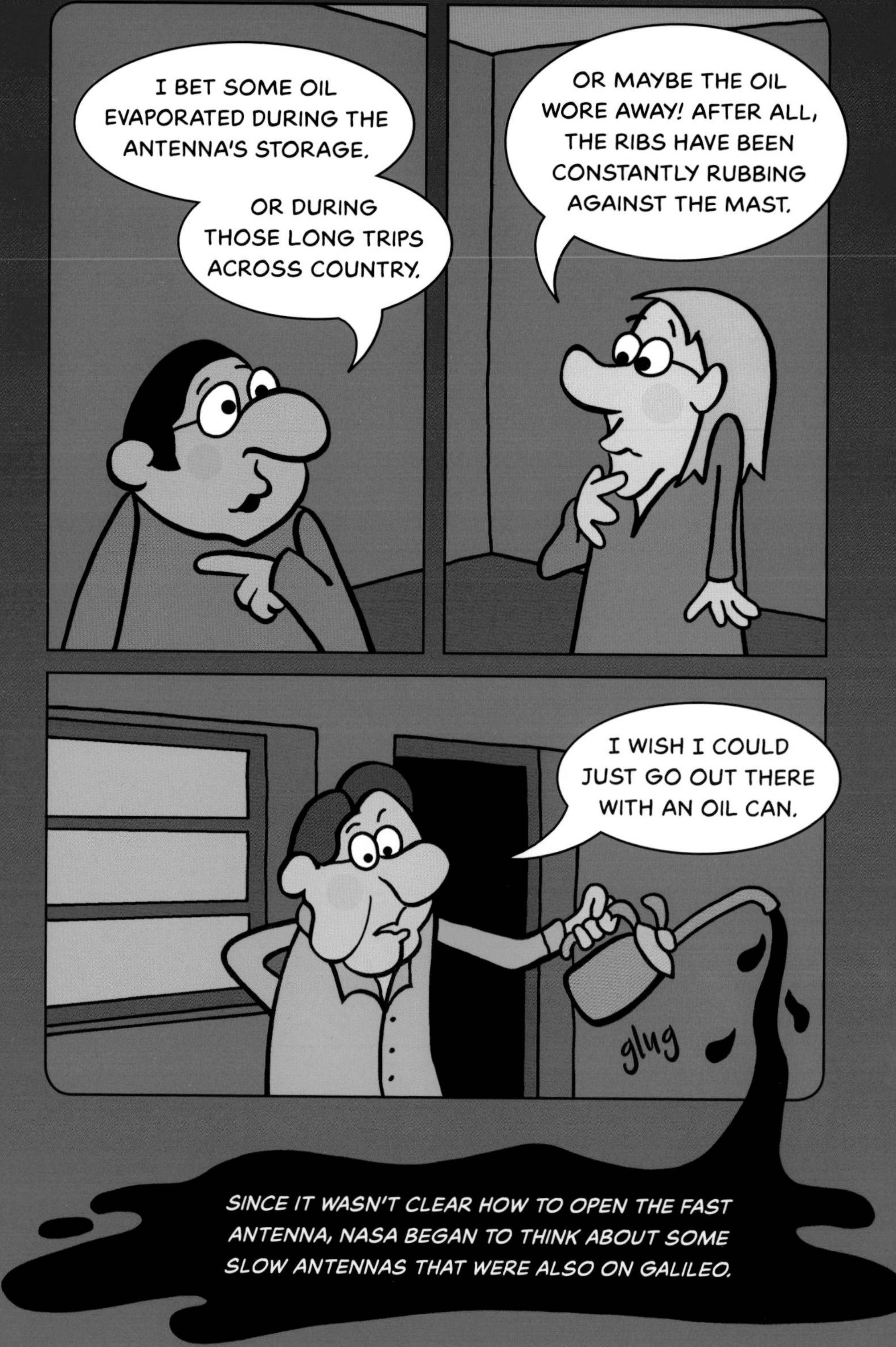
I BET SOME OIL EVAPORATED DURING THE ANTENNA'S STORAGE.
OR DURING THOSE LONG TRIPS ACROSS COUNTRY.
OR MAYBE THE OIL WORE AWAY! AFTER ALL, THE RIBS HAVE BEEN CONSTANTLY RUBBING AGAINST THE MAST.
I WISH I COULD JUST GO OUT THERE WITH AN OIL CAN.
glug
SINCE IT WASN'T CLEAR HOW TO OPEN THE FAST ANTENNA, NASA BEGAN TO THINK ABOUT SOME SLOW ANTENNAS THAT WERE ALSO ON GALILEO.

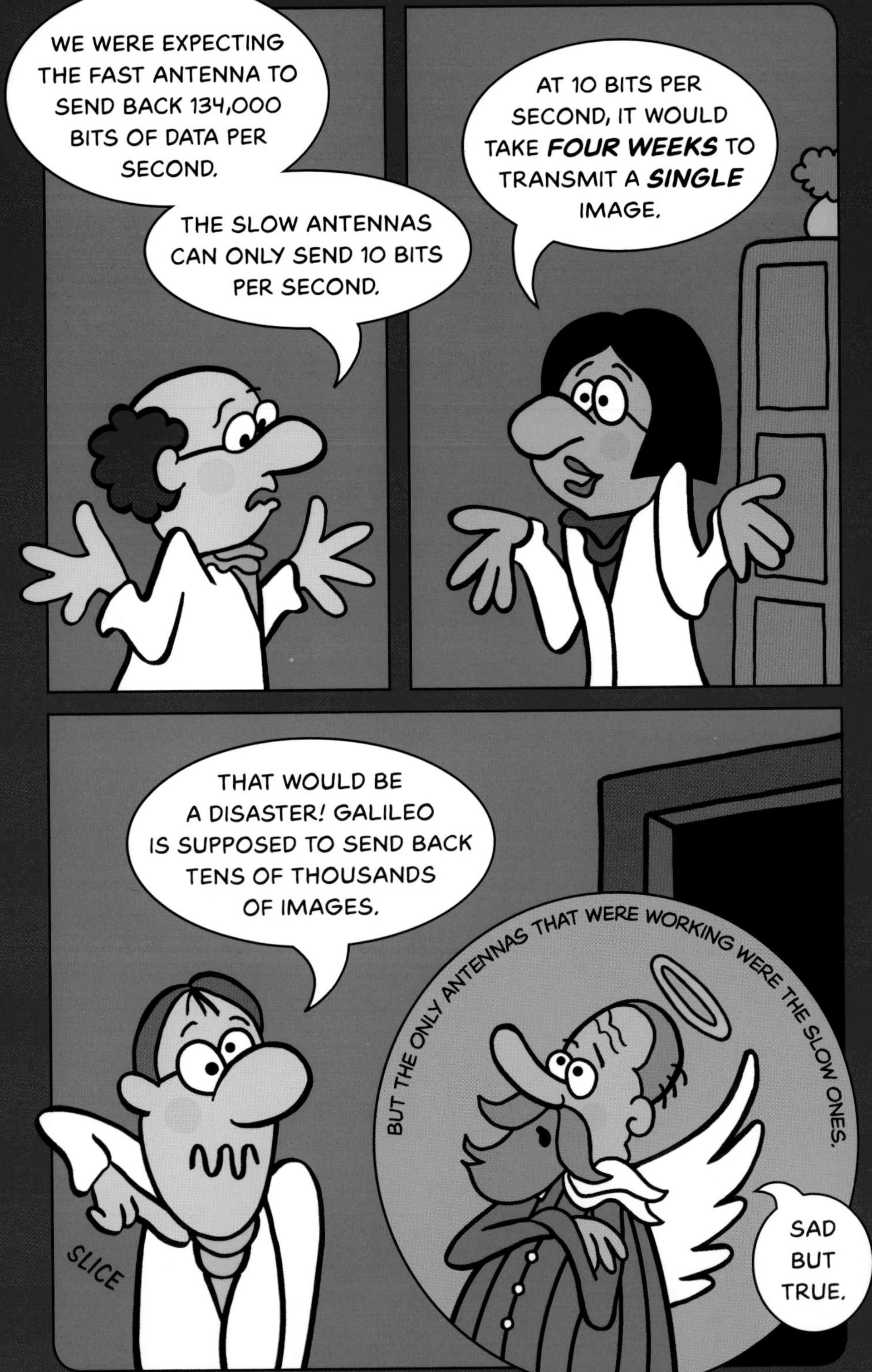
WE WERE EXPECTING THE FAST ANTENNA TO SEND BACK 134,000 BITS OF DATA PER SECOND.
THE SLOW ANTENNAS CAN ONLY SEND 10 BITS PER SECOND.
AT 10 BITS PER SECOND, IT WOULD TAKE FOUR WEEKS TO TRANSMIT A SINGLE IMAGE.
THAT WOULD BE A DISASTER! GALILEO IS SUPPOSED TO SEND BACK TENS OF THOUSANDS OF IMAGES.
SLICE
BUT THE ONLY ANTENNAS THAT WERE WORKING WERE THE SLOW ONES.
SAD BUT TRUE.

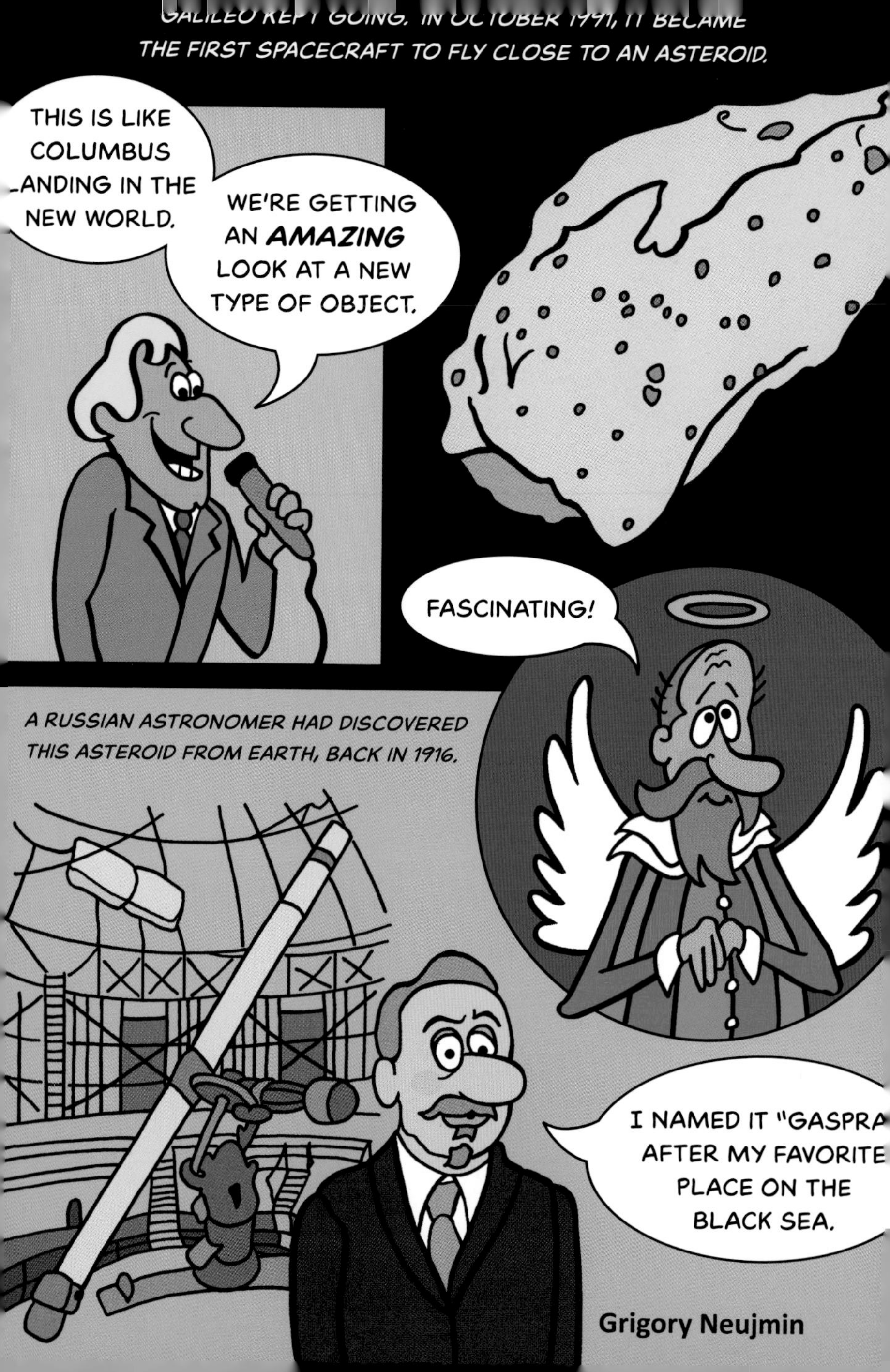
GALILEO KEPT GOING. IN OCTOBER 1991, IT BECAME THE FIRST SPACECRAFT TO FLY CLOSE TO AN ASTEROID.
THIS IS LIKE COLUMBUS LANDING IN THE NEW WORLD.
WE'RE GETTING AN **AMAZING** LOOK AT A NEW TYPE OF OBJECT.
FASCINATING!
A RUSSIAN ASTRONOMER HAD DISCOVERED THIS ASTEROID FROM EARTH, BACK IN 1916.
I NAMED IT "GASPRA AFTER MY FAVORITE PLACE ON THE BLACK SEA.
Grigory Neujmin

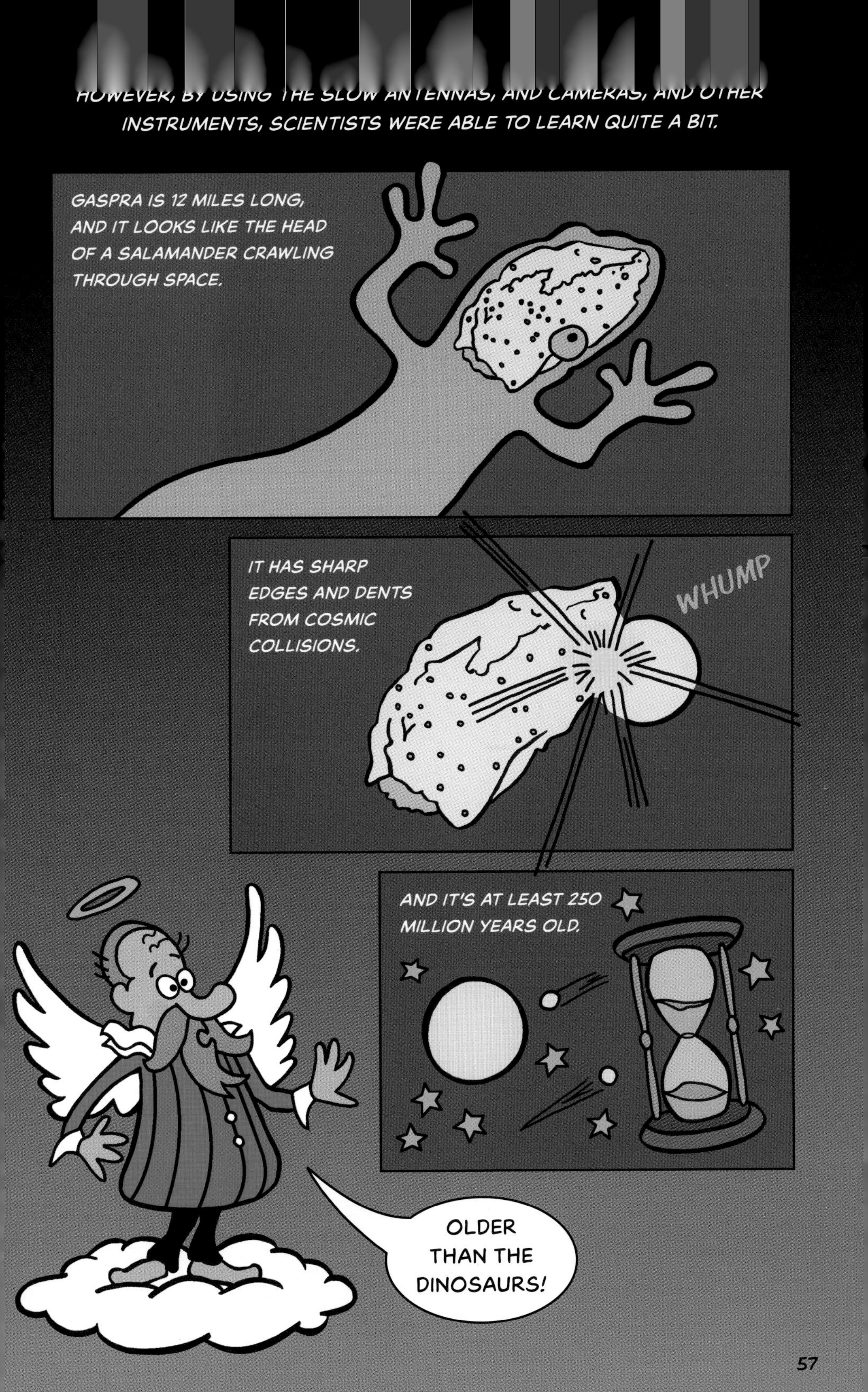
HOWEVER, BY USING THE SLOW ANTENNAS, AND CAMERAS, AND OTHER INSTRUMENTS, SCIENTISTS WERE ABLE TO LEARN QUITE A BIT.
GASPRA IS 12 MILES LONG, AND IT LOOKS LIKE THE HEAD OF A SALAMANDER CRAWLING THROUGH SPACE.
IT HAS SHARP EDGES AND DENTS FROM COSMIC COLLISIONS.
WHUMP
AND IT'S AT LEAST 250 MILLION YEARS OLD.
OLDER THAN THE DINOSAURS!

AFTER GALILEO PASSED GASPRA, IT HEADED BACK TO EARTH FOR THE SECOND TIME.

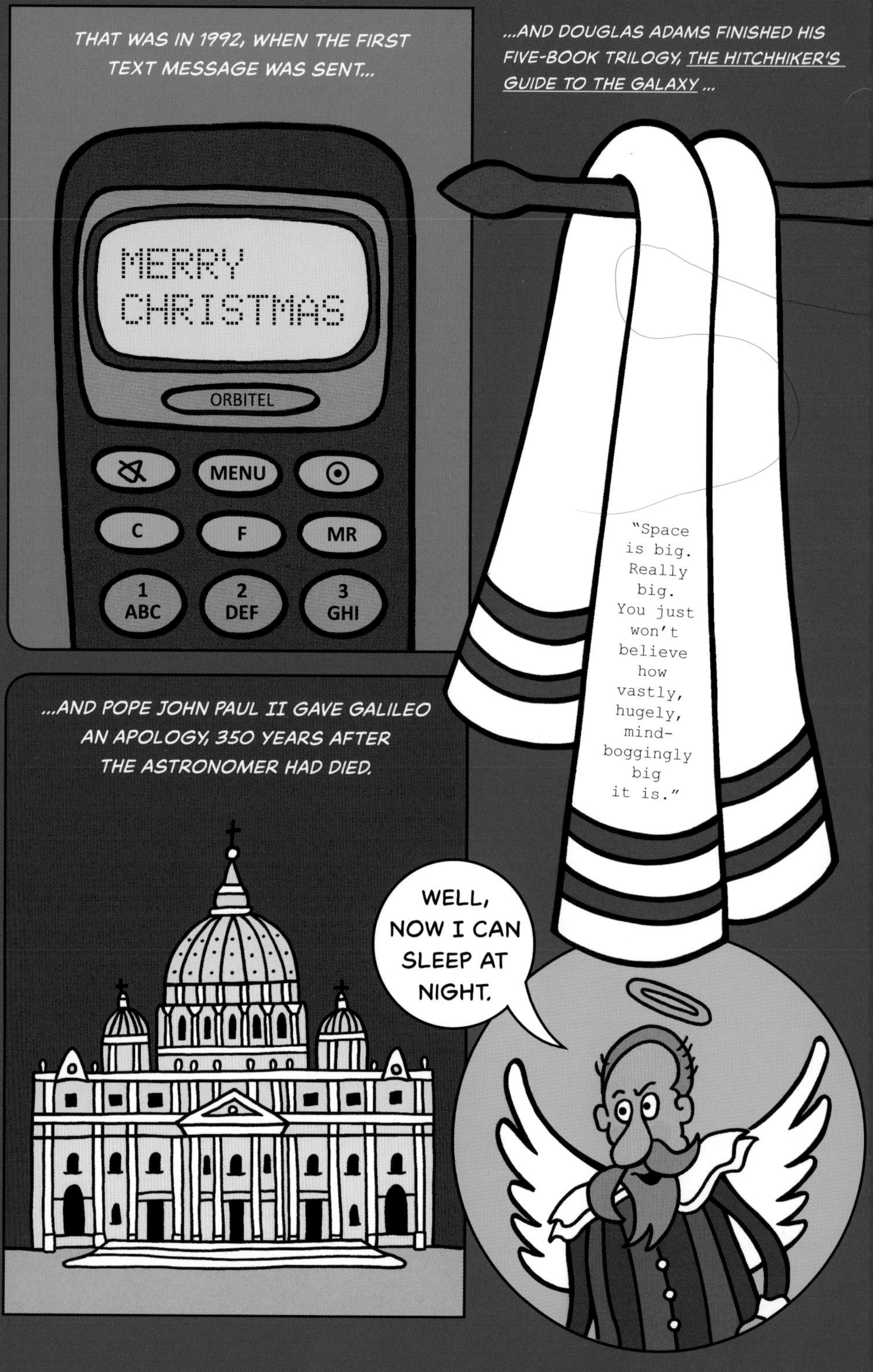
THAT WAS IN 1992, WHEN THE FIRST TEXT MESSAGE WAS SENT...
MERRY CHRISTMAS
ORBITEL
MENU
C
F
MR
1 ABC
2 DEF
3 GHI
...AND DOUGLAS ADAMS FINISHED HIS FIVE-BOOK TRILOGY, THE HITCHHIKER'S GUIDE TO THE GALAXY ...
"Space is big. Really big. You just won't believe how vastly, hugely, mind-boggingly big it is."
...AND POPE JOHN PAUL II GAVE GALILEO AN APOLOGY, 350 YEARS AFTER THE ASTRONOMER HAD DIED.
WELL, NOW I CAN SLEEP AT NIGHT.

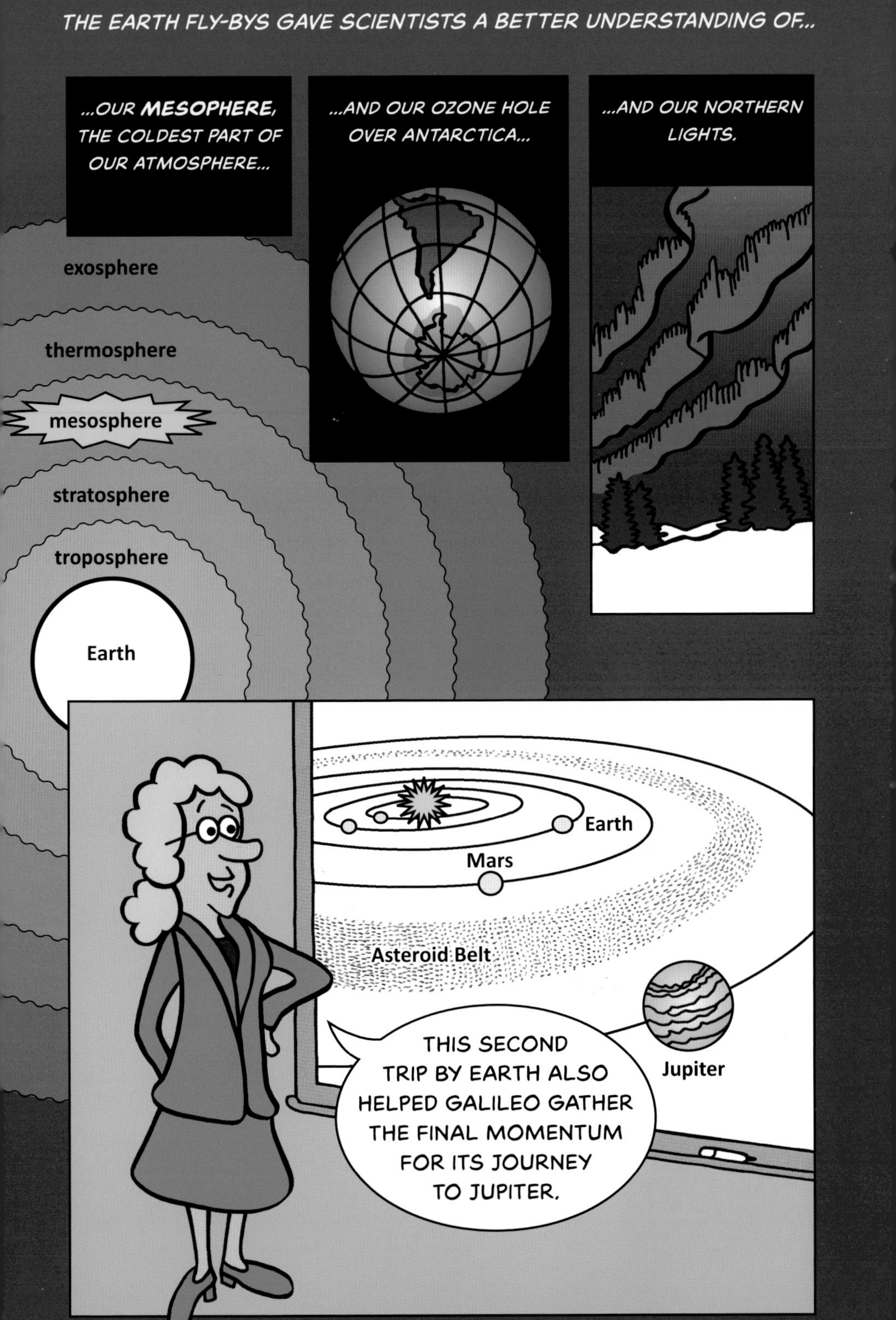
THE EARTH FLY-BYS GAVE SCIENTISTS A BETTER UNDERSTANDING OF...
...OUR MESOPHERE, THE COLDEST PART OF OUR ATMOSPHERE...
exosphere
thermosphere
mesosphere
stratosphere
troposphere
Earth
...AND OUR OZONE HOLE OVER ANTARCTICA...
...AND OUR NORTHERN LIGHTS.
Earth
Mars
Asteroid Belt
Jupiter
THIS SECOND TRIP BY EARTH ALSO HELPED GALILEO GATHER THE FINAL MOMENTUM FOR ITS JOURNEY TO JUPITER.

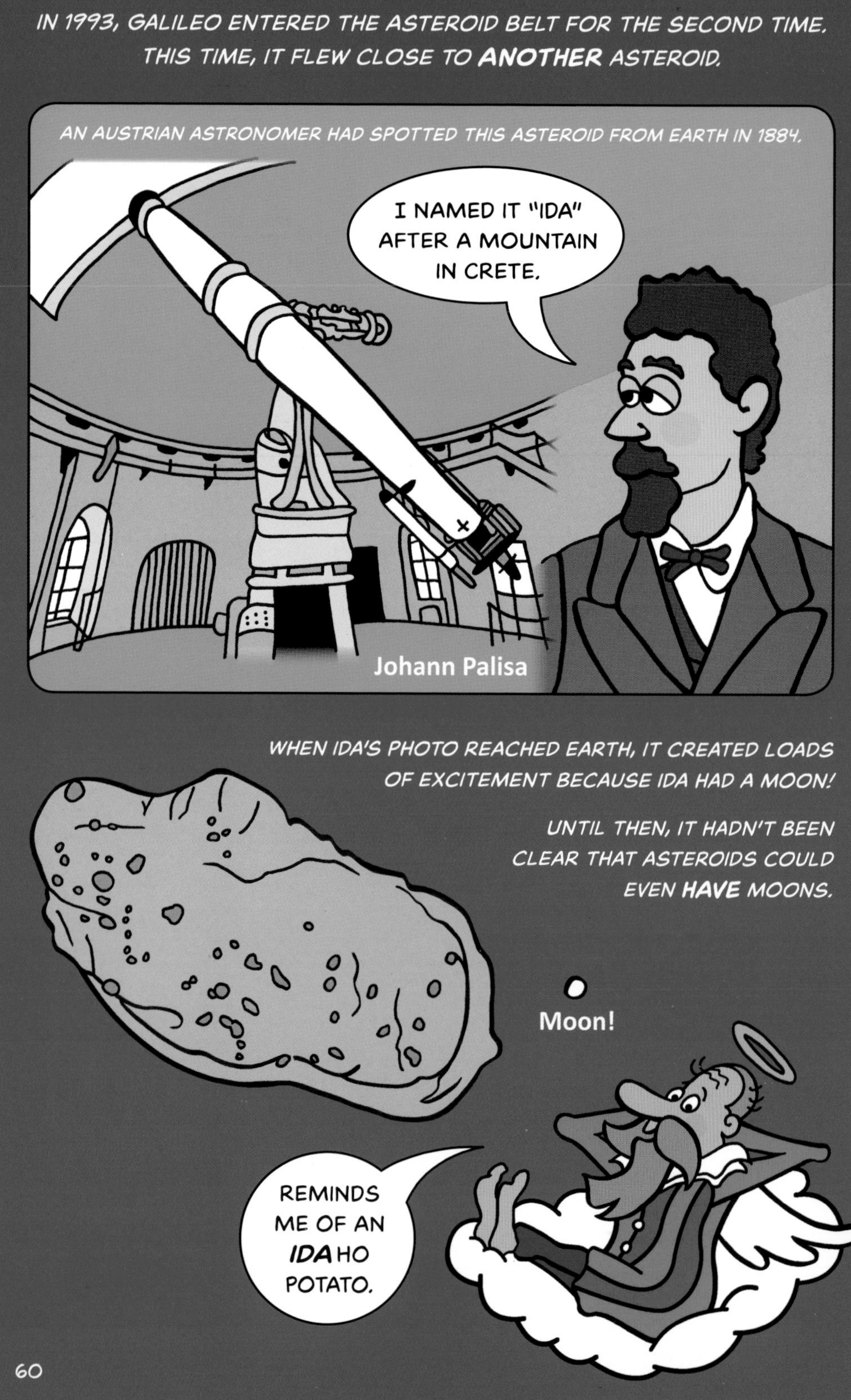
IN 1993, GALILEO ENTERED THE ASTEROID BELT FOR THE SECOND TIME. THIS TIME, IT FLEW CLOSE TO **ANOTHER** ASTEROID.
AN AUSTRIAN ASTRONOMER HAD SPOTTED THIS ASTEROID FROM EARTH IN 1884.
I NAMED IT "IDA" AFTER A MOUNTAIN IN CRETE.
Johann Palisa
WHEN IDA'S PHOTO REACHED EARTH, IT CREATED LOADS OF EXCITEMENT BECAUSE IDA HAD A MOON!
UNTIL THEN, IT HADN'T BEEN CLEAR THAT ASTEROIDS COULD EVEN **HAVE** MOONS.
Moon!
REMINDS ME OF AN ***IDA*** HO POTATO.

DATA FROM IDA AND ITS MOON TOOK A LONG TIME TO REACH EARTH BECAUSE THE FAST ANTENNA STILL WASN'T WORKING.

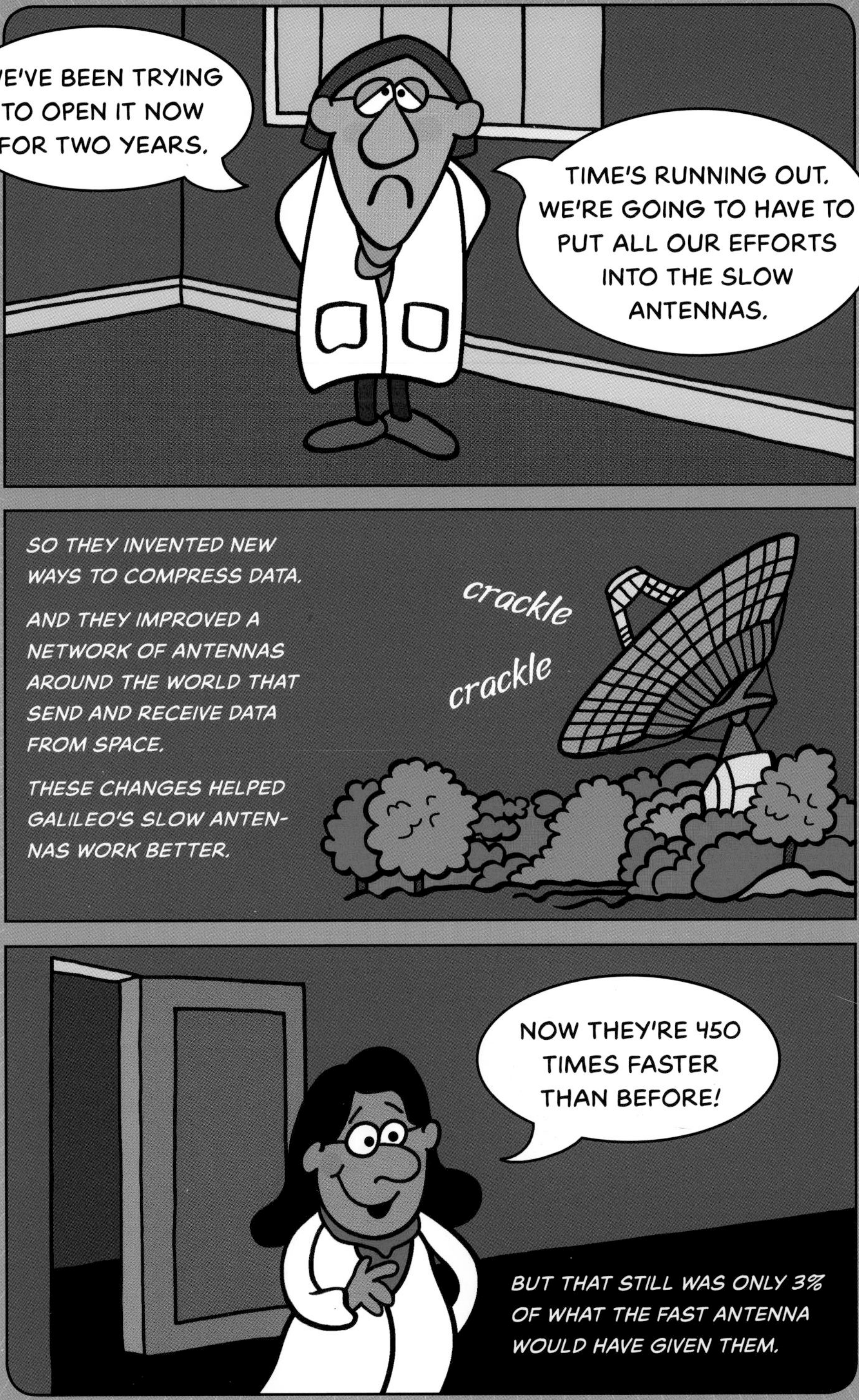
WE'VE BEEN TRYING TO OPEN IT NOW FOR TWO YEARS.
TIME'S RUNNING OUT. WE'RE GOING TO HAVE TO PUT ALL OUR EFFORTS INTO THE SLOW ANTENNAS.
SO THEY INVENTED NEW WAYS TO COMPRESS DATA.
AND THEY IMPROVED A NETWORK OF ANTENNAS AROUND THE WORLD THAT SEND AND RECEIVE DATA FROM SPACE.
THESE CHANGES HELPED GALILEO'S SLOW ANTENNAS WORK BETTER.
crackle
crackle
NOW THEY'RE 450 TIMES FASTER THAN BEFORE!
BUT THAT STILL WAS ONLY 3% OF WHAT THE FAST ANTENNA WOULD HAVE GIVEN THEM.

AS GALILEO FLEW THROUGH THE ASTEROID BELT, LIFE CONTINUED ON EARTH.

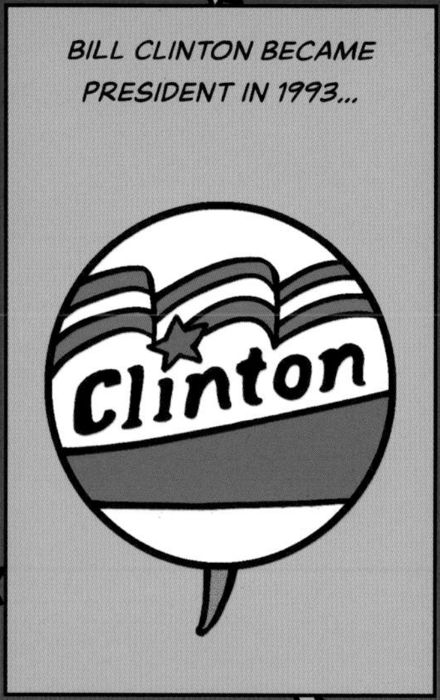
Clinton

BILL CLINTON BECAME PRESIDENT IN 1993...

...AND "CHEERS" WAS ENDING ITS FINAL SEASON ON TV...

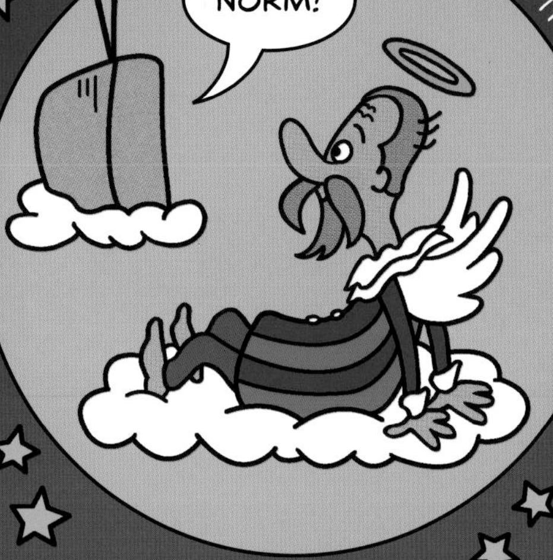
NORM!

...AND THE WORLD WAS FASCINATED WITH A COMET.

ONE SPRING NIGHT IN 1993, THREE ASTRONOMERS WERE SEARCHING THE SKY. THEIR NAMES WERE CAROLYN SHOEMAKER, EUGENE SHOEMAKER, AND DAVID LEVY.

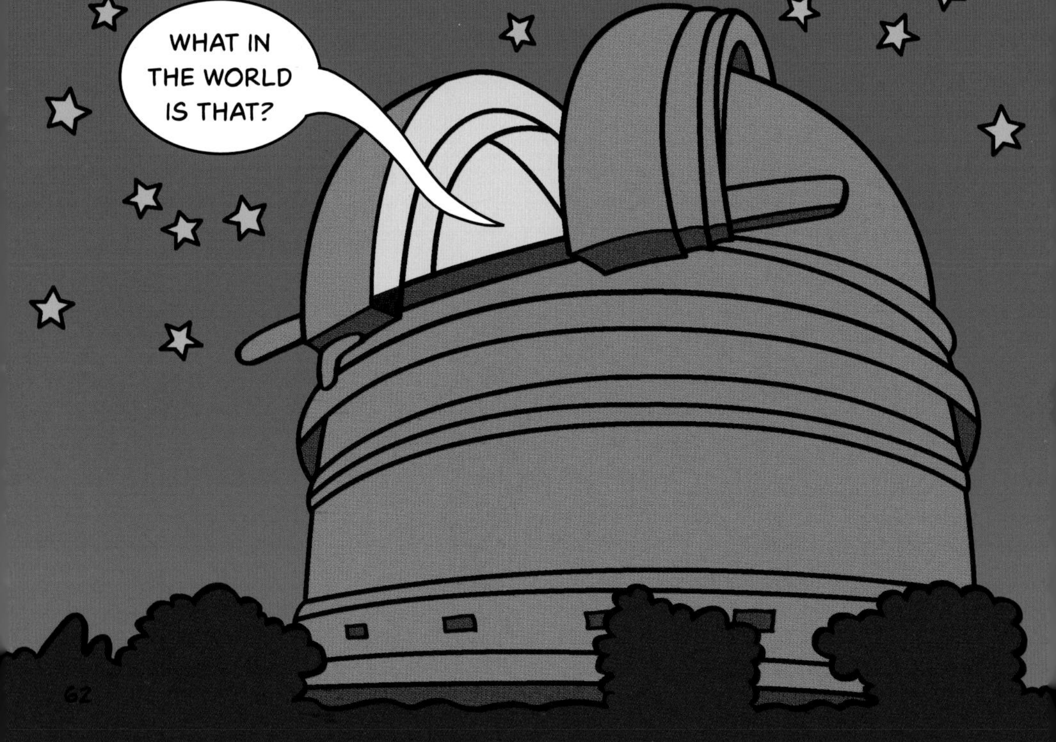
WHAT IN THE WORLD IS THAT?

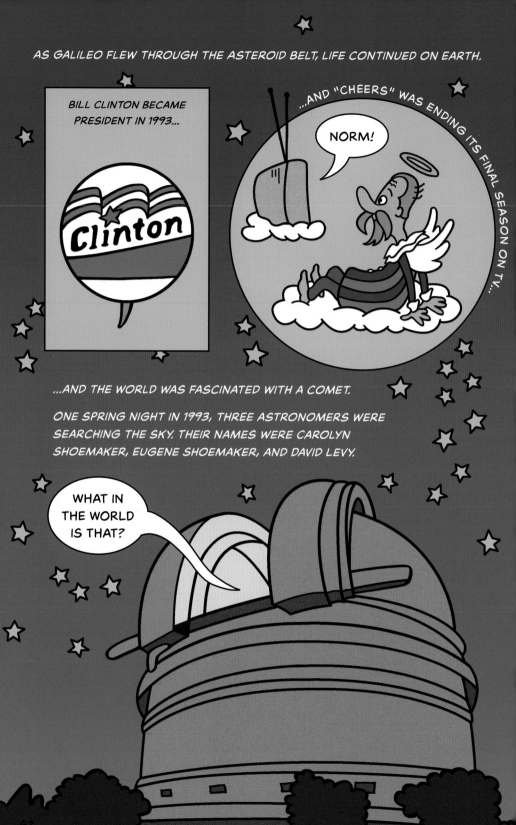

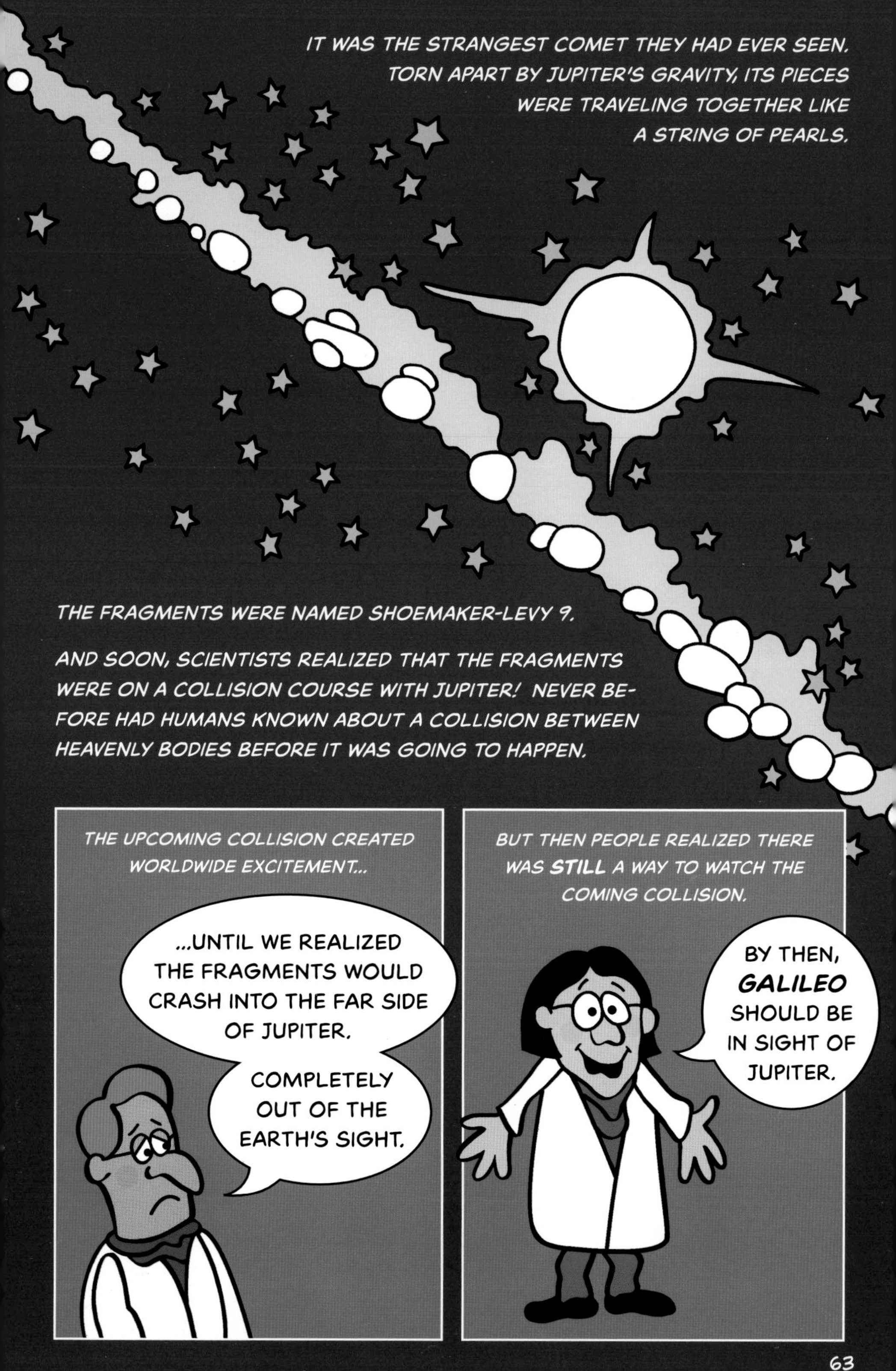
IT WAS THE STRANGEST COMET THEY HAD EVER SEEN. TORN APART BY JUPITER'S GRAVITY, ITS PIECES WERE TRAVELING TOGETHER LIKE A STRING OF PEARLS.
THE FRAGMENTS WERE NAMED SHOEMAKER-LEVY 9.
AND SOON, SCIENTISTS REALIZED THAT THE FRAGMENTS WERE ON A COLLISION COURSE WITH JUPITER! NEVER BEFORE HAD HUMANS KNOWN ABOUT A COLLISION BETWEEN HEAVENLY BODIES BEFORE IT WAS GOING TO HAPPEN.
THE UPCOMING COLLISION CREATED WORLDWIDE EXCITEMENT...
...UNTIL WE REALIZED THE FRAGMENTS WOULD CRASH INTO THE FAR SIDE OF JUPITER.
COMPLETELY OUT OF THE EARTH'S SIGHT.
BUT THEN PEOPLE REALIZED THERE WAS **STILL** A WAY TO WATCH THE COMING COLLISION.
BY THEN, **GALILEO** SHOULD BE IN SIGHT OF JUPITER.

IN THE SUMMER OF 1994, THE COMET'S FRAGMENTS SMASHED INTO JUPITER.

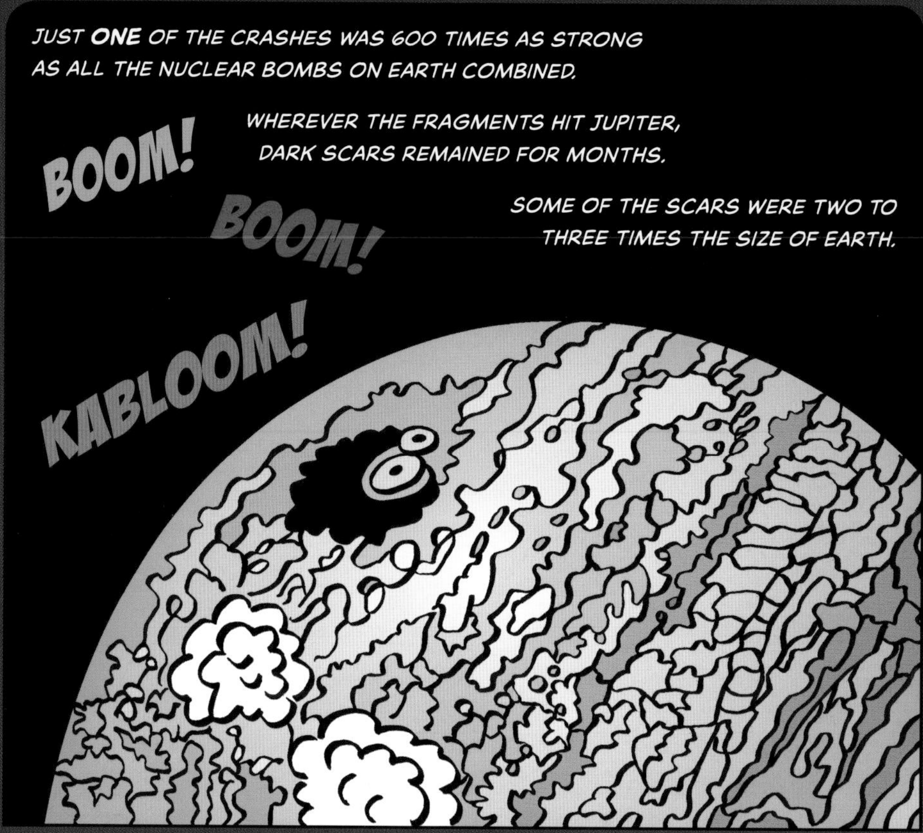
JUST ONE OF THE CRASHES WAS 600 TIMES AS STRONG AS ALL THE NUCLEAR BOMBS ON EARTH COMBINED.
BOOM!
WHEREVER THE FRAGMENTS HIT JUPITER, DARK SCARS REMAINED FOR MONTHS.
BOOM!
SOME OF THE SCARS WERE TWO TO THREE TIMES THE SIZE OF EARTH.
KABLOOM!

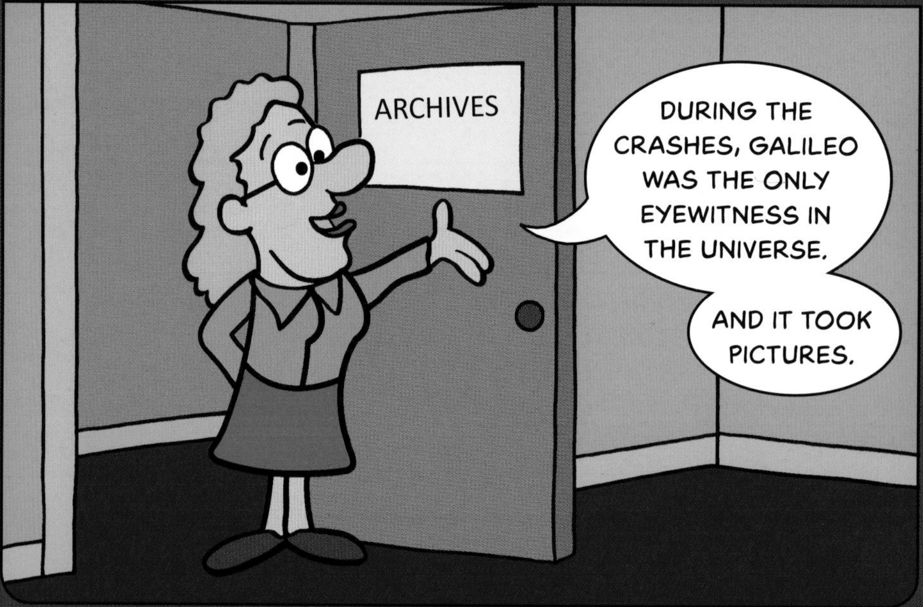
ARCHIVES
DURING THE CRASHES, GALILEO WAS THE ONLY EYEWITNESS IN THE UNIVERSE.
AND IT TOOK PICTURES.

A FEW MONTHS LATER, GALILEO FINALLY REACHED JUPITER. IT HAD BEEN SI
RS SINCE IT HAD LEFT EARTH, AND 20 YEARS SINCE THE PROJECT HAD BEG

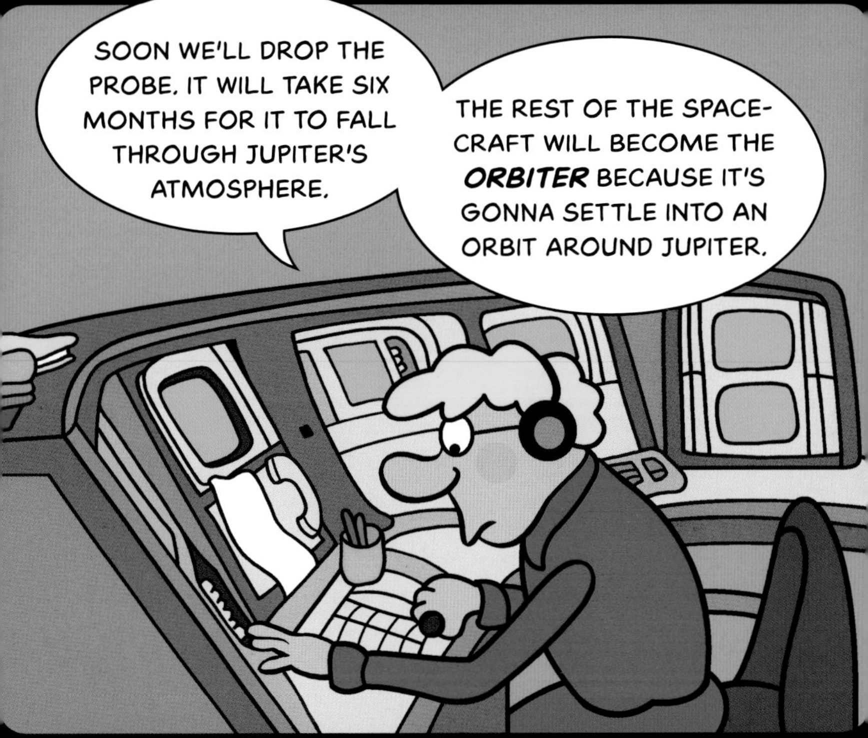
SOON WE'LL DROP THE PROBE. IT WILL TAKE SIX MONTHS FOR IT TO FALL THROUGH JUPITER'S ATMOSPHERE.
THE REST OF THE SPACE-CRAFT WILL BECOME THE **ORBITER** BECAUSE IT'S GONNA SETTLE INTO AN ORBIT AROUND JUPITER.

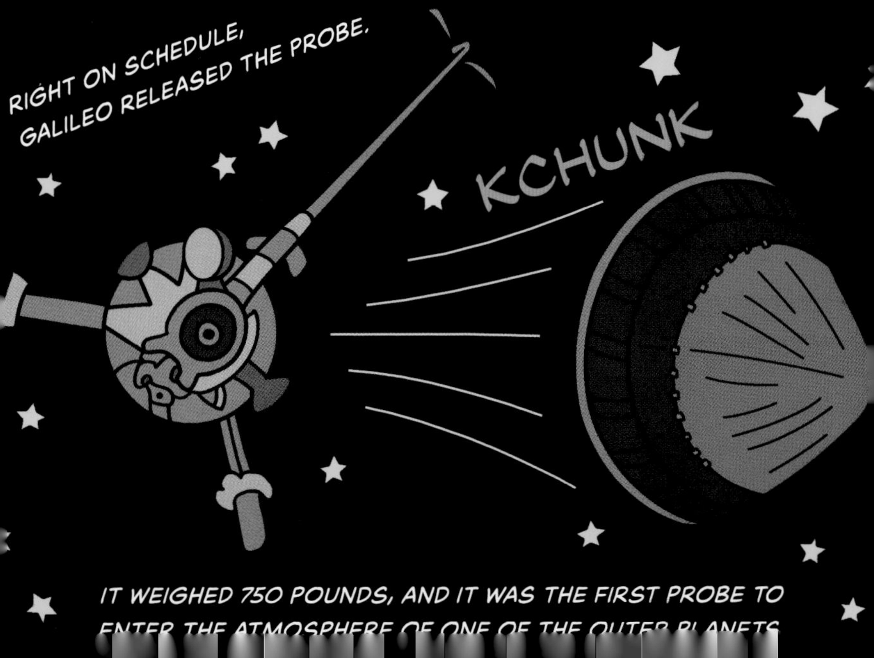
RIGHT ON SCHEDULE, GALILEO RELEASED THE PROBE.
KCHUNK
IT WEIGHED 750 POUNDS, AND IT WAS THE FIRST PROBE TO
ENTER THE ATMOSPHERE OF ONE OF THE OUTER PLANETS.

FOR YEARS, THE PROBE HAD BEEN SITTING IN FRONT OF AN ENGINE, SO NONE OF THE FLIGHT CONTROLLERS HAD BEEN ALLOWED TO START UP THAT ENGINE.

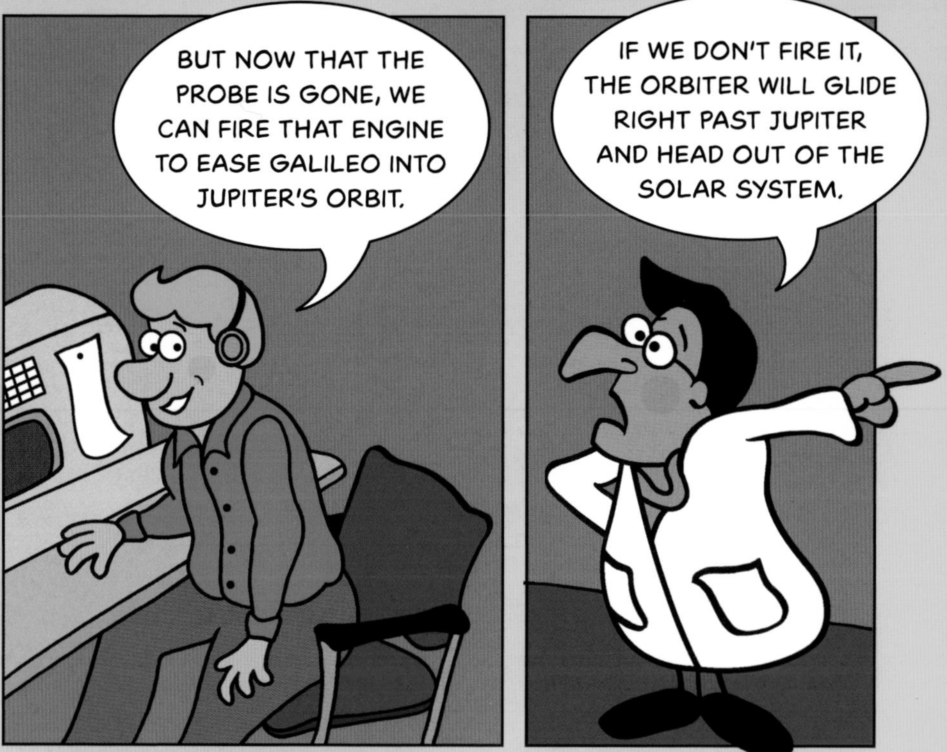

BUT NOW THAT THE PROBE IS GONE, WE CAN FIRE THAT ENGINE TO EASE GALILEO INTO JUPITER'S ORBIT.
IF WE DON'T FIRE IT, THE ORBITER WILL GLIDE RIGHT PAST JUPITER AND HEAD OUT OF THE SOLAR SYSTEM.

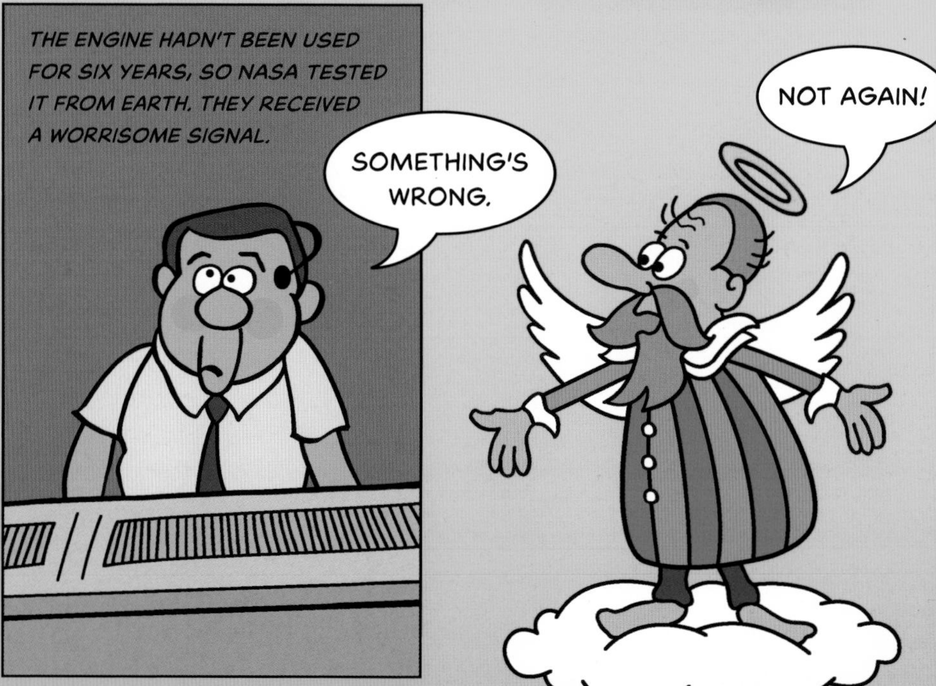

THE ENGINE HADN'T BEEN USED FOR SIX YEARS, SO NASA TESTED IT FROM EARTH. THEY RECEIVED A WORRISOME SIGNAL.
SOMETHING'S WRONG.
NOT AGAIN!

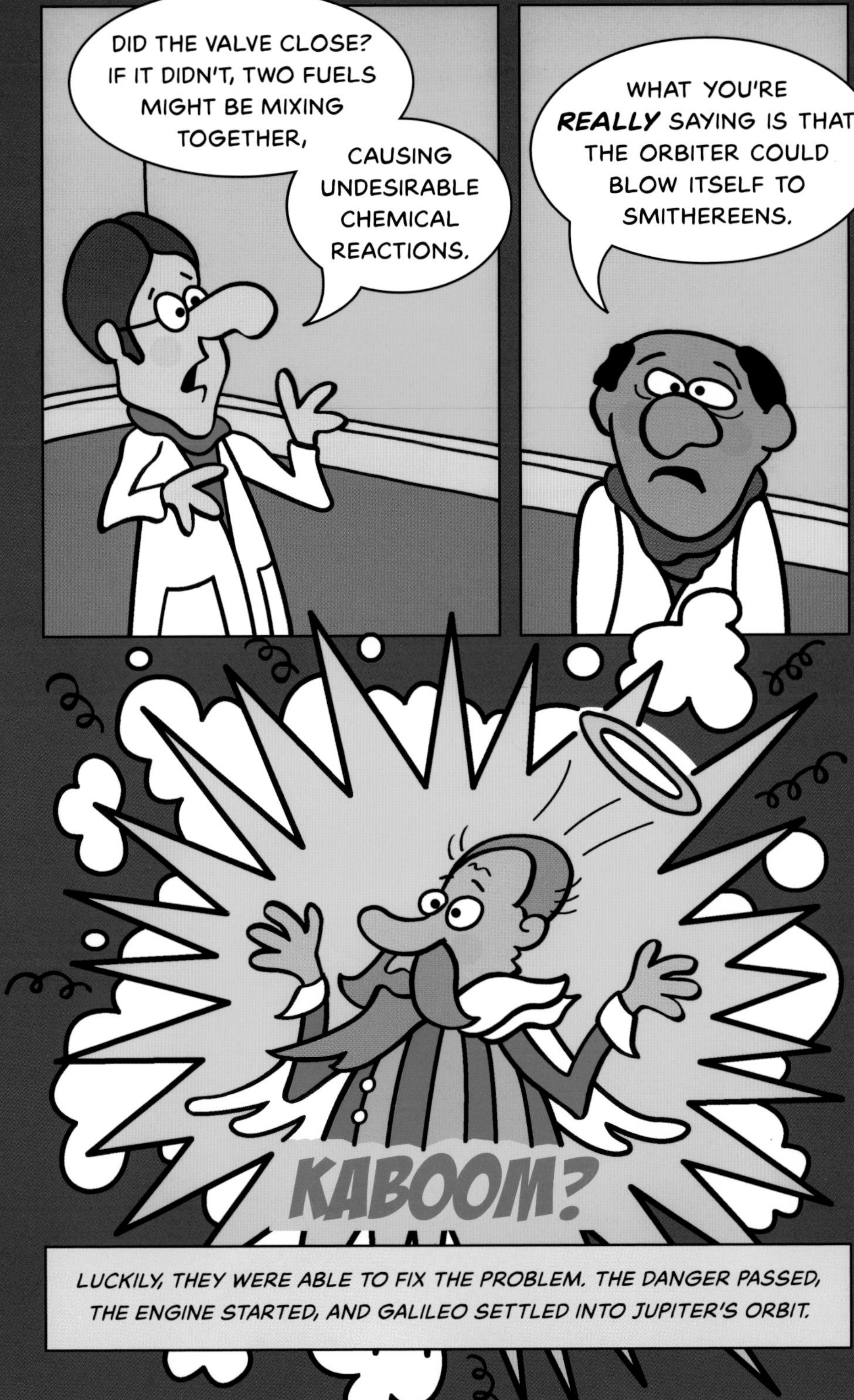
DID THE VALVE CLOSE? IF IT DIDN'T, TWO FUELS MIGHT BE MIXING TOGETHER,
CAUSING UNDESIRABLE CHEMICAL REACTIONS.
WHAT YOU'RE **REALLY** SAYING IS THAT THE ORBITER COULD BLOW ITSELF TO SMITHEREENS.
KABOOM?
LUCKILY, THEY WERE ABLE TO FIX THE PROBLEM. THE DANGER PASSED, THE ENGINE STARTED, AND GALILEO SETTLED INTO JUPITER'S ORBIT.

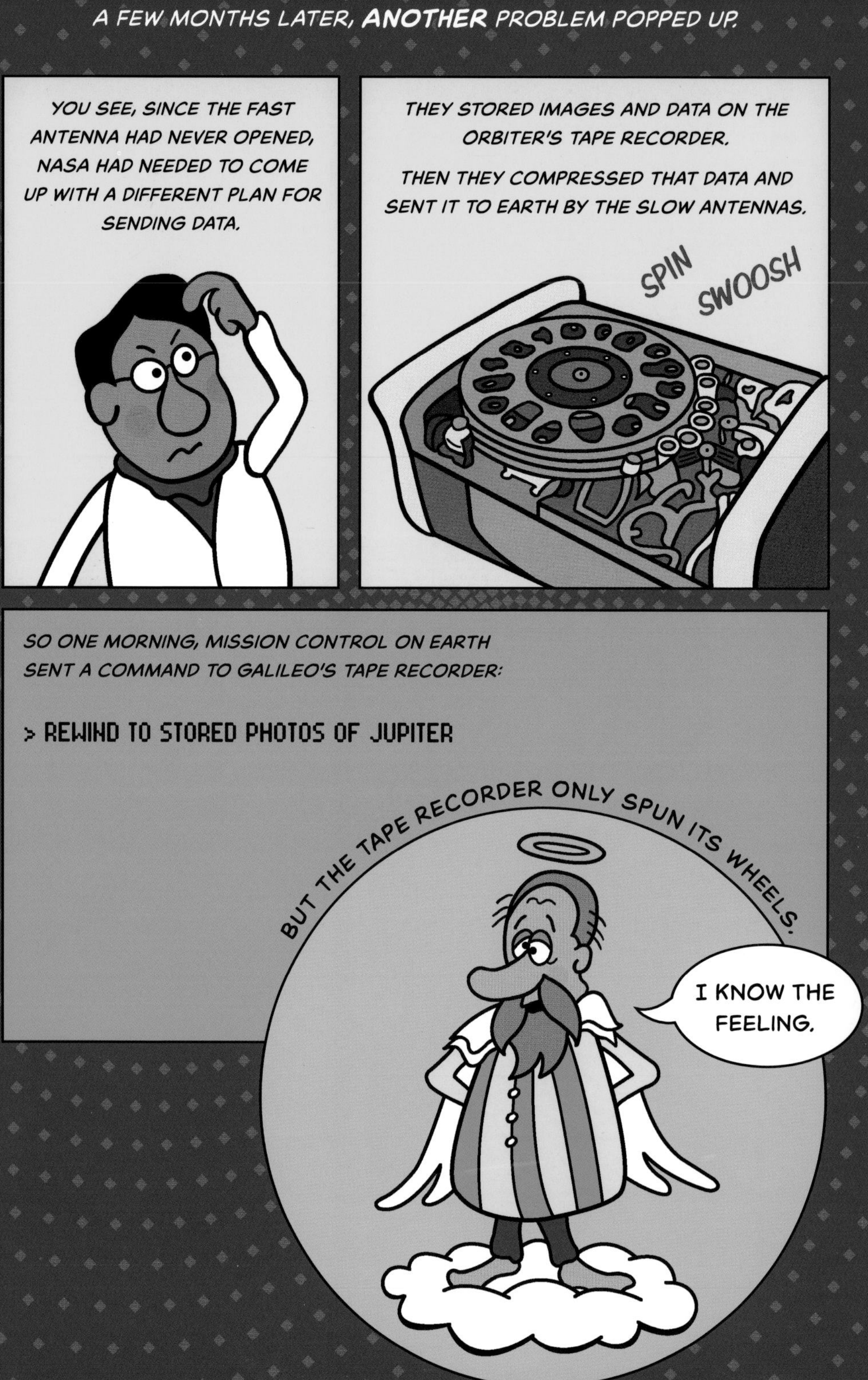
A FEW MONTHS LATER, **ANOTHER** PROBLEM POPPED UP.
YOU SEE, SINCE THE FAST ANTENNA HAD NEVER OPENED, NASA HAD NEEDED TO COME UP WITH A DIFFERENT PLAN FOR SENDING DATA.
THEY STORED IMAGES AND DATA ON THE ORBITER'S TAPE RECORDER.
THEN THEY COMPRESSED THAT DATA AND SENT IT TO EARTH BY THE SLOW ANTENNAS.
SPIN
SWOOSH
SO ONE MORNING, MISSION CONTROL ON EARTH SENT A COMMAND TO GALILEO'S TAPE RECORDER:
> REWIND TO STORED PHOTOS OF JUPITER
BUT THE TAPE RECORDER ONLY SPUN ITS WHEELS.
I KNOW THE FEELING.

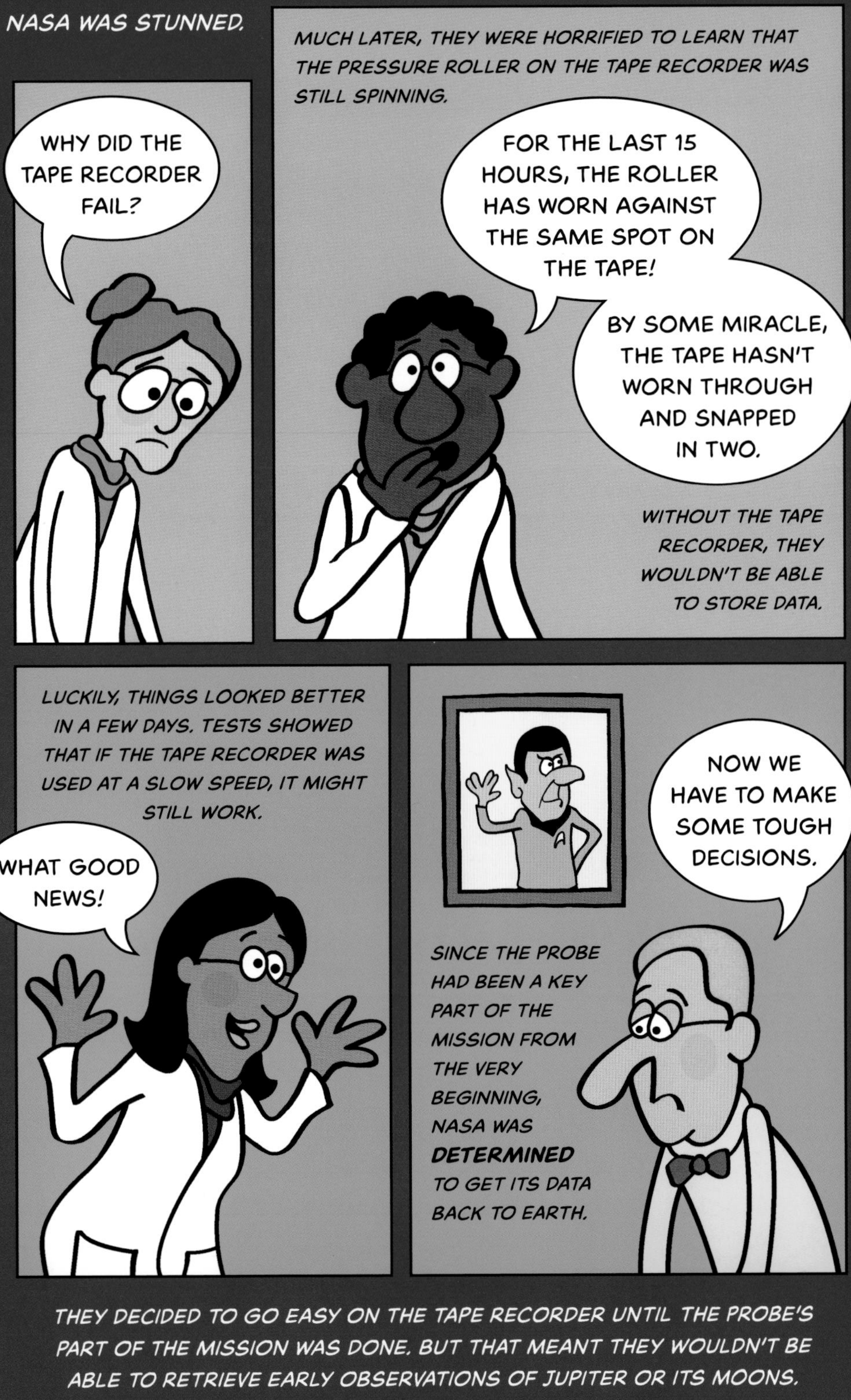
NASA WAS STUNNED.
WHY DID THE TAPE RECORDER FAIL?
MUCH LATER, THEY WERE HORRIFIED TO LEARN THAT THE PRESSURE ROLLER ON THE TAPE RECORDER WAS STILL SPINNING.
FOR THE LAST 15 HOURS, THE ROLLER HAS WORN AGAINST THE SAME SPOT ON THE TAPE!
BY SOME MIRACLE, THE TAPE HASN'T WORN THROUGH AND SNAPPED IN TWO.
WITHOUT THE TAPE RECORDER, THEY WOULDN'T BE ABLE TO STORE DATA.
LUCKILY, THINGS LOOKED BETTER IN A FEW DAYS. TESTS SHOWED THAT IF THE TAPE RECORDER WAS USED AT A SLOW SPEED, IT MIGHT STILL WORK.
WHAT GOOD NEWS!
NOW WE HAVE TO MAKE SOME TOUGH DECISIONS.
SINCE THE PROBE HAD BEEN A KEY PART OF THE MISSION FROM THE VERY BEGINNING, NASA WAS **DETERMINED** TO GET ITS DATA BACK TO EARTH.
THEY DECIDED TO GO EASY ON THE TAPE RECORDER UNTIL THE PROBE'S PART OF THE MISSION WAS DONE. BUT THAT MEANT THEY WOULDN'T BE ABLE TO RETRIEVE EARLY OBSERVATIONS OF JUPITER OR ITS MOONS.

MEANWHILE, THROUGH THE SUMMER AND AUTUMN OF 1995, THE PROBE HAD BEEN FALLING THROUGH JUPITER'S ATMOSPHERE.

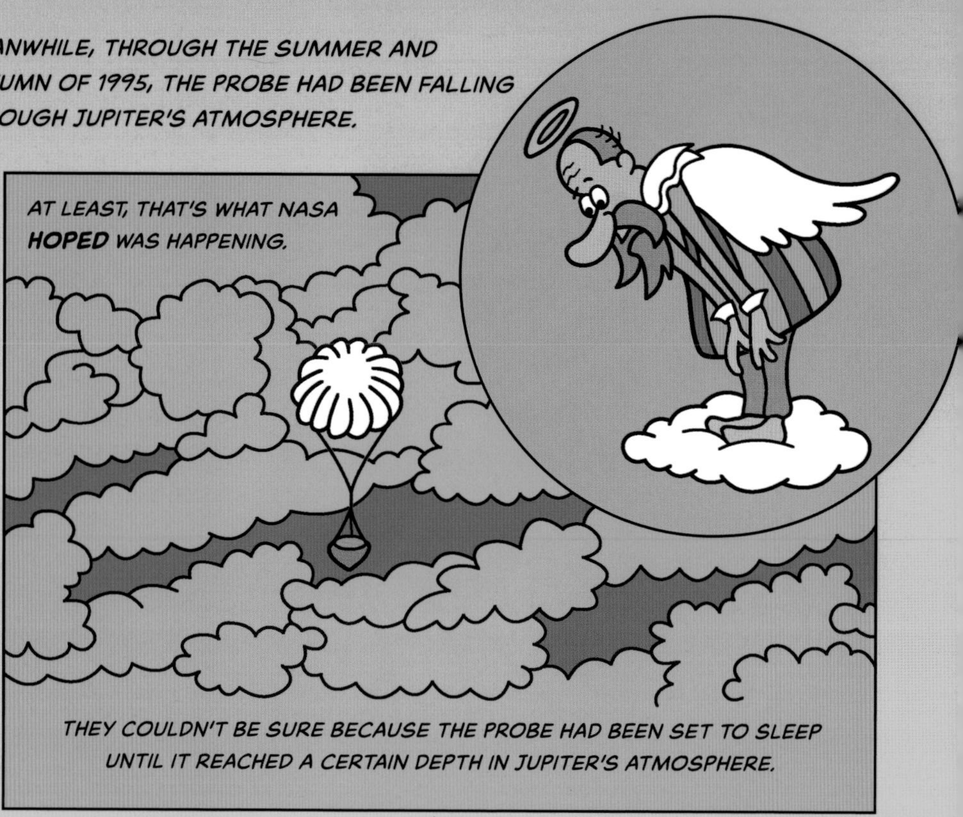
AT LEAST, THAT'S WHAT NASA **HOPED** WAS HAPPENING.
THEY COULDN'T BE SURE BECAUSE THE PROBE HAD BEEN SET TO SLEEP UNTIL IT REACHED A CERTAIN DEPTH IN JUPITER'S ATMOSPHERE.

AS THE SCIENTISTS WAITED FOR THE MONTHS TO PASS, THEY WORRIED.

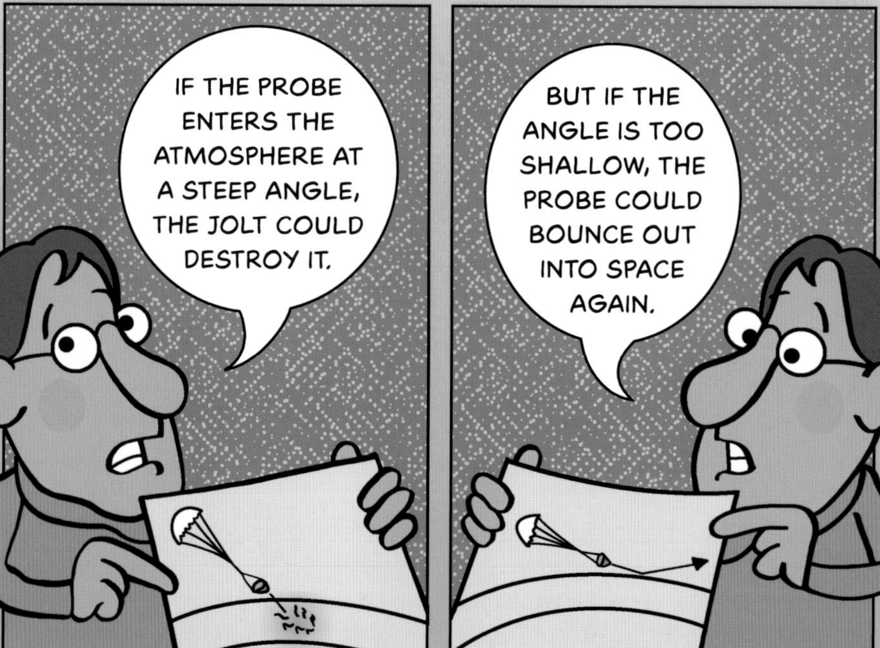
IF THE PROBE ENTERS THE ATMOSPHERE AT A STEEP ANGLE, THE JOLT COULD DESTROY IT.
BUT IF THE ANGLE IS TOO SHALLOW, THE PROBE COULD BOUNCE OUT INTO SPACE AGAIN.

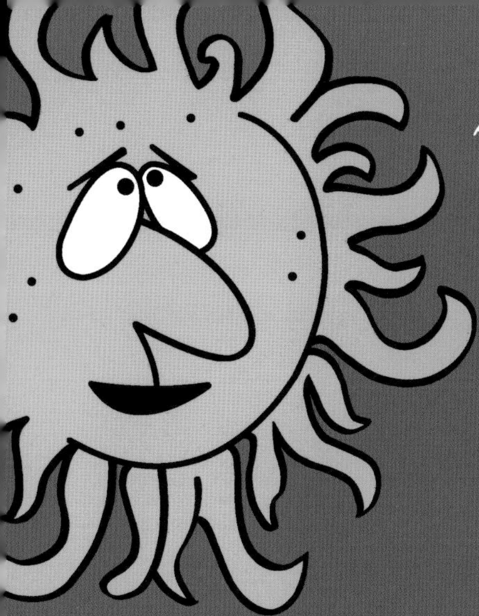

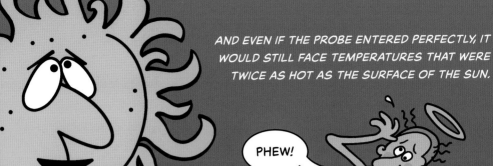

AND EVEN IF THE PROBE ENTERED PERFECTLY, IT WOULD STILL FACE TEMPERATURES THAT WERE TWICE AS HOT AS THE SURFACE OF THE SUN.

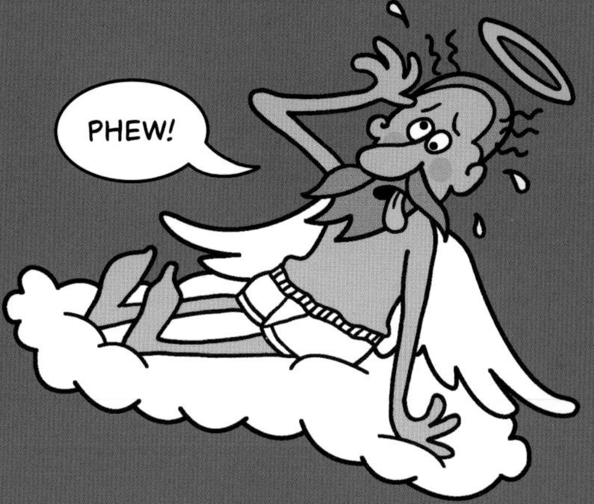
PHEW!

FINALLY, THE DAY ARRIVED WHEN THE PROBE WAS SUPPOSED TO WAKE UP.

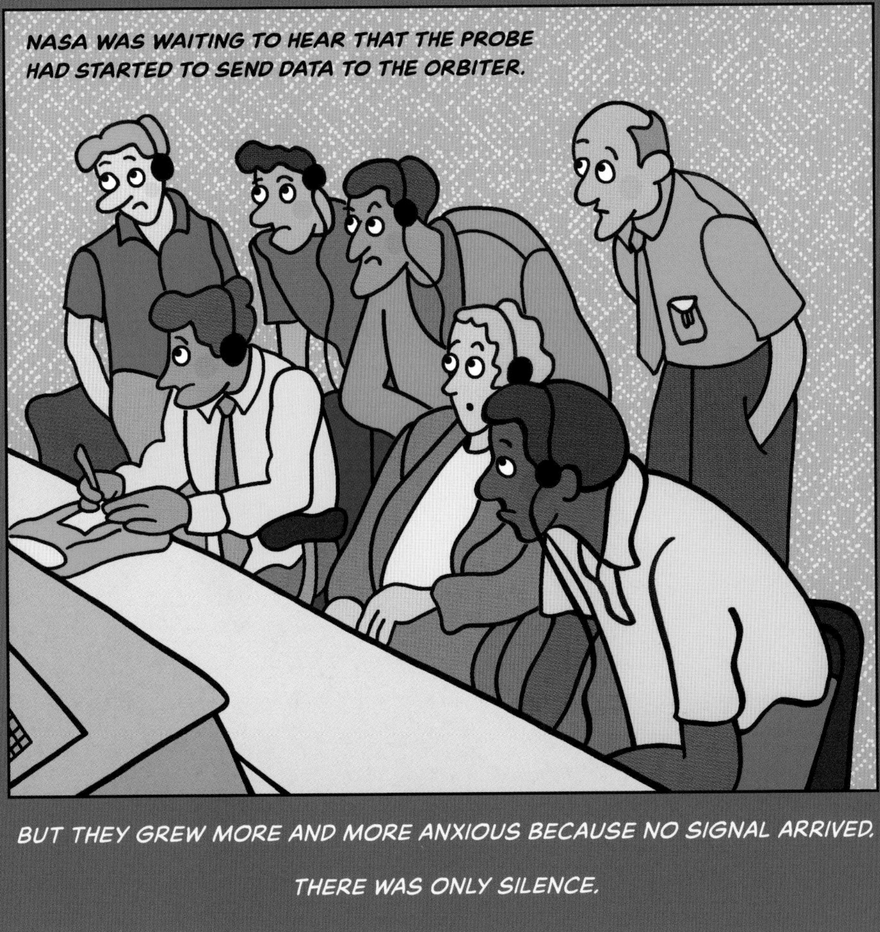
NASA WAS WAITING TO HEAR THAT THE PROBE HAD STARTED TO SEND DATA TO THE ORBITER.

BUT THEY GREW MORE AND MORE ANXIOUS BECAUSE NO SIGNAL ARRIVED.

THERE WAS ONLY SILENCE.

TENSELY, THEY WAITED -- AND WONDERED.

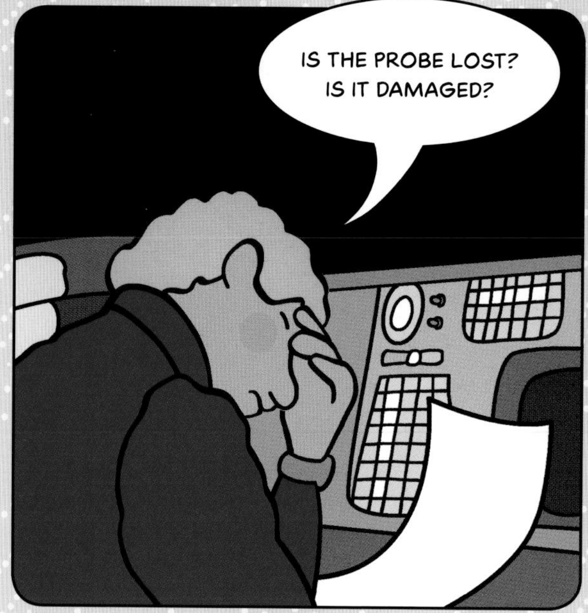
IS THE PROBE LOST? IS IT DAMAGED?

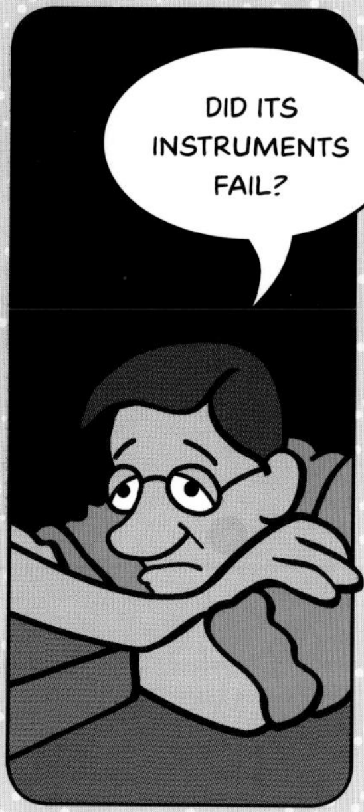
DID ITS INSTRUMENTS FAIL?

FINALLY, A SIGNAL ARRIVED! IT SHOWED THAT THE PROBE HAD BEEN SENDING DATA TO THE ORBITER.

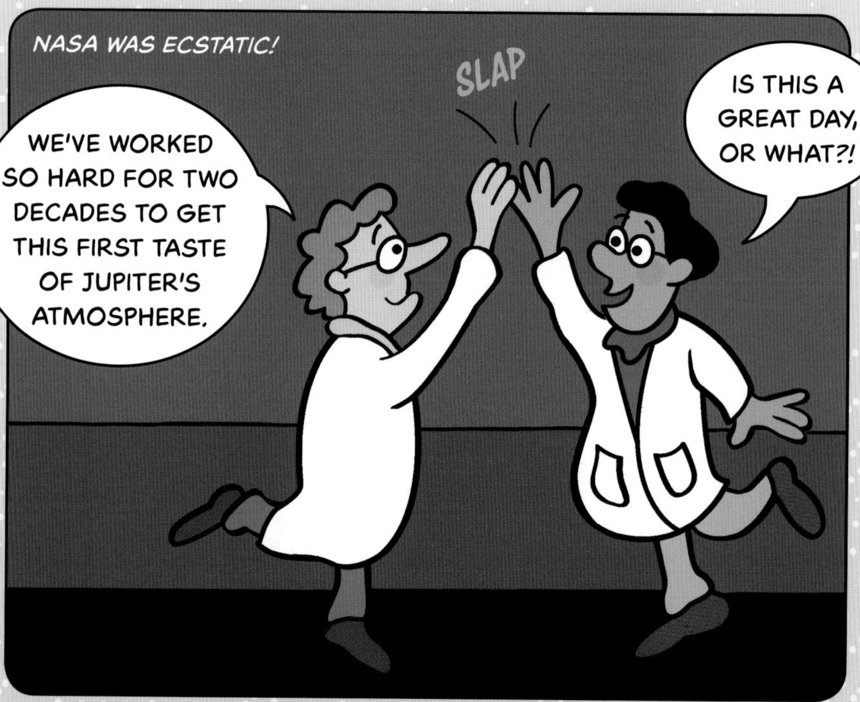
NASA WAS ECSTATIC!
WE'VE WORKED SO HARD FOR TWO DECADES TO GET THIS FIRST TASTE OF JUPITER'S ATMOSPHERE.
SLAP
IS THIS A GREAT DAY, OR WHAT?!

AS THE PROBE FELL, IT COLLECTED DATA ABOUT...

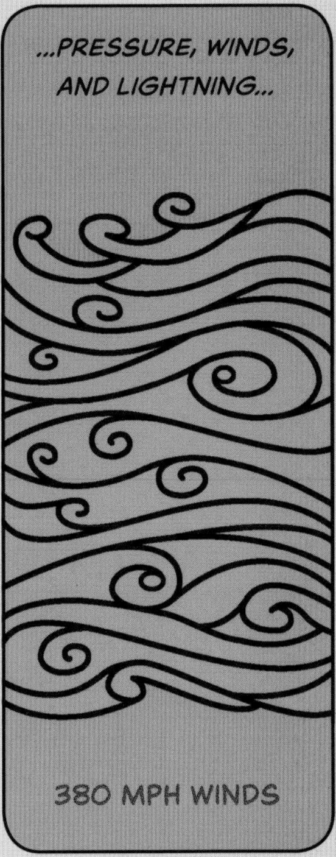
...PRESSURE, WINDS, AND LIGHTNING...
380 MPH WINDS

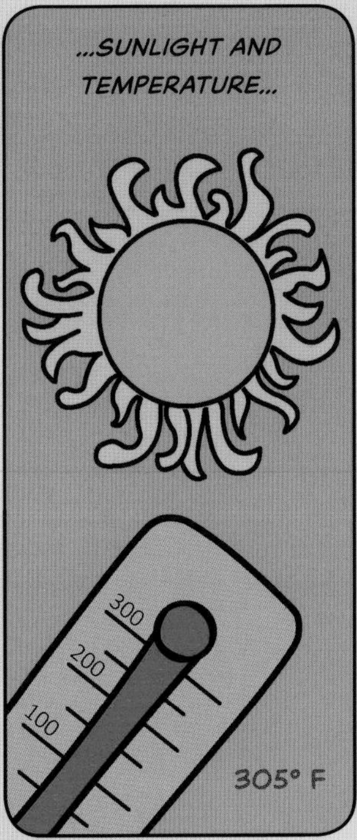
...SUNLIGHT AND TEMPERATURE...
300
200
100
305° F

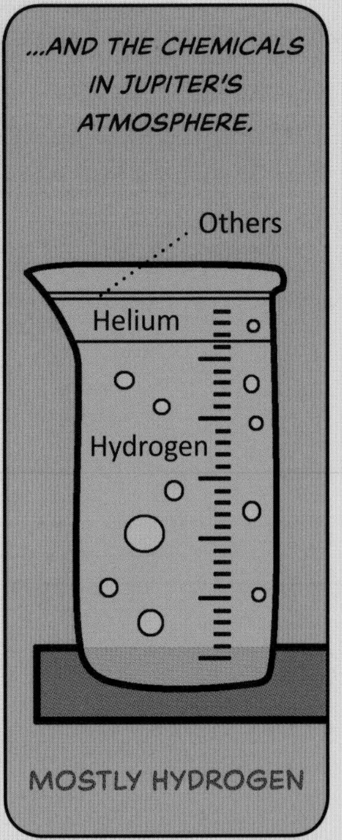
...AND THE CHEMICALS IN JUPITER'S ATMOSPHERE.
Others
Helium
Hydrogen
MOSTLY HYDROGEN

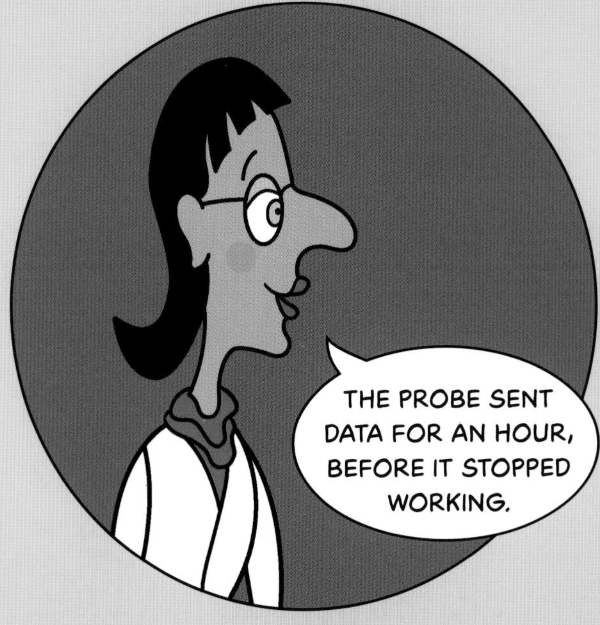
THE PROBE SENT DATA FOR AN HOUR, BEFORE IT STOPPED WORKING.

THAT WAS EXACTLY HOW NASA HAD EXPECTED THINGS TO TURN OUT.

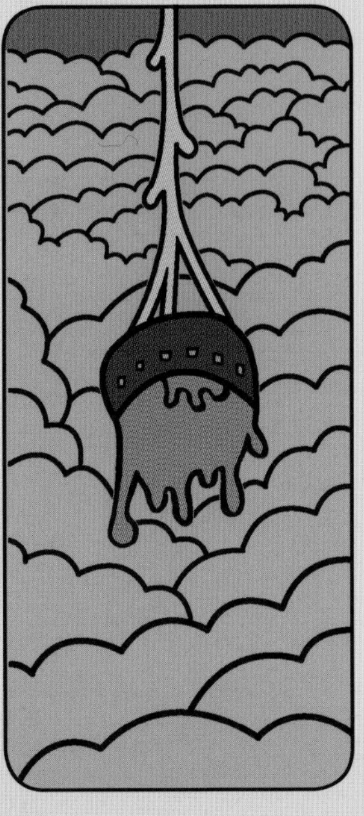

IN THE END, THE PROBE SIMPLY MELTED.

THE GALILEO TEAM TOOK A MOMENT TO REFLECT ON THE MISSION SO FAR.

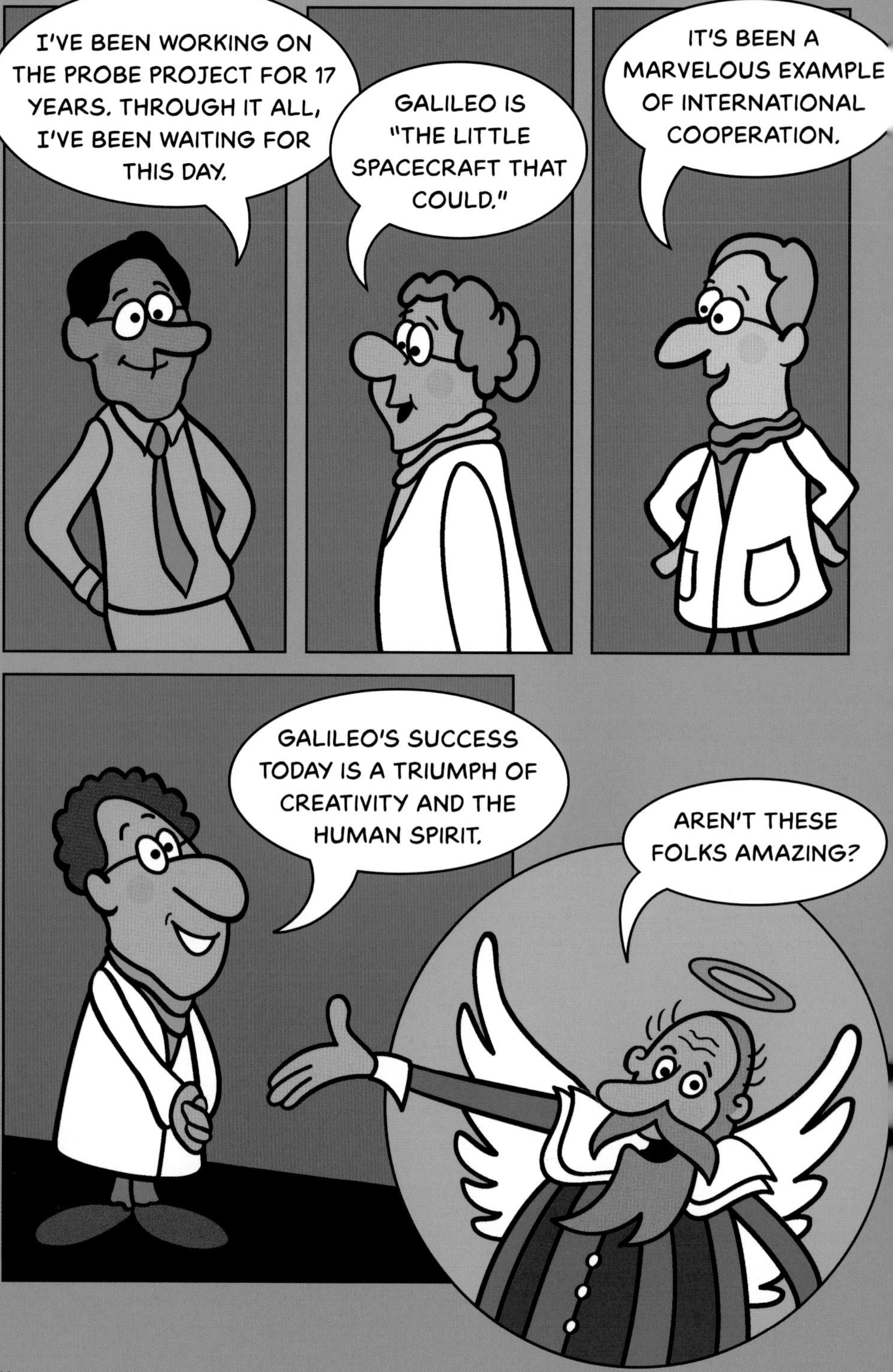
I'VE BEEN WORKING ON THE PROBE PROJECT FOR 17 YEARS. THROUGH IT ALL, I'VE BEEN WAITING FOR THIS DAY.
GALILEO IS "THE LITTLE SPACECRAFT THAT COULD."
IT'S BEEN A MARVELOUS EXAMPLE OF INTERNATIONAL COOPERATION.
GALILEO'S SUCCESS TODAY IS A TRIUMPH OF CREATIVITY AND THE HUMAN SPIRIT.
AREN'T THESE FOLKS AMAZING?

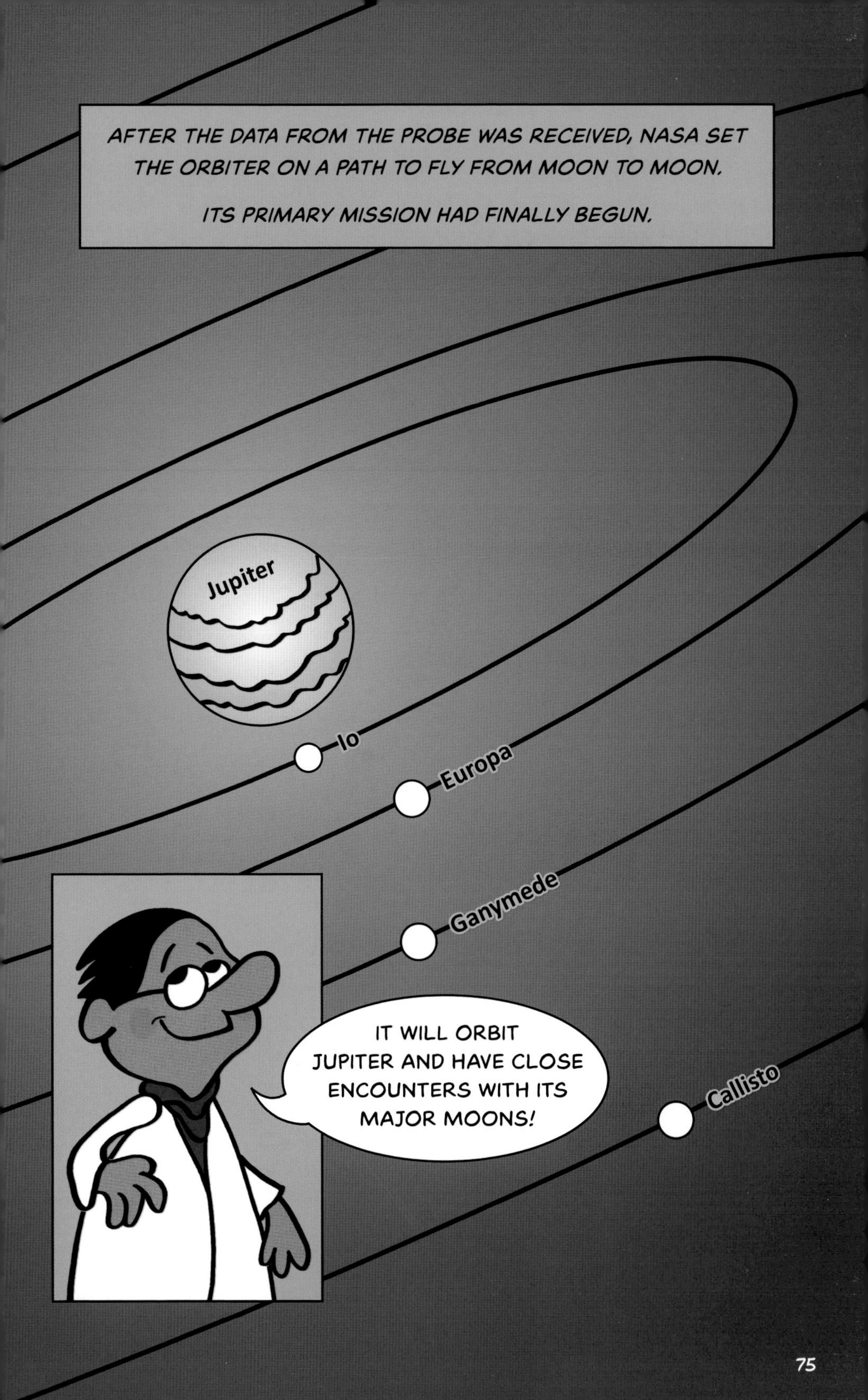
AFTER THE DATA FROM THE PROBE WAS RECEIVED, NASA SET THE ORBITER ON A PATH TO FLY FROM MOON TO MOON.
ITS PRIMARY MISSION HAD FINALLY BEGUN.
Jupiter
Io
Europa
Ganymede
Callisto
IT WILL ORBIT JUPITER AND HAVE CLOSE ENCOUNTERS WITH ITS MAJOR MOONS!

DURING THE PRIMARY MISSION, THE ORBITER SENT
SOME FASCINATING DATA BACK TO EARTH.

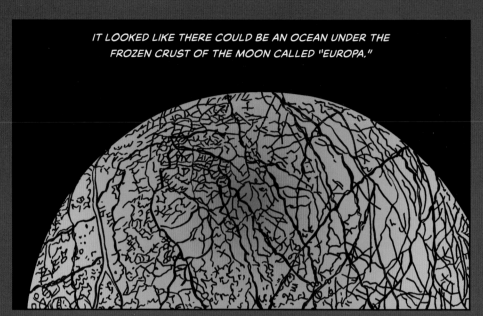

IT LOOKED LIKE THERE COULD BE AN OCEAN UNDER THE
FROZEN CRUST OF THE MOON CALLED "EUROPA."

THE CRUST IS BROKEN UP LIKE ICE FLOES.

IT'S BEEN JOSTLED FROM BELOW BY WARM ICE, OR MAYBE EVEN BY LIQUID WATER.

THAT'S AN ENVIRONMENT WHERE LIFE COULD EXIST.

AND **THAT** CERTAINLY CAUGHT THE WORLD'S ATTENTION!

COULD THERE BE LIFE UNDER EUROPA'S ICE?

IT WAS POSSIBLE.

THE ORBITER'S PRIMARY MISSION WAS SUPPOSED TO WIND DOWN IN 1997, BUT WHEN THAT TIME CAME, IT WAS WORKING FINE, AND IT STILL HAD FUEL.

SO NASA EXTENDED THE MISSION FOR TWO MORE YEARS TO LOOK VERY CLOSELY AT THE MOONS EUROPA AND IO.

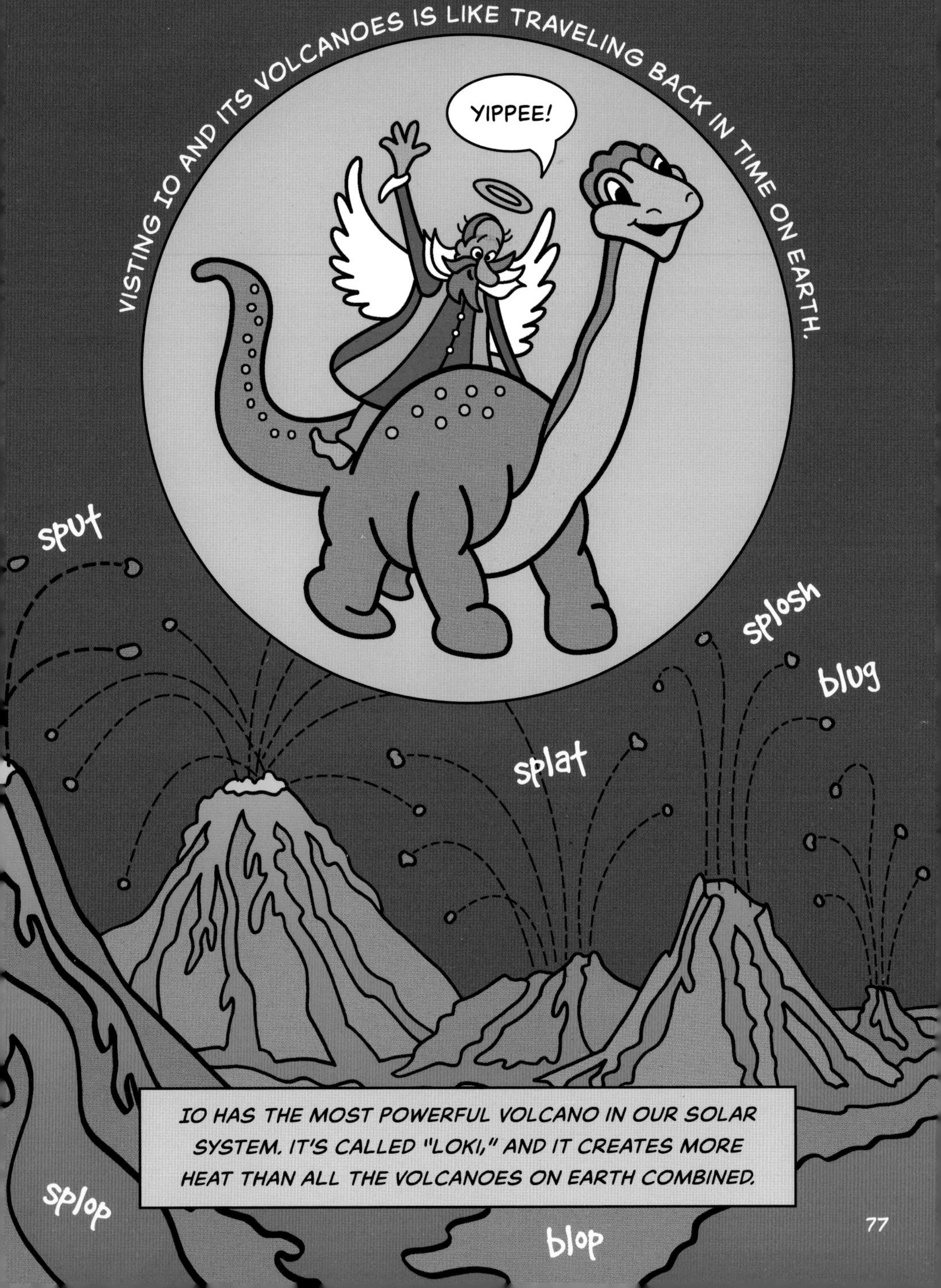
VISTING IO AND ITS VOLCANOES IS LIKE TRAVELING BACK IN TIME ON EARTH.
YIPPEE!
sput
splosh
blug
splat
IO HAS THE MOST POWERFUL VOLCANO IN OUR SOLAR SYSTEM. IT'S CALLED "LOKI," AND IT CREATES MORE HEAT THAN ALL THE VOLCANOES ON EARTH COMBINED.
splop
blop

WHEN 1999 CAME, THE MISSION WAS SUPPOSED TO END.
BUT THE ORBITER WAS STILL WORKING!

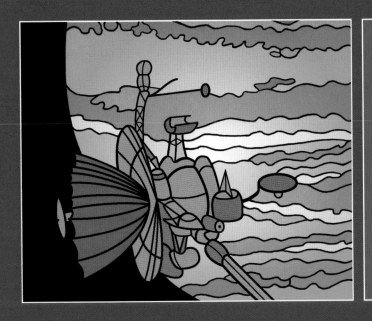

SO THE MISSION WAS EXTENDED AGAIN, UNTIL 2001.

GALILEO COLLECTED DATA AS IT FLEW CLOSE TO EUROPA, IO, AND CALLISTO.

WHEN 2001 CAME, THE MISSION WAS SUPPOSED TO END.

BUT THE ORBITER IS STILL WORKING!

SO THE MISSION WAS EXTENDED AGAIN, UNTIL 2003.

THIS TIME, GALILEO STUDIED THE MOONS IO, GANYMEDE, AND AMALTHEA.

IN ALL, DURING THE PRIMARY AND EXTENDED MISSIONS, GALILEO HAD 35 ENCOUNTERS WITH JUPITER'S MOONS.

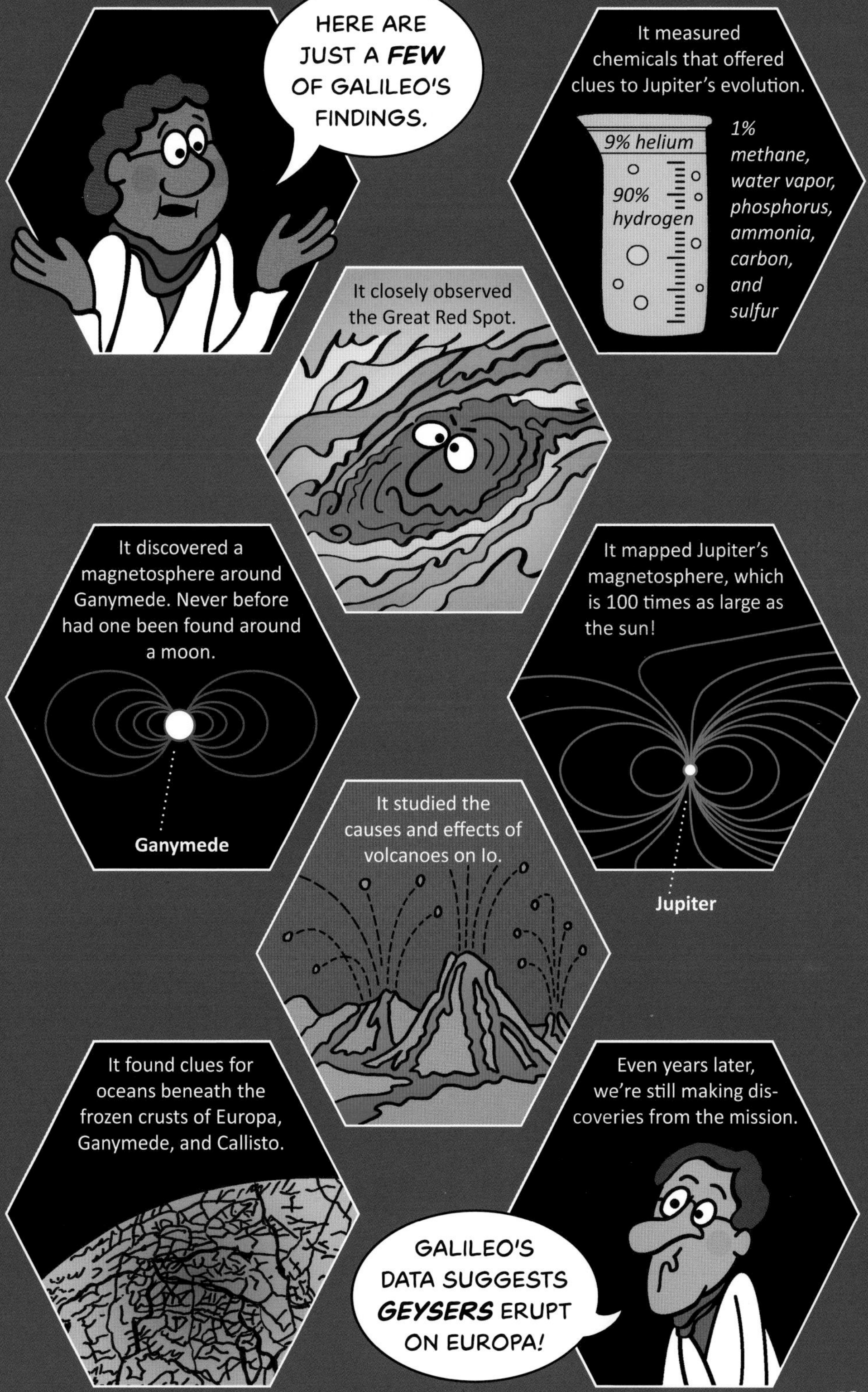

HERE ARE JUST A *FEW* OF GALILEO'S FINDINGS.

It measured chemicals that offered clues to Jupiter's evolution.

9% helium

90% hydrogen

1% methane, water vapor, phosphorus, ammonia, carbon, and sulfur

It closely observed the Great Red Spot.

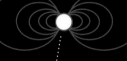

It discovered a magnetosphere around Ganymede. Never before had one been found around a moon.

Ganymede

It mapped Jupiter's magnetosphere, which is 100 times as large as the sun!

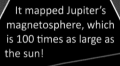

Jupiter

It studied the causes and effects of volcanoes on Io.

It found clues for oceans beneath the frozen crusts of Europa, Ganymede, and Callisto.

Even years later, we're still making discoveries from the mission.

GALILEO'S DATA SUGGESTS *GEYSERS* ERUPT ON EUROPA!

DURING THE EXTENDED MISSIONS, SCIENTISTS TALKED ABOUT HOW TO PROTECT THEIR DISCOVERIES WHILE THEY WRAPPED UP THE ORBITER'S JOURNEY.

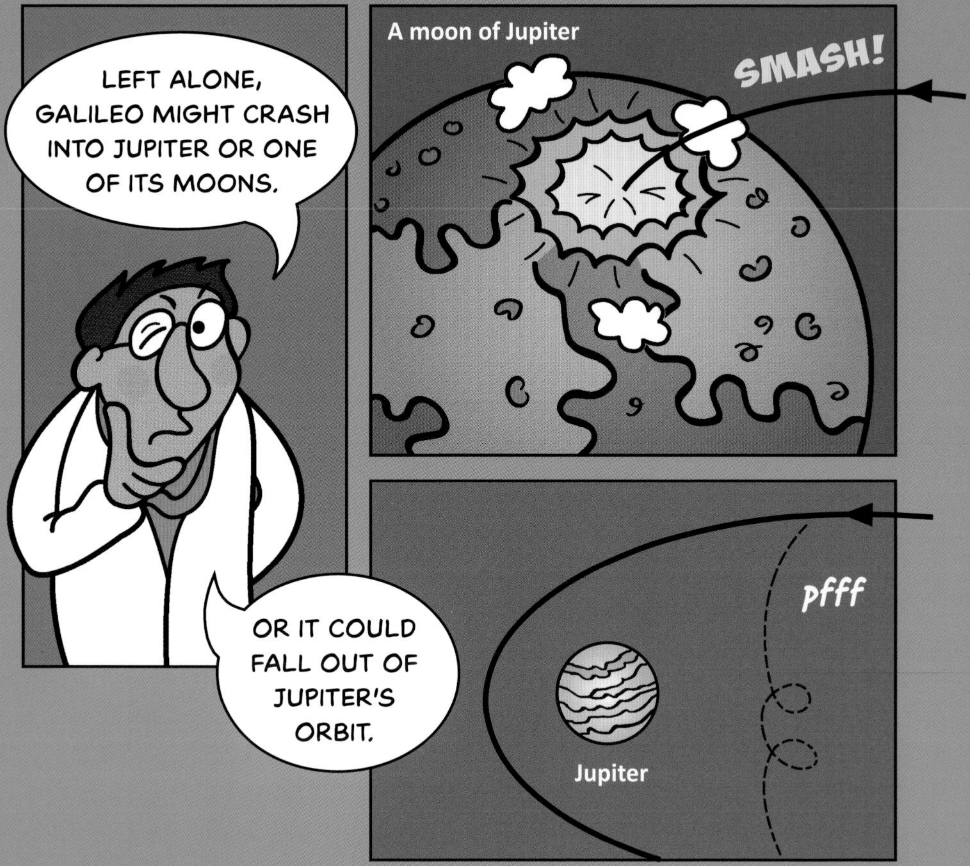
LEFT ALONE, GALILEO MIGHT CRASH INTO JUPITER OR ONE OF ITS MOONS.
A moon of Jupiter
SMASH!
OR IT COULD FALL OUT OF JUPITER'S ORBIT.
pfff
Jupiter

IF IT FELL OUT OF ORBIT, THERE WAS A TINY CHANCE IT COULD RETURN TO EARTH.

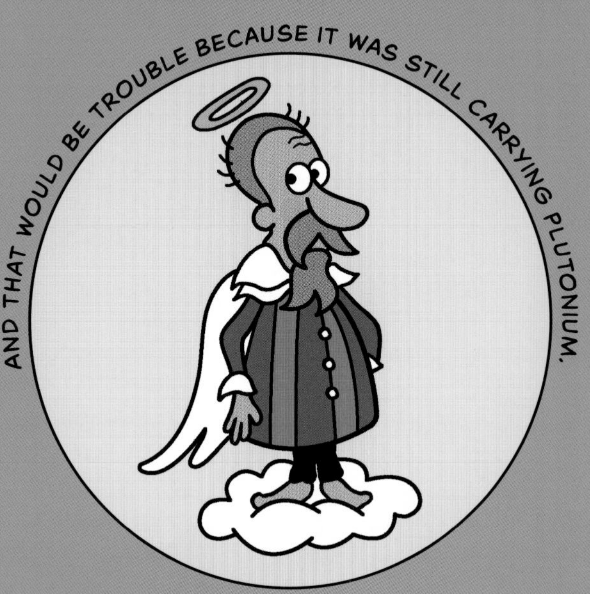
AND THAT WOULD BE TROUBLE BECAUSE IT WAS STILL CARRYING PLUTONIUM.

EVERYONE AGREED THAT THEY SHOULDN'T LET THE ORBITER CRASH INTO EUROPA OR ANY OF THE OTHER MOONS THAT MIGHT CONTAIN LIFE.

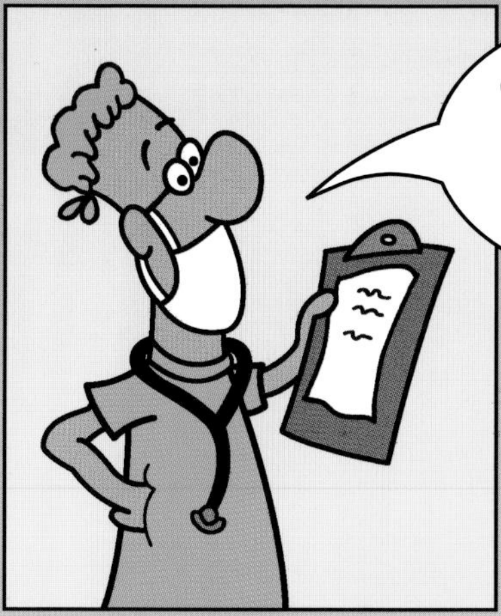
GALILEO WASN'T STERILIZED BEFORE IT LEFT EARTH.

THAT MEANT ITS EARTH MICROBES COULD OVERRUN INDIGENOUS MICROBES, IF THERE WAS ANY POSSIBILITY OF LIFE ON THOSE MOONS.

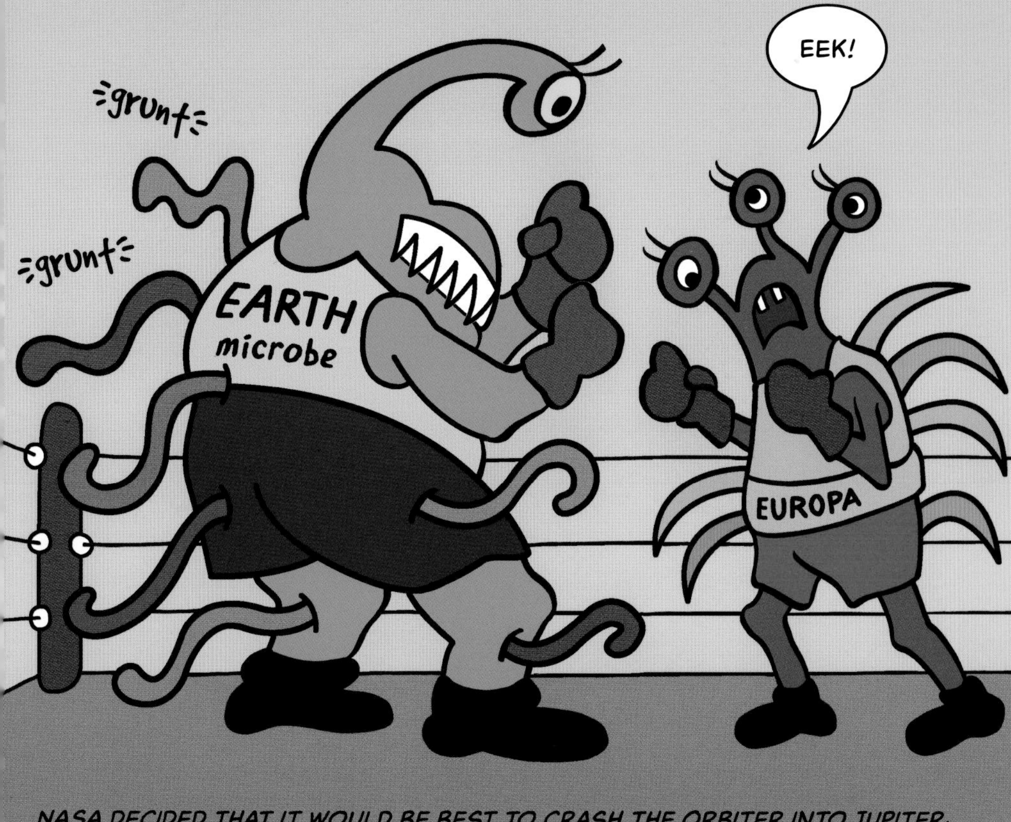
EEK!
grunt
grunt
EARTH microbe
EUROPA

NASA DECIDED THAT IT WOULD BE BEST TO CRASH THE ORBITER INTO JUPITER, WHICH DIDN'T HAVE ANY OF THE CONDITIONS THAT SUPPORT LIFE.

AND BY 2003, THAT PLAN WAS BECOMING NECESSARY...

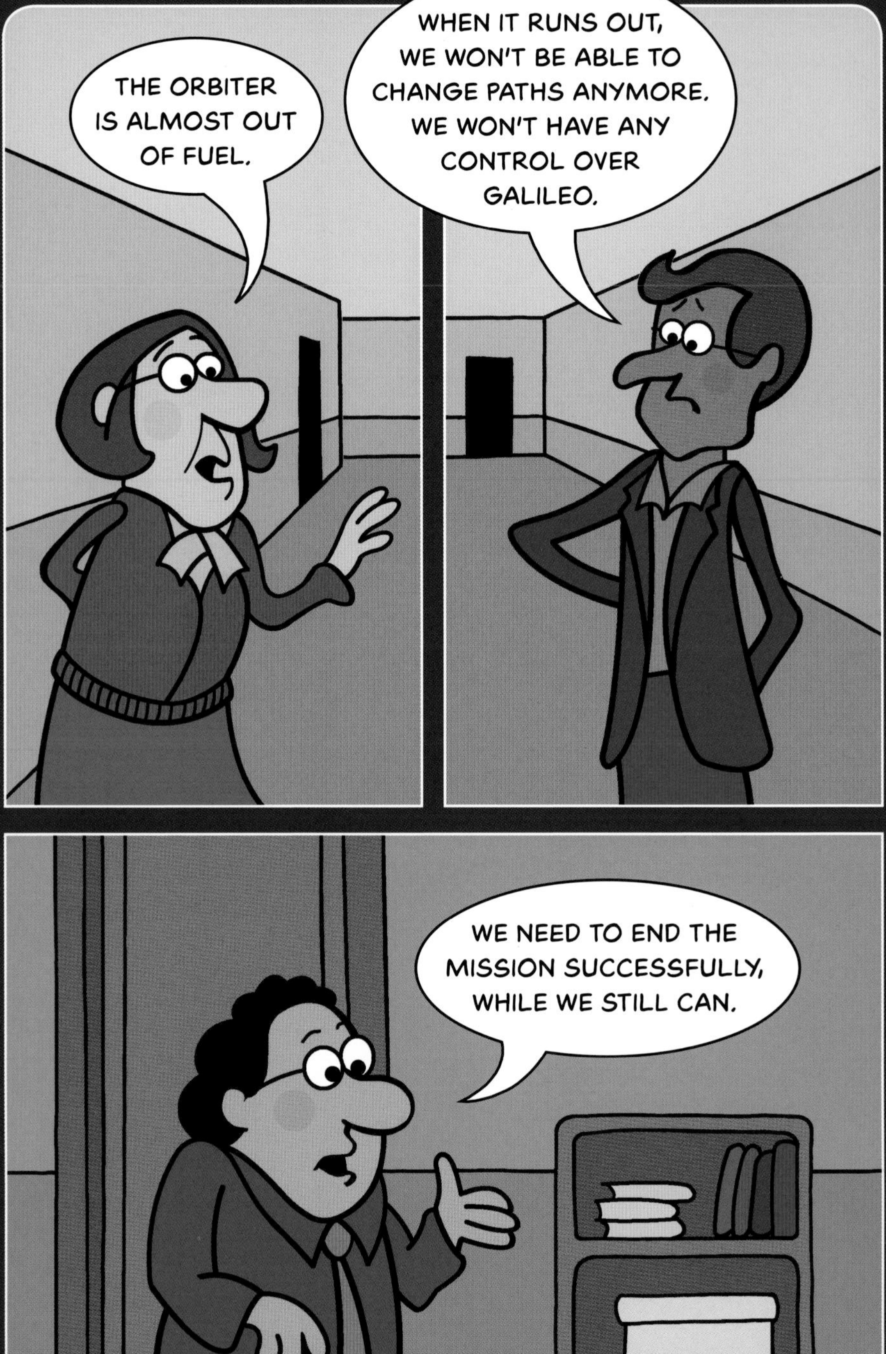
THE ORBITER IS ALMOST OUT OF FUEL.
WHEN IT RUNS OUT, WE WON'T BE ABLE TO CHANGE PATHS ANYMORE. WE WON'T HAVE ANY CONTROL OVER GALILEO.
WE NEED TO END THE MISSION SUCCESSFULLY, WHILE WE STILL CAN.

AND SO THEY SET THE ORBITER ON A COLLISION COURSE WITH JUPITER.

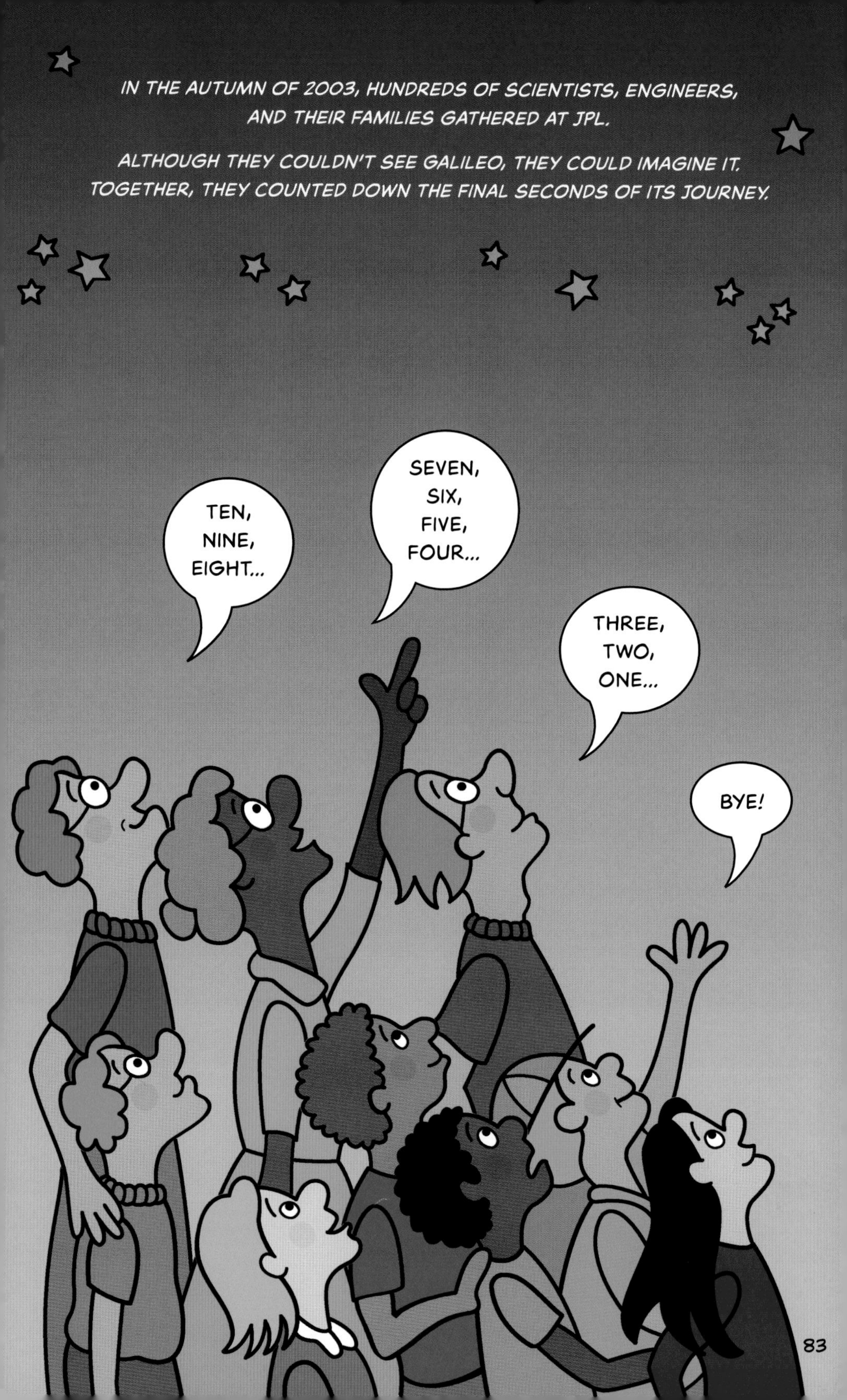
IN THE AUTUMN OF 2003, HUNDREDS OF SCIENTISTS, ENGINEERS, AND THEIR FAMILIES GATHERED AT JPL.
ALTHOUGH THEY COULDN'T SEE GALILEO, THEY COULD IMAGINE IT. TOGETHER, THEY COUNTED DOWN THE FINAL SECONDS OF ITS JOURNEY.
TEN, NINE, EIGHT...
SEVEN, SIX, FIVE, FOUR...
THREE, TWO, ONE...
BYE!

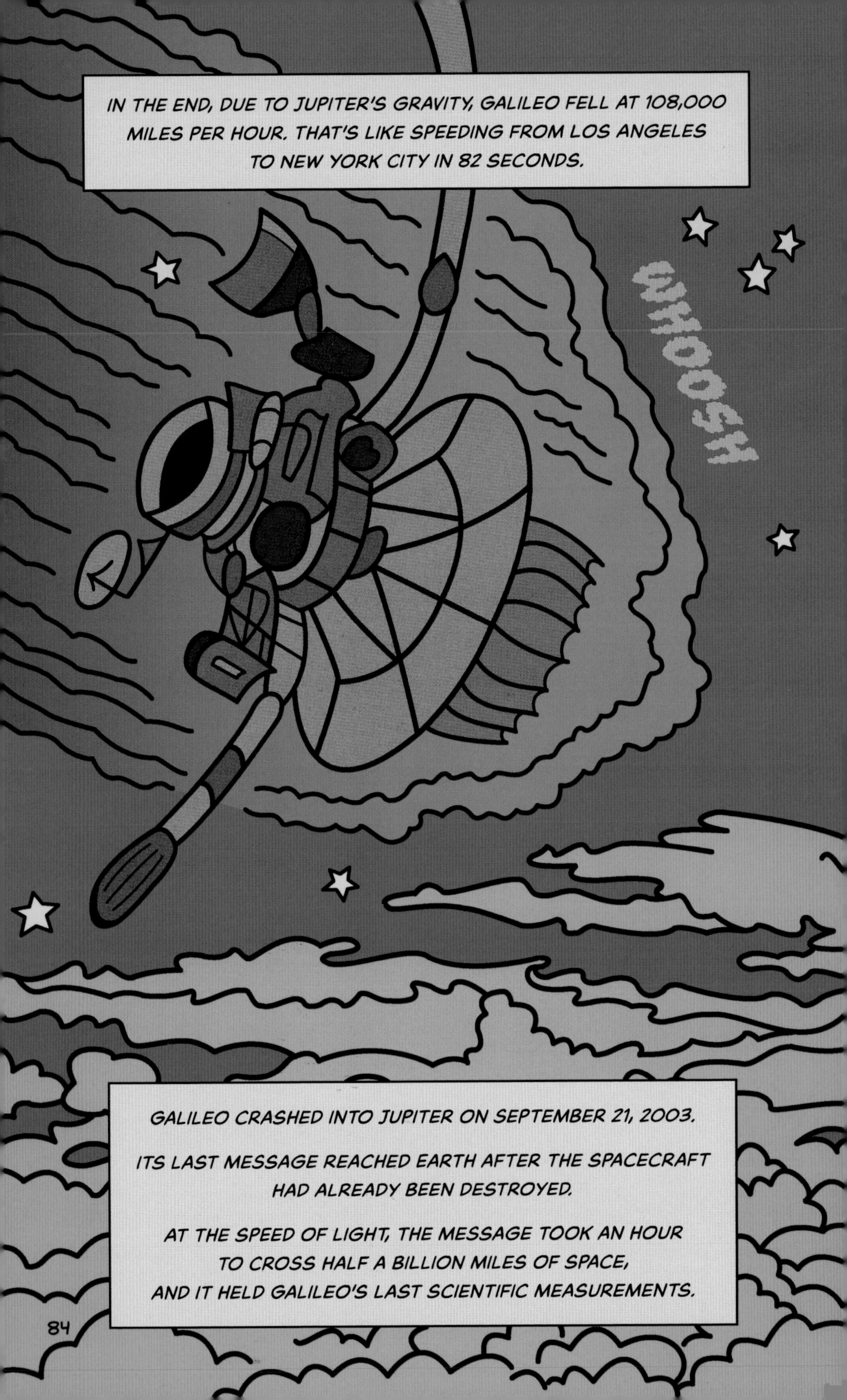
IN THE END, DUE TO JUPITER'S GRAVITY, GALILEO FELL AT 108,000 MILES PER HOUR. THAT'S LIKE SPEEDING FROM LOS ANGELES TO NEW YORK CITY IN 82 SECONDS.
WHOOSH
GALILEO CRASHED INTO JUPITER ON SEPTEMBER 21, 2003.
ITS LAST MESSAGE REACHED EARTH AFTER THE SPACECRAFT HAD ALREADY BEEN DESTROYED.
AT THE SPEED OF LIGHT, THE MESSAGE TOOK AN HOUR TO CROSS HALF A BILLION MILES OF SPACE, AND IT HELD GALILEO'S LAST SCIENTIFIC MEASUREMENTS.

THE GALILEO MISSION TURNED OUT TO BE ONE OF NASA'S HARDEST PROJECTS.

FOR A QUARTER OF A CENTURY, THE PEOPLE ON THE MISSION USED THEIR IMAGINATIONS TO OVERCOME TOUGH PROBLEMS, SOME OF WHICH CAME UP WHEN THE SPACECRAFT WAS MILLIONS OF MILES AWAY.

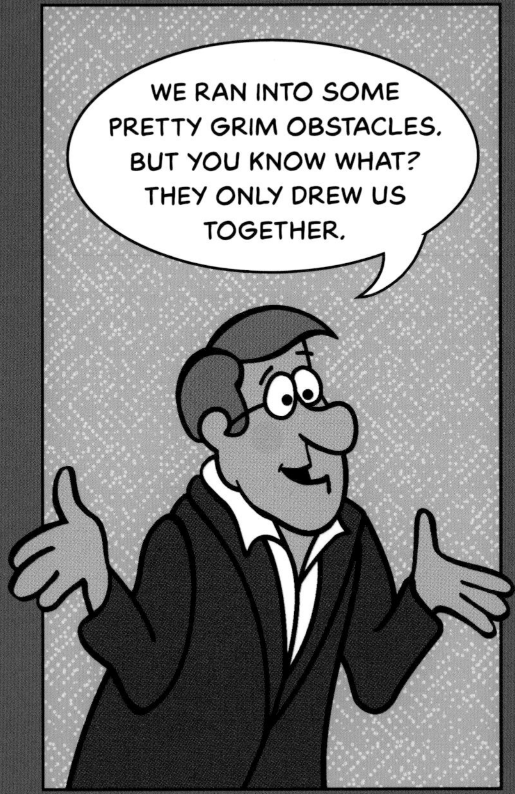
WE RAN INTO SOME PRETTY GRIM OBSTACLES. BUT YOU KNOW WHAT? THEY ONLY DREW US TOGETHER.

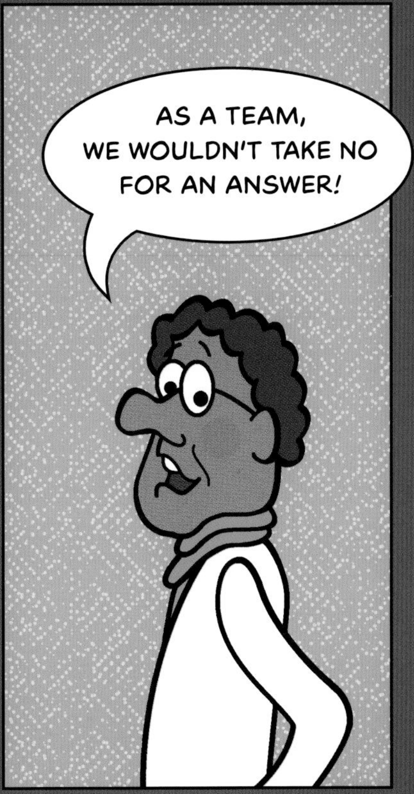
AS A TEAM, WE WOULDN'T TAKE NO FOR AN ANSWER!

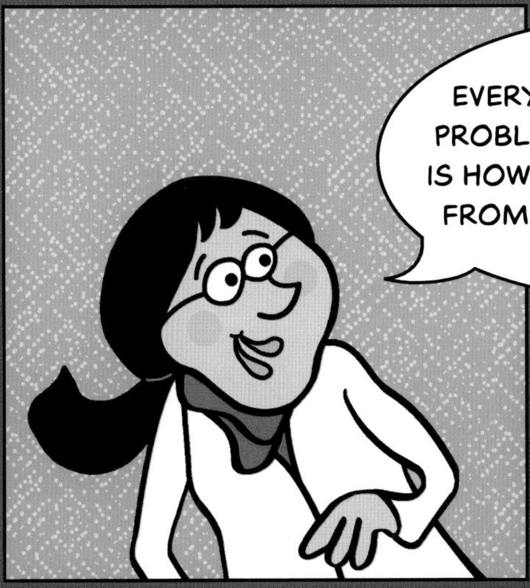
EVERY JOURNEY HAS ITS PROBLEMS. WHAT COUNTS IS HOW WELL YOU RECOVER FROM THOSE PROBLEMS.

GALILEO RECOVERED OVER AND OVER AGAIN.

WITH BRILLIANT BREAKTHROUGHS AND UNEXPECTED DISCOVERIES, IT WAS A SPECTACULAR MISSION!

NOW THAT YOU'VE READ THIS STORY, WHY DO **YOU** THINK THE GALILEO TEAM KEPT GOING?

HAVE YOU EVER KEPT GOING, EVEN THOUGH IT WAS TOUGH?

HOW DO YOU USE **YOUR** IMAGINATION TO SOLVE PROBLEMS?

WHAT SPACE MISSION WOULD BE MOST EXCITING TO **YOU**?

DO YOU EVER DREAM OF UNKNOWN WORLDS?

CAN YOU SEE YOURSELF SETTING SAIL FOR THE PLANETS?

WHEN YOU LOOK UP AT THE STARS, WHAT DO **YOU** IMAGINE?

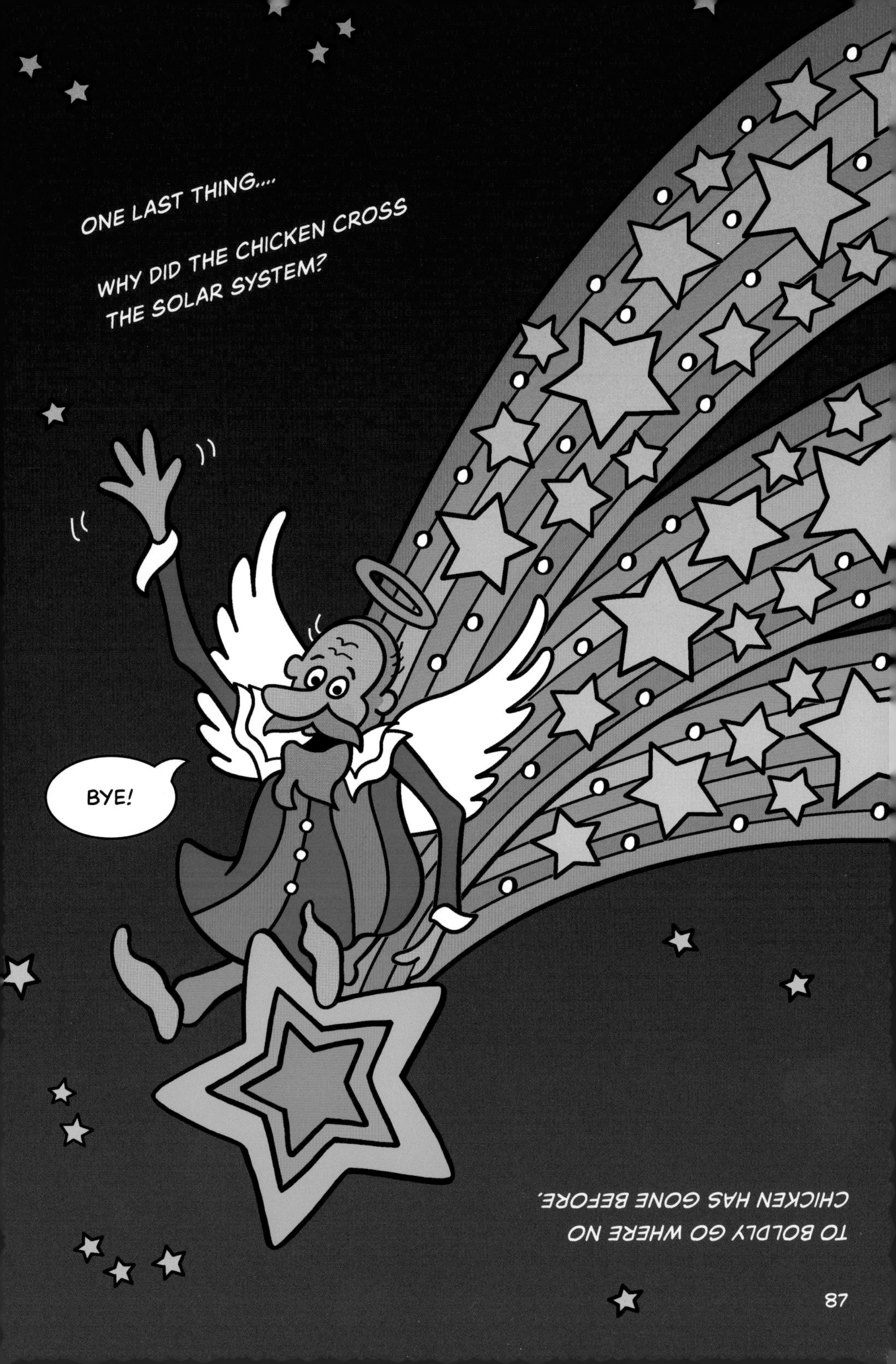
ONE LAST THING....
WHY DID THE CHICKEN CROSS THE SOLAR SYSTEM?
BYE!
TO BOLDLY GO WHERE NO CHICKEN HAS GONE BEFORE.

BIBLIOGRAPHY

CASANI, JOHN (GALILEO PROJECT MANAGER), INTERVIEW BY JOHN KRIGE, MAY 18, 2009, PASADENA, CALIFORNIA.

CRAWFORD, J. CRAIG. "GROUP SAYS GALILEO FUEL OLD, DANGEROUS." *ORLANDO SENTINEL*, OCTOBER 5, 1989.

DAWSON, VIRGINIA P., AND MARK D. BOWLES. *TAMING LIQUID HYDROGEN: THE CENTAUR UPPER STAGE ROCKET 1958-2002*. WASHINGTON, DC: NATIONAL AERONAUTICS AND SPACE ADMINISTRATION, OFFICE OF EXTERNAL RELATIONS, 2007.

FISCHER, DANIEL. *MISSION JUPITER: THE SPECTACULAR JOURNEY OF THE GALILEO SPACECRAFT*. NEW YORK: COPERNICUS BOOKS, 2001.

GALILEO TO JUPITER: PROBING THE PLANET AND MAPPING ITS MOONS. PASADENA, CALIFORNIA: NATIONAL AERONAUTICS AND SPACE ADMINISTRATION, CALIFORNIA INSTITUE OF TECHNOLOGY, JET PROPULSION LABORATORY, 1979.

HANLON, MICHAEL. *THE WORLDS OF GALILEO: THE INSIDE STORY OF NASA'S MISSION TO JUPITER*. LONDON: CONSTABLE PUBLISHERS, 2001.

HARLAND, DAVID M. *JUPITER ODYSSEY: THE STORY OF NASA'S GALILEO MISSION*. CHICHESTER, UK: SPRINGER-PRAXIS BOOKS, 2000.

HARLAND, DAVID M., AND RALPH D. LORENZ. *SPACE SYSTEM FAILURES: DISASTERS AND RESCUES OF SATELLITES, ROCKETS AND SPACE PROBES*. CHICHESTER, UK: SPRINGER-PRAXIS BOOKS IN ASTRONOMY AND SPACE SCIENCES, 2005.

LOGSDON, JOHN M. "THE SURVIVAL CRISIS OF THE US SOLAR SYSTEM EXPLORATION PROGRAM IN THE 1980S." IN *EXPLORING THE SOLAR*

SYSTEM: THE HISTORY AND SCIENCE OF PLANETARY EXPLORATION.,
EDITED BY ROGER D. LAUNIUS. NEW YORK: PALGRAVE MACMILLAN,
2013.

MELTZER, MICHAEL. *MISSION TO JUPITER: A HISTORY OF THE GALILEO
PROJECT.* WASHINGTON, DC: NATIONAL AERONAUTICS AND SPACE
ADMINISTRATION, NASA HISTORY DIVISION, 2007.

MESTEL, ROSIE. "CAROLYN SHOEMAKER AND 'HER COMET.'" *NEW
SCIENTIST* 143 (JULY 9, 1994): 23.

MOORE, ARDEN. "GALILEO FINALLY HEADS TO JUPITER." *SOUTH
FLORIDA SUN SENTINEL,* OCTOBER 19, 1989.

NILSEN, ERIK N., AND P.A. "TRISHA" JANSMA. "GALILEO'S ROCKY ROAD
TO JUPITER." *ASK MAGAZINE,* NO. 42 (SPRING 2011).

SAGAN, CARL. "BENEFIT OUTWEIGHS RISK: LAUNCH GALILEO CRAFT."
USA TODAY, OCTOBER 10, 1989.

*SPACE EXPLORATION: NASA'S DEEP SPACE MISSIONS ARE
EXPERIENCING LONG DELAYS; BRIEFING REPORT TO THE CHAIRMAN,
SUBCOMMITTEE ON SCIENCE, TECHNOLOGY, AND SPACE, COMMITTEE
ON COMMERCE, SCIENCE, AND TRANSPORTATION, U.S. SENATE.*
WASHINGTON, DC: GENERAL ACCOUNTING OFFICE, 1988.

WIKIPEDIA, THE FREE ENCYCLOPEDIA, S.V. "COMET SHOEMAKER-LEVY
9," (ACCESSED MARCH 12, 2020), HTTPS://EN.WIKIPEDIA.ORG/WIKI/
COMET_SHOEMAKER%E2%80%93LEVY_9

WIKIPEDIA, THE FREE ENCYCLOPEDIA, S.V. "STS-34," (ACCESSED
MARCH 12, 2020), HTTPS://EN.WIKIPEDIA.ORG/WIKI/STS-34

WIKIPEDIA, THE FREE ENCYCLOPEDIA,
S.V. "WANK (COMPUTER WORM),"
(ACCESSED MARCH 12, 2020),
HTTPS://EN.WIKIPEDIA.ORG/WIKI/
WANK_(COMPUTER_WORM)

ACKNOWLEDGEMENTS

HOLLY (THOMASON) TRECHTER HAD THE EXCITING OPPORTUNITY TO DO AN INTERNSHIP AT THE NASA AMES HISTORY ARCHIVES. WITH THE INDISPENSABLE HELP OF HER SUPERVISOR, APRIL GAGE, SHE ARCHIVED THE PAPERS OF JOHN D. MIHALOV (HTTPS://HISTORY.ARC.NASA.GOV/HIST_PDFS/GUIDES/PPO522JM_MIHALOV.PDF).

MR. MIHALOV WAS A CO-INVESTIGATOR ON THE GALILEO PROJECT, AND AS HOLLY READ HIS PAPERS, SHE BECAME FASCINATED WITH THE GALILEO MISSION. SHE WANTED TO SHARE ITS STORY WITH KIDS, SO SHE WORKED WITH HER SISTER, JANE DONOVAN, TO CREATE THIS BOOK.

HOLLY AND JANE ARE THANKFUL THAT THEY COULD USE NASA'S PHOTO ARCHIVES. THEY ARE ALSO INDEBTED TO THE AMAZING APRIL GAGE, WHO ARCHIVES DOCUMENTS AND ARTIFACTS FROM MANY NASA MISSIONS. HER GENEROUS WELCOME AND ENCOURAGEMENT MADE THIS BOOK POSSIBLE.

THE AUTHORS ARE ALSO GRATEFUL TO R. KEVIN OBERMAN, WHO WAS THE DEPARTMENT OF ENERGY ENGINEER WHO RELEASED THE ANTI-WORM FIX DURING THE LOMA PRIETA EARTHQUAKE. MR. OBERMAN READ AN EARLY DRAFT OF THE AUTHORS' DESCRIPTION OF THOSE EVENTS, AND HE KINDLY PROVIDED FEEDBACK.

THIS BOOK ALSO BENEFITED FROM THE LIVELY COMMENTS OF JON THOMASON, KEN THOMASON, KATHY HOFF, LOIS SEAVER, DAVID LEV, AND PAMELA D'ANGELO. HOLLY WOULD ESPECIALLY

LIKE TO THANK HER HUSBAND, DAVE TRECHTER, FOR HIS TENDER PATIENCE AND LOVING SUPPORT.

ANY MISTAKES THAT MIGHT EXIST IN THIS BOOK ARE HOLLY'S AND JANE'S.

FINALLY, THE AUTHORS ARE AWESTRUCK BY THE HUNDREDS OF PEOPLE WHO PUT THEIR HEARTS AND SOULS INTO THE GALILEO PROJECT. THEIR WORK ON THIS COMPELLING MISSION CONTINUES TO HUMBLE AND INSPIRE.

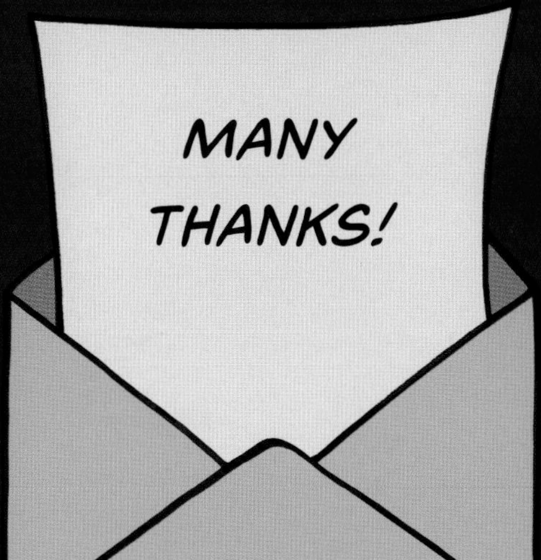
MANY THANKS!